~ Previews ~

Healing with Life Force by Shivani Lucki is a book which will inspire many people to make important life-changing decisions. The hints given there will be of great benefit to all those who are sincerely interested in changing their life from one of pure materialism to one of pure spirituality. This is a change which has to be made by every individual if we want a new world.

I have known Shivani for more than twenty years. She is a true disciple of a realized master, Sri Paramhansa Yogananda. I congratulate her on her initiative in reaching out to the countless souls who are at a loss to know how to get out of the labyrinth of delusion in which they are entrapped.

–**Vanamali Mataji,** *Vanamali Ashram, Rishikesh*

With clarity, precision, and depth of understanding, Shivani has delivered a masterpiece that in my opinion must be made part of medical curriculum. Modern medicine recognizes all diseases as psychosomatic, thus emphasizing the importance of thought patterns engrained in subconscious mind as the origin of ill health. The many case studies presented in the book confirm my experience as a clinical psychiatrist: the practices of affirmations, meditation and positive attitudes not only help patients with disease remission but also prevention. A must read for all who want to live a healthy life in this maddening world.

–**Dr. Mona Choudhary,** *MBBS, MD psychiatry, founder of Parentingmantra.com, New Delhi*

Healing with Life Force highlights a capacity unique to humans: free will. It invites us to apply this instrument to create good habits to replace unhealthy ones and to consciously choose positive thoughts to combat anxiety, negativity, and fear. We discover healing tools we never knew existed. I speak from experience when I say that what you find here will transform you.

–**Dr. Kriti Maroli,** *MDS, Gargaon, India*

This book is a marvelous blend of science and spirituality, both necessary for a perfectly healthy life. Shivani has zealously endowed the Life Force trilogy with the elixir of the transformative self-healing teachings of Paramhansa Yogananda, which she herself has practiced and taught for half a century.

The delightful personal experiences of people from around the world add a dimension of immediacy, demonstrating that the practices in the book are effective even and especially in times of physical and emotional peril. As a teacher of preventive medicine, I know the importance of maintaining a healthy lifestyle. If we adopt even some of the wise suggestions in this book for both our physical and "mental diet," we can develop strong immunity and enjoy better health.

–*Dr .Pallavi Shukla*, *MBBS, MD, PhD, assistant professor, preventive oncology, AIIMS, New Delhi*

This book is the definitive compendium of the teachings on healing of Paramhansa Yogananda, teachings that not only set us on the path of curing ourselves from the fundamental cause of disease—spiritual ignorance—but that provide highly practical and immediately applicable methods that anyone can use in whatever situation life brings. Shivani has spent decades studying, applying and sharing these teachings, and these exhaustive volumes are the fruit of her profound dedication to the path of spiritual healing, as taught by the great masters of Self-realization.

–**Hana Mukti Božanin,** *meditation instructor, english teacher, and translator, Belgrade, Serbia*

HEALING WITH LIFE FORCE

HEALING WITH
LIFE FORCE

TEACHINGS AND TECHNIQUES OF PARAMHANSA YOGANANDA

VOLUME 2 MIND

SHIVANI LUCKI

Healing with Life Force

Volume Two: Mind

©2024 by Shivani Lucki
All rights reserved. Published 2024
Printed in the United States of America

CRYSTAL CLARITY PUBLISHERS
1123 Goodrich Blvd. | Commerce, California
crystalclarity.com | clarity@crystalclarity.com
800.424.1055

ISBN 978-1-56589-048-0 (print)
ISBN 978-1-56589-530-0 (e-book)
Library of Congress Data available.

*Cover layout and interior design by
Tejindra Scott Tully*

Cover image by Apace on Freepik

Please be advised: The content in this book is not intended to be a substitute for professional medical advice, diagnosis or treatment. Always consult with a qualified and licensed physician or other medical care provider, and follow their advice without delay.

My Intuitive
HEALING JOURNEY

I have always been cautious about selecting solutions for my medical care. Before choosing a doctor, I will always do extensive research. Yet I was finding now that neither my carefully chosen endocrinologist, gynecologist, or gastroenterologist could offer solutions to relieve my debilitating symptoms.

For the last nine months I had suffered from hypocortisolemia, a condition where the adrenals don't make enough cortisol, resulting in profound fatigue and acute pain all over my body. I took the medications my doctors prescribed, but I was getting more and more tired, and there were days when I hadn't the strength to get out of bed. Adding to this sad situation, my pancreas began to malfunction.

Not knowing where else to turn, I prayed for guidance.

I am a specialist in reconstructive dental surgery, and one day while practicing in a colleague's studio I was suddenly drawn to the bookshelves that held medical journals and books. Not looking for any book in particular, I reached out and took a random book in hand.

Strangely, it had nothing to do with dentistry, but even before I opened it I knew with a sure intuition that it contained the answers to my health problems. I brought it home and read it from cover to cover that evening. It described a recent area of research called "functional medicine" and described all of the symptoms I was experiencing, as well as the reasons I had become ill, and the therapy that would bring my body back into balance.

The next day I found the phone number of the author, who was president of two Italian associations dedicated to functional medicine. Yet even though he had the most impressive credentials, an intuitive feeling prevented me from calling him. Instead, I googled "functional medicine in Como." Several names appeared, and while none seemed to specialize in my symptoms, I was intuitively drawn to one name. Incongruously, it was an ENT (ear, nose, and throat) specialist, yet I knew somehow that he would cure me.

When I described my symptoms, he suggested a treatment called neural therapy. Surprisingly, I – the careful researcher – immediately agreed to the therapy, not knowing what it was. Back home, I looked it up: "Neural therapy consists of deep injections of procaine diluted with bicarbonate at the orthosympathetic nerve ganglia to calm their activity (and thus dampen the whole hormonal cascade of stresses and catabolism) to promote normal parasympathetic action." This sounded rather frightening, but I knew it was the right therapy for me.

After only a few sessions, all of my symptoms disappeared and I was feeling better than ever. It turned out that this humble ENT was the president of a functional medicine association and that he had written numerous books on it and was a pioneer of neural therapy.

I have returned to work and to my spiritual life with renewed vigor, with a fresh appreciation for the superiority of intuitive guidance over rational research, and with gratitude that I had the courage to follow my intuition.

–**Valentina**, *Como, Italy*

TABLE OF CONTENTS

VOLUME II | MIND

My Intuitive Healing Journey | 3
Foreword | 7
Introduction | 9

Part VI: The Healing Powers of the Mind | 17

Chapter One: We Are What We Think | 19
Chapter Two: Your Mental Diet | 27
Chapter Three: Superpowers of the Conscious Mind | 39
Chapter Four: Willpower | 51
Chapter Five: Visualization | 67
Chapter Six: The Subterranean Subconscious | 79
Chapter Seven: Superconscious Intuition | 107

Part VII: Habits | 127

Chapter One: Habits | 129
Chapter Two: How Habits Are Created | 137
Chapter Three: Discovering Your Habit Allies and Enemies | 145
Chapter Four: Eliminating Bad Habits | 153
Chapter Five: Habit Exchange | 161
Chapter Six: Superconscious Solutions | 173

Part VIII: Scientific Healing Affirmations | 187

Chapter One: The Truth Shall Make You Free | 189
Chapter Two: Choose Your Affirmation | 199
Chapter Three: Affirmation Recipe | 213
Chapter Four: Scientific Affirmation Techniques | 219
Chapter Five: Affirmation in Motion and Music | 227
Chapter Six: Healed by Affirmations | 235

PART IX: DIVINE GRACE | 245

CHAPTER ONE: **Who Is Listening?** | 247
CHAPTER TWO: **Who Is Asking?** | 259
CHAPTER THREE: **Scientific Healing Prayer Demands** | 267
CHAPTER FOUR: **Inner Guidance** | 283
CHAPTER FIVE: **Channeling Healing Energy to Others** | 299

GLOSSARY | 320
BIBLIOGRAPHY | 323
PHOTOS & ILLUSTRATIONS | 327
ABOUT THE AUTHORS | 328-330
IN APPRECIATION | 331

FOREWORD

Dr. Maria Donatella Caramia

Healing with Life Force is imbued with the power and spirit of a great world teacher. The author shares with us the essence of Paramhansa Yogananda's timeless teachings, which were first articulated nearly a century ago, and are even more relevant today.

We now know that our thoughts can change our bodies in accordance with the brain's formidable neuroplastic powers. And we cannot separate these newly discovered truths from the effects of spiritual practices on our minds, emotions, and immune system. The techniques in this volume, particularly the scientific healing affirmations for healing of mind and body, put us in the driver's seat when it comes to maintaining our health and healing ourselves. They enable us to create a reality in which we are strong, resilient, and capable of navigating life with grace and fortitude - one positive thought at a time.

I have long admired Shivani as a personal friend and a profoundly inspiring teacher. She combines keen intelligence with intuition and a generosity that aspires to help everyone be supported, recognized, and healed.

Shivani had the great good fortune to learn the principles and practices of Self-realization from one of the greatest thinkers of our times, Swami Kriyananda, who himself received them directly from Yogananda. She very generously shares the wisdom of these masters, augmenting them with insights that she has gained from fifty years of personal practice.

As you read these pages, I urge you to take the time to follow the exercises, as they will help you exchange harmful habits for healing ones, and receive the unfailing guidance of your own higher Self.

Dr. Caramia is a neurologist, psychologist, professor of humanistic neurology at the University of Rome Tor Vergata.

INTRODUCTION

The book you have in hand is the second volume in the *Life Force* trilogy—*Prana, Mind, Magnetism*—three guidebooks for your journey to better health. Together they represent an overarching view of Paramhansa Yogananda's teachings and techniques for self-healing and Self-realization.

Volume One, *Prana,* takes us back to the very beginning, when Life Force becomes the power that fashions creation. Yogananda shows us how to harness that power and use it to infuse our bodies with vitality. That force also gives rise to the eternal struggle between the soul and the ego, the root cause of all disease. Through the pages and practices of this book, you will learn how to reconcile these two protagonists through techniques of meditation; how to regenerate the cells and organs of your body with Yogananda's Energization Exercises; and how to nourish yourself and keep your body free from impurities with his dietary and detox recipes. A fascinating section in this volume presents Yogananda's techniques for utilizing the sun's power for self-healing.

Volume Two, *Mind,* highlights the superpowers of the conscious, subconscious, and superconscious dimensions of the mind. It offers extensive advice for breaking the stranglehold of negative habits, for using affirmations to carve new thought habits in the brain, and for learning to cooperate with the highest source of healing—Divine Love.

Volume Three, *Magnetism,* reveals how the Law of Attraction operates in our lives: how it draws us into contact with friends from past lives; and how we can use it to attract the economic and human resources for a successful career.

The final chapter of the trilogy demonstrates how we can attune ourselves to the subtle, vibratory healing frequencies of mantra and music; of nature, holy places, and inspiring people. Important techniques are given to reinforce the magnetic aura which protects us from negative influences that threaten our physical, mental, emotional, and spiritual health and well-being.

We are not alone in this quest. Some of those who have come before us, in ages past and in our times, those who have reached the summit of what it means to be a fully Self-realized being, have left for us guidelines for our own achievements.

One such recent guide is Paramhansa Yogananda.

Paramhansa Yogananda

Author of the enduring spiritual classic, *Autobiography of a Yogi*,[1] Yogananda is universally regarded as an enlightened spiritual master of modern times. He had the remarkable gift of distilling the essential wisdom of India's great scriptures and presenting them in what he called "how-to-live teachings," useful and accessible to us today.

Yogananda was born in India in 1893, on the cusp of the beginning of Dwapara Yuga, the Age of Energy, which according to his guru, Swami Sri Yukteswar, started in 1899. Ushering in this new age were the discoveries of Albert Einstein and Nikola Tesla on the nature of matter and energy.

In the first decade of the twentieth century alone, the landmark inventions included radio, radar, and the electrocardiogram, to name a few. Energy now powers all our systems of transportation, communication, and the countless gadgets that simplify and enhance our daily lives.

When Yogananda arrived on the shores of the New World in 1920, around the time the Wright brothers had taken flight and Henry Ford had produced the Model T, the timing was right and people were eager to learn techniques of self-improvement that were based on principles of Energy.

Although Yogananda is not remembered primarily as a miracle healer, in his early lecture tours across America he gave many public demonstrations of the power of self-healing. On October 21, 1924, he held a first "public divine healing meeting" in Portland, Oregon. During a healing program at his headquarters at Mt. Washington in Los Angeles on November 1, 1925, he healed a woman of crippling neuritis, after which she was able to walk without crutches.

In Washington, D.C., in 1927, a reported 5,000 people attended his healing program. It was at this time that he was invited to the White House where he met with President Calvin Coolidge.

Titles of his public talks reflect the scientific spirit of the new age:

Practicing Religion Scientifically
Scientific Spiritual Healing
Law of Attracting Abundance and Health Consciously
The Mind: Repository of Infinite Power
Harmonizing Physical, Mental, and Spiritual Methods of Healing.

When divinely guided, Yogananda would occasionally perform a healing, but his intention as a spiritual guide was to teach others the methods by which they could draw upon the inexhaustible Life Force to heal themselves. The gift that Yogananda gives us in these pages is the key to unlock the mysteries of life.

In addition to the five million copies of his *Autobiography* in circulation, his other books are widely read. Included in these volumes are important writings about health and healing which are not easily available. Of special note are his early correspondence lessons, written by his own hand between 1923 and 1935; the articles he wrote for his organization's magazines (*East-West* and *Inner Culture*), including his "Health, Intellectual and Spiritual Recipes," and his parallel commentaries on the Bhagavad Gita and the Christian Bible.

I draw on these sources abundantly in these books. It is Yogananda's wisdom, in his voice and his words that I strived to convey as compiler, organizer, and annotator. All of his quotations are indicated in the text with a symbol of the spiritual eye.

Swami Kriyananda

J. Donald Walters, later to become Swami Kriyananda, was accepted by Yogananda as a monastic disciple in 1948. On the master's request, Kriyananda carefully studied his writings, especially his commentaries on the Bhagavad Gita and the Christian Bible. He took copious notes of the master's public talks and their private conversations, which he later incorporated in his books *The New Path* and *Conversations with Yogananda*. Yogananda designated him as head of the monks, authorized him as a minister and teacher, and gave him the authority to initiate people into the science of Kriya Yoga. His life work, Yogananda told him, would involve teaching and writing.

During his sixty-five years as a disciple (1948-2013), Kriyananda gave lectures around the world, including daily talks on major Indian television channels. He published approximately 140 books in which he showed how his guru's teachings can be applied to improve and elevate our daily life activities—in business and leadership, relationships, education, music and the arts, and for achieving dynamic health and well-being.[2] Excerpts from these and unpublished articles and letters are included in the text, the Endnotes, and the Appendices.

I was trained by Kriyananda from 1969 until his passing, and have been practicing and sharing these teachings for the past fifty years. In addition to those of Yogananda, I have drawn profusely from Kriyananda's writings. Each of his quotations in the text is indicated with the Joy Symbol.

Interactive

Throughout the three volumes you will find exercises to help you practice what you are learning. Your own experience of the techniques will give you an immediate awareness of their benefits.

Each exercise is aligned with a self-improvement goal, such as identifying our positive and negative, helpful and harmful habits. Doing the exercises at the points indicated will help you bring their benefits into your daily life.

Most of the exercises can be done, at your choosing, as you move through the book. Some of them are writing exercises that you will find in the online Appendices to download and complete electronically, or print and complete on paper.

Value Added: A Treasure Trove of More Inspiration!

Available exclusively for readers of this volume is access to an online site: www.healinglifeforces.com/volume-2/ (or scan this QR code), where you will find:

- Articles by Paramhansa Yogananda and Swami Kriyananda, including previously unavailable material about:
    - Overcoming harmful emotions
    - The significance of dreams
    - How to develop creative intuition

- ➢ How to overcome fear and anger
- ➢ How to eliminate negative habits and create healthy ones
- A class with Shivani in Kriyananda's Superconscious Living Exercises
- Talks by Shivani on "Healing Prayers and Affirmations."
- and much more!

> **You're also invited to join the Online Healing Community** for regular healing tips, interactive sessions, and seminars with the author. Come visit us at *www.healinglifeforces.com*.

Stories

Especially engaging, inspiring, and instructive are the stories that I have included throughout the books from people who have used these techniques for their own healing. Some of the stories are allegorical, some are drawn from mythology, while most of them tell of real-life experiences.

Terminology

Because this is a handbook of spiritually based practices for improving health and finding healing, the central importance of **"Spirit"** cannot be overstated. Regardless of how we personally conceptualize and relate to the Supreme Reality, it must occupy a central position if we hope to understand and make effective use of these principles and practices.

Can an atheist find value in these teachings? Yes, because they are thoroughly grounded in the way human beings are made. Even if we reject the concept of "God," we may recognize the presence of a higher source of wisdom and inspiration. Many scientists, including physicist and cosmologist Stephen Hawking, and science-fiction writers like Isaac Asimov, have denied the existence of God while endorsing and popularizing cosmological principles that touch on the spiritual.

Yogananda urged us to be "spiritual scientists." He said that while the scientist approaches the Infinite from the outside, the spiritual scientist approaches it from the inside.[3]

Psychologist and researcher David DeSteno writes about "the science behind the benefits of religion."

> "I've come to see a nuanced relationship between science and religion. I now view them as two approaches to improving people's lives that frequently complement each other...If we ignore that body of knowledge, if we refuse to take these spiritual technologies seriously as a source of ideas and inspiration to study, we slow the progress of science itself and limit its potential to benefit humanity." [4]

Whether we think of ourselves as scientists, technologists, or believers, we can all experience the practical results of these scientific healing practices.

Energy

Yogananda uses a variety of phrases to refer to energy in its varied forms. His term "Cosmic Energy" refers to the universal energy by which all creation is manifested, and that is the source of all life. He describes this source also as the "Cosmic Electric Force," and the "Cosmic Intelligent Energy." [5]

As cosmic energy descends through the three universes and the three bodies that the soul inhabits (see Part I), it becomes what Yogananda termed "Life Force" or "Life Energy." When it enters the physical body, it becomes the "Lifetronic Force," synonymous with the Sanskrit term *prana*.

When quoting Yogananda directly, I have always used his exact words. In my commentaries and explanations, I generally refer to the healing force in the body as Life Force; interchangeably as *prana*.

Energization Exercises

The primary Life Force healing technique described in these books is a practice that Yogananda developed in the 1920s that he originally called Yogoda Exercises. He later referred to them as Energization Exercises. Citations from Yogananda in the 1920s and 1930s use the term Yogoda, but I refer to them as Life Force Energization Exercises, and often simply as "energization exercises." Instruction in the practice of these exercises, in easy-to-follow videos, is included in the Appendices.

Life Force / **14**

Sanskrit words appear sparingly throughout the text, usually when they capture a concept that is difficult to render in other languages. A glossary of Sanskrit terms is included at the back of each volume.

LEGEND OF CITATIONS

Each citation is referenced in the Endnotes. These are the symbols used within the text.

PARAMHANSA YOGANANDA   **HOLY BIBLE** *(King James)*   **SWAMI KRIYANANDA**

SWAMI SRI YUKTESWAR   **BHAGAVAD GITA**   **MAHAVATAR BABAJI**

Now it's time to start your journey of self-healing. May you make steady progress as you strive to become what Yogananda describes as

"The master of your destiny."

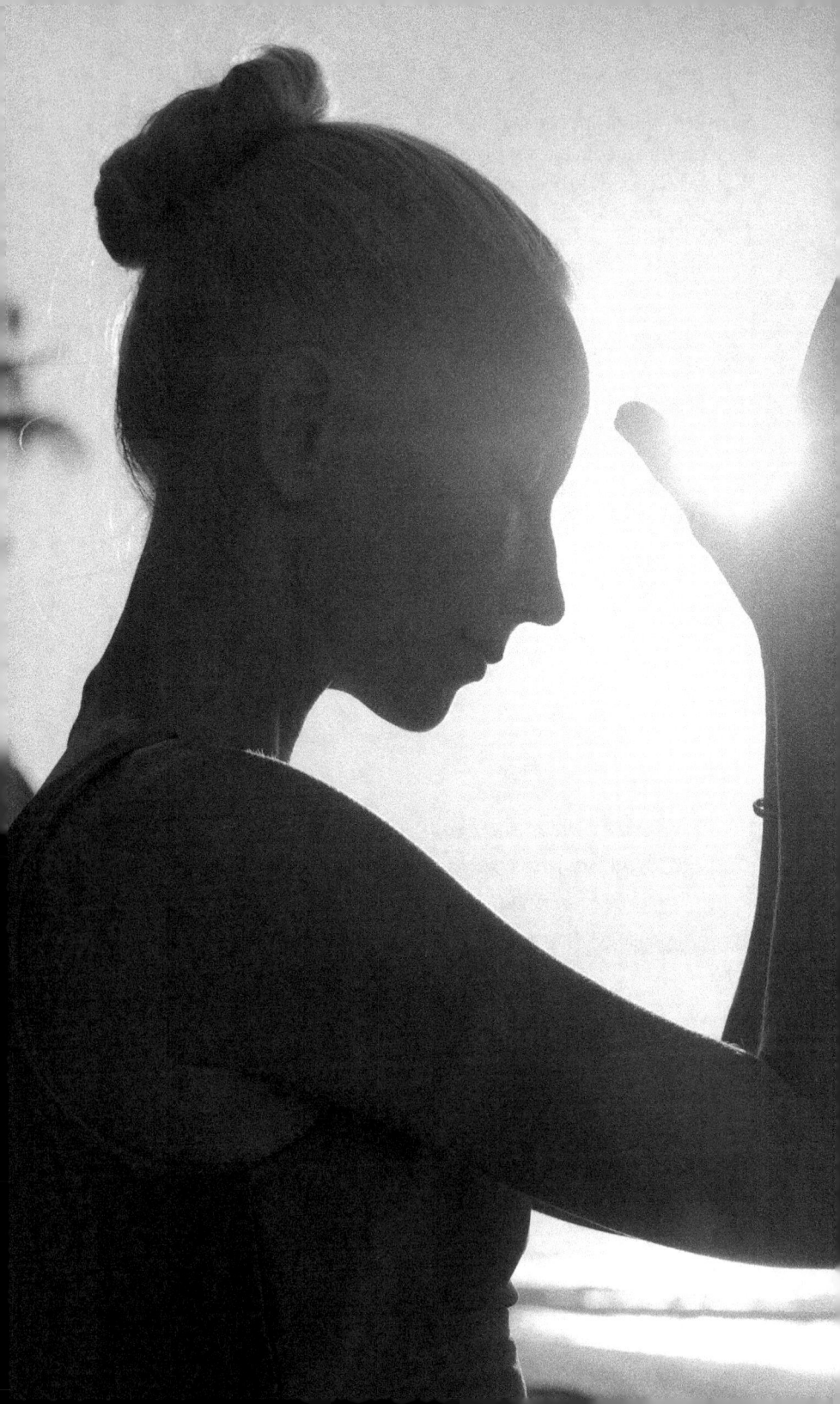

PART VI
HEALING POWERS OF THE MIND

All disease has its roots in the mind…
If the mind can produce ill health
it can also produce good health.[1]

—Yogananda

Thought is the brain of the cells and [of the]
units of Life Force present in every particle
of bodily tissue. Hence, a disease thought upsets
the entire government of the Life Force in
the cells, whereas the thought of health corrects
any disorder in the cellular system.[2]

—Yogananda

❊ Saving Face ❊

Lorraine had been married very happily for thirty years to the beloved pastor of the city's largest Protestant church. She was well respected, a dynamo of compassion and service, and her life was a perfect complement to his.

And now this – out of the blue, a divorce. Ugly thoughts of pain, humiliation, and desperation assailed her. They will talk: How had she not known? They will judge: If she couldn't keep her house in order, how could she counsel others?

Lorraine sought shelter in the fortress of the house that for three decades had served as a warm and loving home. She had counseled and comforted many in similar situations. How valid had her council been?

She resolved to travel, to meet new people and have new experiences. Before embarking, she saw the family physician. As unexpected and shocking as her divorce, there was a facial melanoma that needed urgent treatment.

Why was she now facing a serious illness, so soon after fighting off the gathering clouds of depression? The answer came in a flash of clarity: she had been so fixated on the thought of losing face that she was now literally at threat of losing her face!

She recalled what she had always told others – that life's unavoidable changes are God's way of gently nudging us to grow. As a chapter ends, so another begins. Her prayer was answered – now, knowing the deeper meaning of these events, she no longer feared the thoughts of others, and she was ready to turn the page.

Feeling that the root cause of the melanoma had been removed from her mind, she departed on her trip against her physician's strenuous objections. Travel brought an expanded perspective, and awakened aspects of herself that had long lain dormant. On her return, her doctor confirmed that the melanoma had vanished. Her confidence restored, she resumed her loving service to her many friends in the congregation.

❊ ❊ ❊

PART VI   CHAPTER ONE

We Are What We Think

> Thought has the power of materialization. Change your process of thought. There is no other technique. In this short span of life, by the power of your thought, you can go faster than the airplane, faster than all animals, and be more powerful than any mechanism man has invented. You are made in God's image, and He gave to you the indomitable power of thought.
> —YOGANANDA [1]

While there is a great deal of truth in the adage, "We are what we eat," an even more penetrating saying is "We are what we think." Every great accomplishment has its origin in the mind.

Flying machines existed in Leonardo da Vinci's mind in 1490, but would not take to the air until four centuries later, with the Wright Brothers's first flight in 1903.

In 1964 Eugene Roddenberry imagined the mobile communicator used by the cast of Star Trek. Nine years later, Martin Cooper introduced the first portable telephone.

In a 1898 short story, "From the London Times of 1904," Mark Twain visualized a communications network that scientists could use to share their findings and to work cooperatively. The exact purpose for which the internet was started, in the 1980s.

Astronauts visualize themselves working in space even before they start their training.

Athletes routinely pre-visualize their performances, finding it extremely effective for preparing their bodies and programing their brain pathways for success. They see themselves on the winners' platform and feel the coolness of the medal around their neck.

Tunnels, under-water communications cables, satellites, organ transplants, a tree bearing different varieties of fruit, the Hubble telescope, the Mars rover – all were born first in the fertile mind of visionaries.

The house you now inhabit possibly began its life as your "dream home," which only you believed in.

The mind that can conceive such amazing inventions is capable of helping us to manifest health, success, and happiness.

The quantum mind

The inventor, the scientist, the artist, the athlete – they come to know that the inception of their reality, and the foundation for their success, begins in the mind. According to today's understanding of quantum physics, our subjective mind produces perceptible changes in the objective physical world.

> Your thoughts are a form of energy that transmits a signal from your individual radio tower out to everything and everyone around you....Unlike a radio tower, the energy that comes from your thoughts isn't limited to a geographic location. Your thoughts are connected to the *energy web of all reality*, which is all around us.... The universe reads the vibrational frequency of your thoughts and attracts the people, places and circumstances that make them a reality. ... We all have the capacity and power within ourselves to utilize the energy of our thoughts to shape our reality. [2]

This is the Law of Attraction – the truth that our thoughts, which are patterns of subtle energy, have a power to attract experiences and objects.

> The law of attraction will certainly and unerringly bring to you the conditions, environment, and experiences in life, corresponding with your habitual, characteristic, predominant mental attitude.[3]

In practical terms, the Law of Attraction means that our positive or negative thoughts attract the corresponding results. If during a job interview our thoughts are entirely focused on images of being hired, their energy will influence the outcome. Visualizing ourselves performing well increases the probability of success. But if we fill our mind with thoughts that we are ill and weak, there will be a considerably lower possibility that we will be strong and well.

In this section we will learn techniques for engaging our quantum power of "mind over matter" to help us create and maintain good health.

The psychology of the Vedas

An understanding of how the mind works is part of the rich tradition that comes down from ancient times in India. The scriptures of *Sanatan Dharma** – the Vedas, the Upanishads, the Bhagavad-Gita, the *Yoga Sutras of Patanjali*, and other scriptures and treatises – give detailed guidelines for maintaining a healthy body-mind-soul equilibrium.

Yogananda interpreted this ancient wisdom for the modern age, showing us how the mind can be used as a powerful tool for healing. He introduces us to the four aspects of human consciousness and to the three dimensions of awareness. The techniques he taught, many of which are included in this chapter, are practical means of developing the mind's powers and harmonizing its dimensions.

Patanjali

The four aspects of human consciousness

The mind (as distinct from its physical container, the brain) has four functions: it perceives through the senses, it distinguishes what it perceives, it relates its perceptions to the individual, and it assigns a degree of desirability or lack of desirability to the objects of its perceptions.

As the physical brain functions in more or less the same way in all human beings, the mind functions similarly in all humans. The manner in which each individual chooses to utilize these universal mental capacities is a matter of free choice, which will be influenced by the totality of his previous individual choices (his karma) and his current environmental and familial circumstances.

---

*Sanatan Dharma means that truth which is eternal, and which is expressed in varying ways in all the great religions of the world. –Kriyananda, Swami, *Keys to the Bhagavad Gita*, 2.

Perception. We perceive the world through our five senses. Our physical perceptions supply the mind with data from the external world. What the mind can perceive depends on what it can see, hear, smell, taste, and touch. In Sanskrit, this function of the mind is called *mon*, or *manas*. This is the stage at which the mind sees a horse but doesn't define it – so far, the mind merely perceives a visual image of a horse.

Discrimination. Once the mind perceives something, it tries to make sense of it by using the faculty known in the Vedas as *buddhi*. This is the aspect of the mind that becomes aware of something and tries to identify it and understand whether it is beneficial or harmful. At this stage the mind identifies the object of perception: "That is a horse."

Personalizing. From its countless perceptions, the mind tries to discern which are useful to help it obtain its desires and ensure its survival. This function is called *ahankara* and denotes the egoic will. The egoic mind now defines its relationship to the horse: "This is *my* horse."

Feeling or emotion. The final function of the mind is known as *chitta*, which is the mind's capacity to assign an emotional value to its experiences, labeling them as either pleasing or displeasing. The feeling aspect of the mind is a two-edged sword. On one hand, when the feeling is impartial and impersonal, it works in harmony with *buddhi*. But when the feeling is ego-directed, it traps us in desires and personal attachments. "I *like* my horse!"

To summarize: *manas* connotes sensory awareness: like a mirror, it receives and reflects impressions from the senses. These impressions are then interpreted by the intelligence, *buddhi*, reacted to by the feelings, *chitta*, and finally assigned a value by the personal will, *ahankara*.

The three dimensions of the mind

As the mind coordinates its perceptions, degrees of awareness are created. In psychology, much is made of the **subconscious** level of awareness, especially the darkness that supposedly lurks there. But Yogananda emphasizes the usefulness of the subconscious mind: it serves as a place to store our **memories** and **habits**. When we are able to manage our subconscious memories and habits wisely, they serve as powerful tools for self-healing; but if we aren't careful, they can trap us in unwholesome habits and unbridled emotional reactivity.

We are most familiar with the **conscious mind** with its executive abilities to reason, analyze, and organize. In the next chapter, we will explore the superpowers of the conscious mind – *concentration*, *willpower*, and *visualization* – and discover how we can work with them to improve our health and wellbeing.

Less well known is the dimension of **superconsciousness**, a state of awareness that is superior to and independent of the physical senses and mental reasoning. Its superpower is *intuition*, an invaluable tool in our quest for health and healing, which we will discuss in the third chapter.

The descent of consciousness

COSMIC CONSCIOUSNESS

SUPERCONSCIOUSNESS

"The tree of superconsciousness has its roots in Cosmic Consciousness. Its trunk consists of superconsciousness and its branches consist of superconscious perception, subconscious perception, and conscious perception. This tree of superconsciousness, when perceived, will be found to bear fruits of superconscious intuition." [4]

SUBCONSCIOUSNESS

"The subconscious mind is the memory repository for the conscious mind. Being automatic, it reproduces good and bad memories equally. Hence the subconscious mind must be trained through the conscious mind." [5]

CONSCIOUSNESS

The ordinary tree of consciousness has its roots in the intelligence in the brain. Its trunk consists of the mind and its branches consist of reason, will, and feeling. The conscious mind, dependent on the intellect, seeks reasonable solutions to its problems. It is subordinate to superconsciousness, not superior to it.[6]

Interplay between the three dimensions

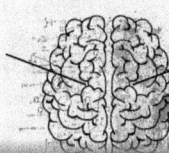

SUPERCONSCIOUS MIND

INTUITION, UNLIMITED PERCEPTION,
UNIVERSAL KNOWLEDGE, EVER-NEW JOY

↑ ↓

LOGICAL MIND — REASON, ANALYSIS, ORGANIZATION

SENSE PERCEPTIONS — SIGHT, HEARING, SMELL, TASTE, TOUCH

CONSCIOUS MIND

↓ ↑

SUBCONSCIOUS MIND

MEMORY, IMAGES, HABITS

Each of the dimensions of consciousness perceives reality in its own way. We bring all of them to bear on the innumerable decisions we must make each day.

The **subconscious**[7] mind is active when we are sleeping, but its labors aren't confined to our slumbers. During waking hours, the subconscious will bypass the rational conscious mind and impose automatic reactions based on our past experiences.

For example, if when walking you see a dog and in the past you have been bitten by a dog, a subconscious reaction might make you tense your muscles ready to flee, or, more constructively, tell you to cross the street and avoid the dog.

Our subconscious impressions can collaborate with the conscious mind, submitting memories that are useful in the present.

It is surprising and humbling to realize how many of our decisions are dominated by these subtle influences.

The **conscious** mind dominates our waking hours. It operates on the basis of the information it receives from the five senses, but also from external sources. While the conscious mind is influenced by our subconscious memories, it can turn the tables and impress new thoughts and behaviors on the subconscious, using its powers of concentration, will, visualization, and imagination.

The **superconscious** is always awake, perceiving reality from a multi-dimensional vantage point, much as the view from a helicopter is broader and more inclusive than the view from the ground. Superconscious perceptions are accessible to the conscious mind when our thoughts and emotions are calm.

We can achieve the state of inner harmony that Patanjali defines as yoga – *"Yogas chitta vritti nirodh"* ("Yoga is the neutralization of the vortices of emotional feeling") by stilling the waves of agitated thoughts and emotions so that the conscious mind becomes the receptacle of superconscious perception.

> The superconscious... represents a much higher degree of awareness. Indeed, it is the true source of all awareness. The conscious and subconscious minds filter that higher awareness, merely— stepping it down, so to speak, like the transformer that converts a high voltage to a lower and makes it available to our homes.[8]

In the chapters that follow, we will consider each level of consciousness and learn to use its unique powers to improve our health.

PART VI   CHAPTER TWO

Your Mental Diet

> There is no disease of the body apart from the mind. –SOCRATES

Psychological diseases give birth to physical diseases. In fact, most physical diseases derive their roots in the mind through disease convictions.[1] –YOGANANDA

While we know that material foods supply the body with energy, we must also remember that good thoughts are nourishing food for the mind, and thoughts of any other nature are poisonous to the health of body and mind. Have you ever analyzed your magnetic mental diet? It consists usually of the thoughts which you are thinking as well as the thoughts you are receiving from the close thought contact with your friends. Peaceful thoughts and peaceful friends always produce healthy, magnetic minds.[2] –YOGANANDA

Most people cannot heal themselves because their own thoughts are poisoned by the habit of thinking of chronic sickness...Thought is the brain of the cells and units of Life Force present in every particle of bodily tissue. Hence, a disease thought upsets the entire government of the Life Force in the cells, whereas the thought of health corrects any disorder in the cellular system. –YOGANANDA [3]

Every cell of the physical body is conscious: our cells breathe, respond to information, and interact with other cells. However, they do not have a mind of their own—they obey the thoughts coming from the command center of the brain.

Each of our thoughts either opens channels for a flow of healing life force, or closes them. Positive thoughts – "I feel great today!" – prepare the cells to receive healing energy. Negative thoughts – "This is all too much for me!" "I'm no longer as strong as I was!" – block the flow of healing energy.

When these thoughts are accompanied by mental images and emotions—an enthusiastic smile and uplifted arms, or a sad, hunched-over posture and sense of defeat— the effect on the flow of energy is even stronger.

We essentially create our health profile one thought at a time.

Just as in time we develop certain eating habits, we also have recurring habits of thought that Yogananda calls our "mental diet." These habitual thoughts, formulated by the conscious mind, are then stored in the subconscious, where they influence how we perceive ourselves and others.

The following story tells how Hana almost allowed a negative thought to ruin her day.

❊ The Ringtone of Negativity ❊

The virulence of the Covid virus, and the resulting pervasive atmosphere of fear and uncertainty, were deeply unsettling for me. To hold these feelings at bay and keep my consciousness elevated, I made a conscious effort to expose myself to uplifting vibrations as much as possible. I listened to Radio Ananda almost around the clock, finding that it helped keep me calm and centered.

There was a day when I felt especially positive, secure, and held safely in the hands of Divine Mother and my Master. My husband and my son and I had visited our local Ananda center to clean and say hello to the space that for several weeks had not seen people gathering for meditation. We had just finished when I got a call from a person with whom I had had a difficult business relationship.

She called me often, and the conversations were so unpleasant that I dreaded hearing the phone ring. So as not to be constantly on edge, I changed the ringtone for everyone else, leaving a separate warning tone for her alone.

Although it was her ringtone, I answered, and we had a brief and not entirely unpleasant conversation. But afterward, I realized that my negative reaction to having her intrude on my happy day was unsettling.

We set off for home on foot, and as we walked I suddenly became aware that I was no longer feeling safe and secure. It was as if I had somehow become porous, and the fears that Covid had given rise to were entering my consciousness.

Fortunately, the uplifting effects of our time at the meditation center, combined with my efforts to maintain a positive state of mind, helped me be aware of what was happening. It wasn't that the objective situation had suddenly become more threatening or worrisome, but by allowing myself to harbor negative thoughts I had opened doors to a whole universe of negativity. –**Hana**, *Belgrade, Serbia*

Self-fulfilling prophecies

A habitual negative mindset can affect our health drastically. People who have nothing good to say about others, and who indulge in spewing negative, provocative, or violent words and emotions into their surroundings, weaken their immunity and open themselves to illness.

> Doctors have found that people with high levels of negativity are more likely to suffer from degenerative brain diseases, cardiovascular problems, digestive issues, and recover from sickness much slower than those with a positive mindset.[4]

Words and emotions of fear and anxiety not only close the flow of life force, they create a magnetism that will inevitably draw negativity to us.

Perhaps I am not the only one who, as a child, feigned a fever when I didn't want to go to school, only to find that I actually had a fever! Here is a story about someone who did not want to go to court.

✺ FROM PANIC ATTACK TO HEART ATTACK ✺

On the day before the hearing, my client called to say that he was on the way to the hospital with chest pain and would be unable to appear in court. At the hospital, he was admitted with a heart attack.

I was representing the client at his arraignment on charges of drug possession, in the tribal court of a Native American reservation. Several days before the hearing, he had written to say that he did not want to appear, because he was afraid of going to jail. I did my best to reassure him that we would find a reasonable solution. But his anxiety only increased, and that evening he called and said that he was considering suicide as an alternative to jail. I tried to calm him, then I called social assistance.

Shortly thereafter, he had the heart attack.

In court the next day, I was able to negotiate a sentence without jail time. When he received the news, his condition rapidly improved and he was released from the hospital.

The situation turned out well for my client, and was deeply instructive. I realized how our fears over a perceived unwelcome future can lead to serious physical consequences. I also realized how anxious I habitually became before I had to appear in court, and how the anxiety caused me to be nauseous and short-tempered with my husband and children. It showed me how I had been sabotaging myself.

This was before I found my spiritual path and began to experience the miracles that meditation and inner stillness could bring into my life. That long-ago courtroom experience brought me a step closer to the path that would offer me tools to meet my life's lessons with grace and acceptance, and to control my thoughts and emotions so that they might bring only positive results. –**Ryanna**, *from a Native American Indian Reservation*

✺ ✺ ✺

Our mental diet exerts the greatest influence on our health. Yet we are so blindly unaware of these habitual subconscious thoughts that when they appear on the field of conscious awareness, we are reluctant to acknowledge them.

Discover your mental diet

In J.R.R. Tolkien's *The Lord of the Rings*, Gollum is a fearsome character when we first meet him. He lives in a deep cave, in darkness, and possesses a ring of great power. When Gollum is constrained to leave the cave to seek the lost ring, he is revealed in the light of day as no longer a fearsome monster but a pitiful, weak, conflicted, and ineffectual being.

Habits of negative thinking, feeling, and reacting will only continue to wreak havoc on our health for as long as they remain hidden in the dark recesses of the subconscious mind.

> To change one's life truly, one must dig down into his subconscious thought patterns, and redirect them.[5]

When we fail to recognize our subconscious thought patterns, they acquire a power that can become difficult to redirect. Our journey of self-healing now brings us to the need to unmask these pernicious thoughts and bring them into the light of our conscious awareness, where we can get a handle on them and change them.

SELF-EXAMINATION

Take some time to examine your subconscious thought habits. You will find an exercise called **"My Mental Diet Profile"** in the online Appendices for this chapter where you can download it to your computer. Responding to the questions will help you understand how your thoughts are influencing your health.

The following guidelines will help you complete the exercise.

My physical constitution

We all have our own unique ways of thinking about our bodies. These thoughts contribute to consolidating physical conditions of strength or weakness and good or poor health. Indicate on the worksheet the words that you believe define your physical condition.

My energy level

The energy that is available to us is not limited by our physical constitution. A short, thin body can be a vehicle for tremendous energy, as witnessed by many female Olympic gymnasts. Next to each of the points in this section, note whether you think of yourself as having low, medium, high, or exceptional energy.

My talents and capabilities

Each of us is born with tendencies that we have acquired over many lives, and that we may or may not have continued to develop in this life. We have also acquired new experiences and knowledge along the way. What are your innate and acquired talents? What are you able to do easily, and what are you unable to do that you would like to do?

My mental powers

In this section, jot down whether you think of yourself as having low, medium, high, or exceptional mental abilities. In Chapter Three we will discuss how to improve our mental powers.

My emotional nature

Our emotional experiences of the past are stored in the archives of the subconscious mind. When the circumstances are right, they emerge to silently influence our conscious awareness. We have mentioned the impact of these hidden memories on our physical and mental health. Whereas our emotional reactions differ depending on the situation, we yet have general emotional inclinations which can become our default reaction in a variety of circumstances.

See which words in this section describe your habitual conscious responses, and consider how these reactions impact the dynamic of situations.

My thoughts about others

How we think of and feel about others, even if we never express our thoughts, is bound to affect them, even as our thoughts about ourselves affect us.

When we put people in a box mentally, the energy of our thoughts and feelings is bound to affect them: "Why do they *always* behave like that?" or "They'll never be able to make this project work."

Our positive thoughts also affect others – "She has all the energy and talent she needs to make this project a roaring success!"

Of course, our habitual thoughts and feelings about others affect us as well. Kindness, consideration, compassion, and generosity make for good health, while negative, judgmental thoughts weaken our own energy field and health.

On the worksheet, note some of your thoughts about the people in your world.

The following story is from the life of Saint Thérèse of Lisieux.

❋ The Disgruntled Nun ❋

There was a warm, if impersonal camaraderie between the cloistered nuns. There were hardships they all faced – inner temptations, and harsh physical conditions.

One of the nuns was decidedly unsupportive and went out of her way to be unpleasant and hurtful in many petty ways. The sisters avoided her as much as possible.

But Sister Thérèse felt that it was uncharitable and unchristian to withhold her love from someone who was clearly suffering for having lost her vocation. Thus she looked for a way to reach out to her.

When she asked Jesus in prayer for his counsel, she heard his voice inside her: "Find something admirable about that sister."

For months she observed the nun quietly, but found nothing in her behavior that was worthy of admiration.

One day, as the sisters were returning to their duties after lunch, Thérèse noticed the nun leaving by the back door, carrying something in her apron. Outside, she dropped the bread crumbs she had swept from the table and called the birds to come for them.

At last! This disgruntled nun was kind to the birds, a small enough gesture but nonetheless worthy of admiration. Thérèse never mentioned the nun's act of kindness to the sister or the others. Yet whenever she saw her, she offered a silent prayer: "Lord Jesus, thank you for the example of my sister, she is kind to the birds."

In time, the nun's behavior began to change. She became more cooperative and supportive, more sincere in her devotions, and more ardent in her prayers. A single, persistent if unspoken prayer of admiration had softened her hardened heart.

When the formerly unpleasant nun left the world, she had become a model of kindness. Her passing was exalted, and the nuns all rejoiced.

> **How others see me**
>
> Even as our thoughts influence others, their thoughts will also impact us. Jot down some of your perceptions of how others see you, positively or negatively. Whether their perceptions are true or mistaken, they will affect us energetically. By becoming aware of negative thought forms that are projected toward us, we can find ways to protect ourselves, which we will discuss in detail in Volume Three.

✵ In the Presence of Mine Enemies ✵

The company needed to downsize, but instead of letting the senior staff go with severance benefits, they tried to force us to quit.

In my case, they almost succeeded.

I had always done good work that I was proud of. Now I found myself transferred to a new area where I had no experience. I was placed with a supervisor and colleagues who were hoping to see me walk out the door. The hostile environment and the negative thoughts about me were taking a toll. Day by day the atmosphere became heavier. I was filled with doubts and fears, seeing enemies everywhere, and my self-esteem and professional dignity were being eroded.

Needing to get some distance, I took my accumulated sick leave to pick up the spiritual weapons I had gathered since finding my destined path. As I prayed and meditated I began to see the situation as an opportunity to become stronger. I practiced the Energization Exercises more consciously and strongly. I spent more time in the cave of deep inner calmness in meditation. I practiced the self-healing affirmations, which had been only mentally interesting to me until now.

As I regained my courage, I willfully stopped thinking of myself as a helpless victim. I had tools and I knew how to use them. Once I was in a more positive frame of mind, I began looking for practical solutions, including a more harmonious and fulfilling job.

When I returned to work, I brought my weapons of inner calm and my shield of affirmation.

With a positive attitude, I tried to surround my colleagues with consideration and friendship, even though they were not friendly with me. The tension in the office began to relax, and in time I was even able to feel love for those who were hostile to me. My heart became lighter, and some of the "enemies" began to change their attitude. By the time I left for a more satisfying job, we were sincerely able to wish each other well. –**Paola**, *Varese, Italy*

Environmental influences

The subconscious is very impressionable. Like a sponge, it absorbs thought forms from the environment – even those not directed at us personally.

Even the temperature influences our behavior subconsciously. A study in *Lancet Planetary Health* reported that when the temperature rises or falls outside our comfort zone, the prevalence of hate speech on social media increases.[6]

One of Yogananda's most oft-quoted sayings is: **"Environment is stronger than willpower."**

> Environment and the company you keep are of paramount importance. Your outer environment, in conjunction with your inner environment, through your habits, controls your life and molds your tastes and habits...Through reaction to our outer environment, from early childhood on, our inner mental environment is formed. This inner mental environment of thought and mental habits almost automatically guides our actions.[7]

Life Force / **36**

Toxic mental and emotional environments are as detrimental to our health as exposure to the chemical toxins in our food, air, and water. Negativity in the media and the arts, and regular exposure to false or exaggerated news reportage and imagery, have been shown to increase anxiety, stress, and even the incidence of suicide.

> Consuming the news can activate the sympathetic nervous system, which causes your body to release stress hormones like cortisol and adrenaline. Then, when a crisis is happening, and we are experiencing this stress response more frequently… physical symptoms may arise. Some of the most common symptoms are fatigue, anxiety, depression, and trouble sleeping.
>
> This emotional toll and negative effect on the psyche were demonstrated in a study that found people who watched negative material, as compared to those who watched positive or neutral material, showed an increase in both anxious and sad moods after only 14 minutes of viewing television news bulletins and programs." [8]

Collective thoughts cause natural disasters

Yogananda made some startling statements in an article that he published in the September-October, 1926 issue of *East-West* magazine.

> Nature's calamities are occasioned by the sum total of the multitudinous wrong human thoughts. Every event in Nature is the outcome of the thoughts of creation. We are all indissolubly linked together and bound up in a common fate. Our thoughts help to bind or to liberate the world at large… We are not the creatures, but the creators, of this universe. Our thoughts and deeds have contributed throughout the ages to the making of tidal waves, of forest fires, of volcanic upheavals, no less than they have flowered forth in spiritual giants, in innocent children and in the soft petals of the flowers.

CHAPTER 2: *Points to Remember*

- Our mental diet consists of our recurring thoughts about ourselves, about others, and about our life.

- These habitual thought-forms determine the condition of our health.

- Each thought either strengthens or weakens the flow of life force.

- Even those thoughts that we do not transform into actions emit an energy field that affects ourselves and others.

- We are positively or negatively affected by the thought forms prevalent in our environment.

PART VI CHAPTER THREE

Superpowers of the Conscious Mind

The mind, which is the creator, designer, architect, and the supreme builder in the body, is the supreme power to effect healing.[1] –Yogananda

We should take care not to make the intellect our god; it has, of course, powerful muscles, but no personality. –Albert Einstein

Yogananda used to say, "The greater the will, the greater the flow of energy." We can apply this principle to the task of keeping the body in good health and healing our illnesses.[2] –Kriyananda

The life force in the body has the absolute power to construct or destroy the body. But the life force can only perform according to the will of the bodily owner. Most people don't know that their will can command the body to perform miraculous changes in it.[3] –Yogananda

✺ **Monkey business** ✺
By Swami Yogananda[4]

Tej Bahadur, a young business man in India, spent considerable amounts of his hard-earned money on business trips to London. He was obsessively frugal, but no matter how many times he cut down his overhead, he was never satisfied.

A friend who knew about his cost-saving endeavors came to him one day and excitedly said, "Come to the banks of the river Ganges. I have found a man who can levitate and walk on water, and who is willing to teach the method to a worthy student."

Tej Behadur was duly impressed. "I will ask him to teach me levitation, and travelling thus to London I will save a lot of money."

He immediately wended his way toward the river bank and requested the yogic master to teach him levitation, whereupon the latter agreed. "Son, every night dim the light in your bedroom, lock the doors, and sitting erect on a straight chair facing the East with closed eyes, mentally chant the holy word of the Cosmic Vibration, AUM for an hour. At the end of one month, you will be able to race over the waters."

As he was leaving, the master called him back. "I forgot to tell you something. While you are mentally chanting AUM and are concentrating, be sure not to think of a monkey."

"That is simple," said the business man. "Of course I won't think of a monkey," and after saluting the saint he returned home.

That evening Tej Bahadur followed the Master's instruction and sat to meditate. No sooner had he begun, however, than the thought struck him like a thunderbolt: "I must not think of a monkey."

After ten minutes he had thought of all the varieties of monkeys in South America, India, Africa, Sumatra, and countless other places. He willed himself to banish the thoughts of monkeys which, in a fast-moving procession, were leaping through the window of his helpless mind.

At the end of an hour, he found himself thinking of nothing but monkeys. With each succeeding day he found that he was frantically trying not to think of the millions of monkeys which were jumping into his mind.

Frustrated, he returned to the master and said, "Holy Sir, take back your lesson on levitation! You have taught me to meditate upon monkeys, instead of how to levitate."

> The saint laughed merrily and said, "Son, I tried only to show you how untrained and slavish your mental state of concentration is. Unless you learn to make your mind obey you, you cannot achieve success in any endeavor. First learn to attain mental control, then use that power to achieve small things, then try bigger and bigger achievements until your inner power becomes developed enough to levitate, or to accomplish even greater spiritual miracles."

Our most powerful tool for self-healing is the mind. While life force is the medium through which healing occurs, it is the mind that activates, or in the case of disease disactivates, that flow.

The conscious mind is the workshop where we plan our lives. **Concentration**, **willpower**, and **visualization** are the three superpowers of the conscious mind. Mental strength comes from the mind's ability to perceive clearly, to apply clear reason to its perceptions, and to organize and execute plans for obtaining its goals.

Concentration

Concentration plays an essential role in our physical and mental health and is a major component of the Law of Success.* It is the superpower behind every self-healing technique. When we do the Life Force Energization Exercises, our willpower opens doors for cosmic life force to flow into the body through the medulla oblongata – but it is the one-pointed, deeply concentrated mind that directs the healing power to the area in need. †

Concentration is a built-in faculty of the mind, but it needs to be awakened and exercised regularly. Yogananda offers a two-pronged approach to develop our powers of concentration:

---

* The need for concentration to achieve success and prosperity in all areas of life is discussed in Volume Three.

† For an explanation of the Life Force Energization Exercises, see page 275 in Volume One.

> Mental efficiency depends upon the art of concentration. Man must know the scientific method of concentration, by which he can disengage his attention from objects of distraction and focus it on one thing at a time. By the power of concentration, man can use the untold power of mind to accomplish that which he desires, and he can guard all doors through which failure may enter.[5]

The key concepts in Yogananda's definition are "distraction" and "attention." Our inability to concentrate is due to the mind's tendency to wander. The mind is curious – it loves to explore a variety of directions, sometimes all at once. But when we indulge this tendency, the mind's power becomes dispersed and ineffectual. The sun's rays can warm the soil, but when focused through a magnifying glass, they can light a fire.

Distractions come in a variety of guises. Spiritually, they are *maya*'s frontline soldiers, sent to weaken our minds by keeping them scattered in a variety of pursuits.

We would do well to see them for what they are, and not let them capture us: the beep that announces an email message, an invitation to go out for pizza, the urge to add the newest films on Netflix to your watch-later list, the temptation to address a problem with a project of lesser priority. Our daily lives are filled with such tempting distractions—we have become so thoroughly enamored of them that we think them benign, or inconsequential. But every time we allow ourselves to be tempted by the siren allure of distractions, our power of mental focus is diminished.

Acknowledge your regular distractions

As you engage in your daily activities and duties, what are the distractions that typically tempt you to scatter your focus? Jot down a short list of the recurring distractions in your life, and be on the lookout for them. Once they are identified, we can fire-up the mind's second superpower – willpower – to banish them from the circle of our attention.

The distraction fast and the concentration feast

- Turn off the phone.
- Turn off the news and social media by shutting down your internet browser.
- Clear the clutter from your desk and work space.

Ensure that you won't be disturbed. If the project will demand your focused attention for an extended period, compose a courteous autoresponder in your email app. Inform friends and co-workers that you'll be unavailable – put a note on your door, and post it to your social sites.

- Determine that you are going on a distraction "fast" for a fixed period, perhaps an hour.
- During this time, resist all mental distractions and the temptation to multi-task.
- When other projects arise, jot them down for consideration at the end of your distraction fast.
- Use your willpower to stay focused on the task at hand, without physical or mental tension.
- When you encounter a block, stand up, walk around, and do some deep breathing by an open window. Vigorously rap your head and forehead with your knuckles, then massage your scalp.
- Mentally affirm and visualize the task successfully completed, imagining your feeling of satisfaction.

The mind enjoys concentrating, in the same way that fit muscles enjoy exercise.

At the end of your distraction fast, it's a good idea to take a short break. If you've been sitting at a desk, stand up and move around. Go outside and do some of the exercises recommended in this book. Drink some water, then continue your concentration feast. You may want to review what you've accomplished so far, before moving forward.

One thing at a time

When we focus the laser beam of our attention on one thing at a time, it can penetrate to the heart of the challenge before us. Here are some helpful guidelines:

- Start the day by prioritizing your activities, then re-prioritize them as needed during the day.

- Have a clear, doable goal in mind for each of the day's activities.

- Break down the goals you won't be able to achieve in a single sitting into smaller, interim goals.

- Address no more than one task at a time, and determine to complete it or to reach a given milestone in a fixed time.

Be here now!

The unfocused mind likes to wander in memories of past events, or to race into the future, leaving the present moment unattended. When we are fully aware in the present moment, we become aware of a much broader range of options.

Whatever I do in life, I give it my full attention.
Like a laser beam, I burn from before me
all problems, all obstructions! [6]

The memory bridge

Memory retention is one of the positive side effects of concentration. Memories are stored in the subconscious mind, but they are placed there through conscious mind's ability to focus the laser beam of our full, one-pointed attention on the tasks at hand. They can then be retrieved at will.

> In order to write, think, and feel, one must be able to work in the precious material recalled to the conscious mind by the power of memory. Memory is that faculty of the conscious mind which, through the help of the subconscious mind, can reproduce any past conscious human experience. [7]

We can strengthen our concentration by making a special effort to remember people's names, faces, and details about them. When meeting someone for the first time, give them your full attention, even if the encounter lasts only a few seconds. Repeat their name at least three times in your conversation, and as you do so, associate the name with something or someone you know. Use these mental associations to reinforce the memory.

For example, if you meet someone whose name is Celestine, you could associate it with "celestial" and imagine a cloudless blue sky. The name David might elicit "He fought Goliath," and an image of the statue of David in Florence.

You can apply the same trick to remember important details about people, places, and facts. It only requires a few seconds of your full attention, plus a word association and an image.

A helpful and entertaining way to exercise your power of concentration and memory is to memorize the shopping list. A classic technique is to create a short story and see yourself acting in it. "When I go to the farm, I see them milking the cows (milk), then I walk over to the chicken coop (eggs) to see if they have enough to make egg salad sandwiches (bread) to go with a green salad (lettuce) and carrot juice (carrots)."

There are countless opportunities to strengthen our attention by exercising it. While listening to the speaker at a conference, or in a conversation, resist the temptation to think of your own thoughts and opinions and to prepare a response or question. Instead, apply one hundred percent of your attention to what is being said. You will be amazed to see how your comprehension, and your relationships, will improve.

The following is compiled from Yogananda's suggestions for developing a strong supportive memory.[8] Practicing some or all of the exercises will energize the mind, increase your intelligence and creativity, and keep the brain active, lucid, and engaged throughout your life. You might like to try some of them even now.

- Gently strike all over the skull and forehead with the knuckles of the fingers of both hands for two minutes, concentrating on each hit made by them. With eyes closed, imagine each blow to awaken the sleeping brain cells and stimulate the convolutions in the cerebrum.

- Every morning rub the whole scalp and roots of hair pressingly with the tips of all the fingers of both hands.

- Insert the fingers of both hands at the roots of your hair and graspingly pull them and relax—several times. Then comb your hair or scalp pressingly and gently with a fine comb.

- Massage the area of the medulla oblongata, a point in the brain connected with memory,[9] in the way taught by Yogananda, at night before retiring and again in the morning.*

- Deep attention is a strong force that develops memory. Pay strict attention to the thing that you want to remember.

- Perform every action, insignificant or important, with quick, alert attention. Attention is the needle that cuts the grooves in the record of memory cells.

* *"Bend head down, chin touching chest.* Touch the three middle finger tips of one hand with those of the other hand, then pressingly place these six fingers on the medulla. Give a circular massage from left to right, five times. Then keep[ing] the fingers well pressed on the medulla, bend head backward as far as possible toward the spine, *tensing the [back of neck]*. Relax. *Then quickly drop head toward the chest,* still keeping fingers in position. Exercise three times." –*Yogoda Course,* Lesson 2.

- You must link one idea with another. Connect certain things with certain other things. Everything has some point of contact with or similarity to everything else in the universe.

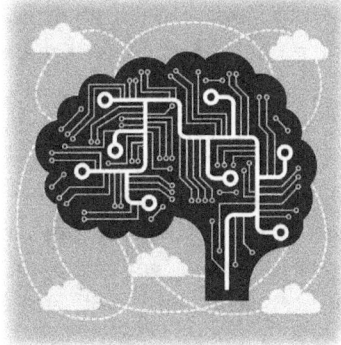

- Every night try to remember in detail all that happened during the past week. Do the same at the end of each month and year; try to remember in detail all the principal events of the month or year in connection with yourself, your city, your country, and the world.

- During the period preceding sleep at night and the state following sleep at dawn, command your subconscious mind to be attentive to all life's activities and to retain all valuable experiences.

- The art of visualization is very important in developing memory. A good practice is to look steadily at a certain object, or at some scenery, or in a store window, then turn away quickly and see how many of the details you can enumerate. The deeper your impressions, the more details you will be able to remember. This is a splendid practice for developing memory of important details.

- The greater the preservation of the vital essence in the body, by sex discipline and by normal use in married life, the greater will be the power of your memory, intelligence and spiritual perception.

- Every day try to memorize some poem and to reproduce it in writing after a week or fortnight, in your leisure moments.*

---

* Yogananda especially recommended memorizing and daily repeating aloud his poem "Samadhi," which you will find in the Appendices.

Mental relaxation

Long, uninterrupted periods of mental work that calls for deeply focused attention can lead to mental tension and strain that inhibits mental productivity and leads to diminishing returns.

It helps to take regular breaks to relax and refresh the mind. Three excellent ways to restore and relax the mind without becoming distracted are 1) the breathing exercises (pages 182-186 in Volume One) 2) rapping the head with knuckles (mentioned earlier); and 3) physical movement. The Superconscious Living Exercises (p. 231) also nourish and invigorate the mind.

Before starting an activity that calls for concentration, it's advisable to take a few moments to relax the mind and body, using the breath to center your energy and attention.

> "By proper breathing exercises and attaining breath calmness, one can attain great concentration." [10]

Once you are feeling calm, set a time limit for the activity, so as not to exhaust your mental powers.

*Practice meditation**

Many classic meditation practices involve focusing the mind on a single object such as the flame of a candle, a mandala or icon, or more inwardly, the movement of the breath. Daily practice for even as little as fifteen minutes is priceless training for the mind. When you meditate, resist the temptation to let the mind wander – bring it back patiently, calmly, impersonally, without judgment. To accomplish this, willpower must be brought to bear, as discussed in the next chapter.

---

* Suggested meditation practices are given in Part II, Volume One. You will also find recommendations for meditation courses in the Bibliography.

Points to Remember about concentration

- When you need to concentrate, start by removing distractions.
- Set a time frame during which you will refuse to be distracted.
- Keep your brain energized by periodically rapping your head and forehead vigorously, then massage your scalp.
- Prioritize the day's activities, then focus on doing one thing at a time.
- Improve your memory by giving your full attention to the present moment.
- Meditation practice improves the mind's ability to concentrate.

PART VI   CHAPTER FOUR

Willpower

> The power of a strong will,
> guided by divine wisdom, is unlimited.
> To its possessor nothing is impossible.[1]
> —YOGANANDA

An essential ingredient for health, happiness and prosperity, will-power is one of the superpowers of the mind, in many ways its most important.

> The factor of will is paramount in life.
> Without it evolution is impossible.
> It is the dynamo of existence.
> Will rules supreme in every sphere.
> Will is the initiator. Will is the executor.
> Will is the genius-maker.
> It creates things that are worth-while.
> Intellect is its servant.
> Man cannot think without willing to think;
> far less can he act without willing to act.
> Will may be blind without intellect,
> but intellect is powerless and
> worthless without will.
> Will is the chief condition of growth.[2]

In Parts III and IV we discussed willpower in relation to the Life Force Energization Exercises. Willpower is such an important instrument for self-healing that it bears mentioning again.

Willpower defined

Yogananda defines willpower as **"desire plus energy, directed toward fulfillment."**

There is a considerable stretch of road between a "wish" and a firm intention. Wishes are vague, wispy, elusive. We wish many things: to be strong, clever, kind, healthy, and to overcome our bad habits and character flaws. We can wish away a lifetime without changing ourselves, unless we can form a firm, determined desire to change and summon a willingness to undertake the required actions.

Before we can infuse our desires with power, we need to gain clarity about our goals. Clearly visualizing a goal will give direction to all our efforts and open a clear path from desire to fulfillment.

By repeatedly applying the power of our thoughts and dedicating ourselves to completing the necessary actions to achieve our desired goal, we generate a palpable magnetic power. As we repeat and refine our efforts, the magnetic field grows, drawing to us everything we need to reach our shining goal.

This is the power of will. It is the difference between "I wish" and "I *will*."

Take a few minutes to gain clarity about your current goals for improving your health.

- What do you desire to accomplish within a month? Choose one priority.

- Write it down, close your eyes, and visualize yourself having achieved that goal. How does that feel?

- What do you desire to accomplish within a year? Choose three priorities.

- Write them down in order of priority, and do the same visualization exercise for each of them, trying to imagine the feeling of their accomplishment.

- As you visualize, mentally repeat this affirmation: "What I do today will create a new and better future, filled with inner joy." [3]

*Willpower and the spiritual eye**

Willpower is a "spiritual muscle." Located in the astral body at the sixth chakra, it corresponds to the point between the eyebrows, the frontal lobes in the physical body.

> The point midway between the eyebrows
> is described as the seat of the intellect,
> of willpower, and—in superconsciousness—
> of ecstasy and spiritual vision.[4]

Yogananda refers to this point as the "spiritual eye, the "eye of intuition," the "eye of wisdom," and the "Christ eye." Stimulating this center increasing the power of our will, enabling us to turn our wishes into accomplishments. Yogananda teaches that keeping our concentrated attention at the spiritual eye in meditation and during our daily activities is the fast track to spiritual progress and success.

> "If you want to make very rapid progress on
> the spiritual path," [Yogananda] used to tell us,
> "keep your mind always centered there."[5]

> The more you concentrate at the Christ center,
> the more rapid will be your spiritual progress.[6]

> If one constantly keeps his mind concentrated
> on the point between the eyebrows (at the
> Christ Center) and sees there the Spiritual Eye
> and commands it to recharge the body
> with strength, it will do so. By doing this,
> people would cease growing old.[7]

Keeping our attention at the spiritual eye during all our daily activities requires a serious commitment, and lots of practice.

* You will find more about the spiritual eye in Part II, Volume One.

> **TRY THIS**
>
> ### Eyewitness
>
> - For five minutes immediately after your morning meditation, keep your attention at the spiritual eye. During that time, imagine that each thought, each conversation, each sensation (tasting food, speaking, listening, moving about) is proceeding from the spiritual eye.
> - Do the same for the first five minutes of your work day—think, listen, speak, feel from the spiritual eye.
> - Another opportunity to stimulate this center is when you are doing the Life Force Energization Exercises, and when you are doing any physical exercise.

In time, this way of perceiving life will transform your every experience.

What weakens our willpower?

In Part III we discussed the attitudes that prevent us from developing the full potential of our will. Because will-weakening attitudes are omens of illness, let's look at them again.

Passivity and procrastination. When we fail to engage our full attention and energy, or when we procrastinate, the strength of our will wanes and begins to atrophy, consequently weakening our resistance to disease.

In my association with Swami Kriyananda, I saw that whenever there was something that needed doing, he attended to it immediately. He asked the same of us, and over the years I was largely able to overcome my former habit of putting things off, and to experience a much more dynamic level of energy and wellbeing. I keep the title of one of his many books stored in my mind as a personal prod to action: *Do It NOW!**

I make a practice of immediately attending to the next task, such as washing the dishes after dinner. If I'm engaged in doing important tasks and I can't immediately attend to other requests that come

---

* Kriyananda later revised this book and re-issued it with the title *Living Wisely, Living Well.*

knocking, I will take a moment to schedule a time to do them. Unattended tasks can trap considerable amounts of our energy; they are like a weight on our shoulders that makes moving ahead much harder.

Doubt is another willpower thief. Once we have set a course of action to improve ourselves, the rational mind will raise all manner of reasonable doubts and hesitations as to its advisability. Our forward progress may be slowed and even derailed. Many people never succeed because their willpower and enthusiasm are stolen by doubt.

✻ STUCK IN THE MUD ✻

It was a tense moment for the foreign visitors in Pakistan – another skirmish with India, with planes flying overhead and bombs dropping. Hurriedly they herded into a bus under the cover of night.

With its headlights turned off, the bus plodded over the back roads through the moonless night. While crossing a shallow stream, the bus became stuck. "Everyone get out and push!" the driver shouted. The bus emptied instantly as the passengers put their shoulders to the task.

But the bus didn't budge. An acquaintance of mine rose from his labors for a moment to gather his breath and observe the scene, whereupon he began laughing heartily. The bus had both forward and posterior doors, and passengers had existed through each, half of them pushing from the front while the others were pushing from the rear.

Alerted by my friend to their folly, they united their efforts and were quickly back on the road to safety.

I've always delighted in the story's symbolism. When we are trying to push ahead, our doubts push us back, rendering us immobile.

When doubts try to block your progress, firmly tell them to stand aside – you'll deal with them once you are riding a powerful current of willpower and energy toward success. By then, their false reasonings will be exposed for what they are.

Overeating. When we give the body too much food, a great deal of our energy is diverted to digestion that would otherwise be available for accomplishment.

Creative work is nearly impossible after a big feast. Until the body recovers from its digestive labors, we must set our creative resolutions aside. Yogananda recommended eating smaller, more frequent meals instead of large meals two or three times a day.

Bad habits. An astonishing amount of willpower gets trapped by bad habits. In time, unhelpful habits can paralyze the will and alter the body's chemistry, making us vulnerable to physical disease and depression. The best time to stop a habit is at the start, before it can spiral into a full-blown addiction. Once clear of a habit, we find its energy available for achieving our worthy goals.*

How to strengthen the power of will

A strong will is our best ally for health and self-healing. It is the miracle-working superpower of the mind.

> Strengthen your will and determination in everything. Your body will then be internally vibrating with life current. A man of strong will, by his highly vibrating mind, can shake out disease, failure, and ignorance, but the will vibration must be stronger than the vibration of physical or inner disease. The more chronic the disease is, the stronger, steadier, and more unflinching should be the determination, faith, and effort of the will to get well.[8]

A weak muscle gets stronger when we use it. So, too, we can strengthen our mental willpower muscle by using it every day.

We can do nothing without willpower. The problem is that we perform most activities with mechanical will. In an earlier chapter, we learned that exposing the body to sunlight charges it with healing life force – and that the effects are greatly amplified when we draw

---

* We will consider how to master our habits in Part VII.

the sun's rays into our bodies with conscious will, instead of baking passively on the beach. To get the most out of our willpower, we need to engage it with deliberate, focused attention.

Yogananda recommended that we practice the following actions and attitudes. He taught that cultivating any of them (or a combination) will transform our willpower into a superpower.

Practice willingness. Change is never easy. The ego finds security in keeping things as they are.

The willingness to step up to a challenge or to alter a course of action or opinion is mightily opposed by the force of routine and the ego's natural inclination to laziness.

> Habitual unwillingness is a common human condition, suggesting to the mind endless mountain ranges of problems in the discharge of the simplest duty. For just as willingness draws a constantly fresh supply of energy to the body, so also does unwillingness block that supply. "The greater the will, the greater the flow of energy." The corollary of that axiom is, "The greater the unwillingness, the feebler the flow of energy." [9]

Years ago, I decided to stop resisting any activity that I was called upon to do. It was a turning point – since I decided to be one-hundred-percent willing to say "Yes!" to life, I have experienced good health and unprecedented levels of creativity and joy. When we stop blocking the flow of life force with unwillingness, we discover that it has no bounds.

> Willingness must be cultivated deliberately. It is an attitude of mind, and depends not on outward conditions. Most people are willing or unwilling depending on their likes and dislikes. This habit tends to develop a bias toward

unwillingness, which gradually becomes chronic, and attracts to itself chronic failure. Don't wait for favorable circumstances to awaken willingness in you. Train yourself in the attitude of saying yes to life! Often by this simple attitude you will find Success arriving, unexpected, at your door!" [10]

Yes, we can!

The next time the unwillingness monster raises its head, affirm out loud and with conviction: "We can and will do this." The "we" in this case refers to your own willpower combined with the readily cooperative divine will.

Do something new, something creative.[11] It takes very little willpower to keep following the path that we've always walked, or that others have walked before us. But unthinking, automatic routines blunt our willpower.

It's one of the dangers of habits. While good habits can free our energy and attention, they can also become a comfortable substitute for the dynamic creativity that expands our awareness and happiness. If we don't yet have the courage or willpower to break out of our deep-seated routines, we can still apply our willpower to do new things on a scale that we can manage.

Our creative breakthroughs don't have to be earthshaking, or upend our life. It could be doing something simple to help others, or exploring an art form that has long called to you.

Although "creativity" generally evokes images of artists at work, it is simply the act of creating, or thinking something new. We can be creative in our decision-making – discovering out-of-the-box solutions that open fresh possibilities. We can bring creativity to bear in our relationships as well (as we will consider in Part X).

We can be endlessly creative at home – cooking, hosting, decorating, flower arranging. At work, we can activate our creativity to find the right words to transform a deadly dull financial report into an enjoyable, enlightening document. We can bring creativity to writing a letter. Creativity is the habit of bringing refreshingly original responses to every challenge. It is an opportunity to use the muscle of our will to tap into the power that creates and sustains the universe.

The point is to bring a sense of adventure even to our daily activities.

Affirm each morning

Today I will try to do little things in an extraordinary way.

I will try to do something useful which no one else has done; something that will show that God's creative principle works in me.

I will strive to manifest the almighty power that is within me, so that on the stage of life I can fulfill my destiny.

Today I will plow the garden of life with my new creative efforts.[12]

Keep a journal

Yogananda recommended writing a journal as a good way to use creative willpower to gain insights about our life. Keeping daily journal entries and reviewing them over time is a wonderful aid for increasing our self-awareness, and for evaluating the attitudes and actions that have brought us greater health, happiness, and success.

- Before retiring for the night, review the highlights of that day, those moments that spontaneously come to mind. Reflect on how they fit into the context of your life's journey.

- Keep a journal page for each day, and write your thoughts about these or other reflections:
    - What did you learn about yourself or about others?
    - What were the day's questions and answers?
    - What were the changes in direction?
    - What decisions did you make?

Do something that challenges you. In youth, we enjoy testing our abilities, and society's boundaries. As the years pass and we settle into comfortable routines, we are more inclined to shy from exploring our abilities and expanding them.

> Very easily... people fall into the habit of thinking they know already how things ought or ought not to be. They identify happiness with fixity instead of accepting life's natural flow. They become in time what I call "psychological antiques"—wanting nothing moved, nothing changed, nothing even improved.[13]

Setting and overcoming challenges engages and strengthens our will.

Challenge yourself

To create dynamic willpower, determine to do some of the things in life that you thought you could not do.

Attempt simple tasks first.

Then, as your confidence strengthens and your will becomes more dynamic, you can undertake more difficult accomplishments.

Be sure that you have made a good selection, then refuse to submit to failure.[14]

❈ The Spontaneity Challenge ❈

My work as a teacher of spiritual practices challenges me daily – it is such a fact of my life that if there is a day without a challenge, I invent one.

When I lead classes in the Ananda Yoga postures, I challenge myself to let go of any egoic desire to control the session, and I use my willpower instead to open doors of inspiration.

As the session progresses, I allow the sequence to develop as it will. I trust the process, as I have seen that the right postures for a particular group will reveal themselves spontaneously, along with the right inspiration for the rhythm of the practice and the intonation of my voice.

I use this creative approach whenever I lead classes in any subject, and when I write emails or talk with people. I find that when I can give myself to the flow of creative inspiration, I can be a better channel of inspiration for others.

Along the way, my will and willingness are strengthened as I experience the joy of connecting to a much greater source of creativity. –**Ahimsa**, *Ananda Assisi*

Keep good company. We are not always aware of how profoundly we are influenced by our environment, and especially by the company we keep. Cultivating the company of strong people will inevitably strengthen our own willpower and motivation.

> "The company you keep cannot but influence you, especially if you keep that company by choice."[15]
>
> "Environment," Paramhansa Yogananda used to say, "is stronger than willpower." By environment he meant, above all, good company. This truth applies universally, at least up to the time when one has developed the inner strength to remain untouched by all outer circumstances.[16]

> Always remember that good company is a stronger influence than your willpower.[17]

✺ Resurrected ✺

My business was on a downward spiral, my health was alarmingly precarious, and my spiritual life was hanging by a thread. I had trouble breathing, trouble sleeping, and I had no idea if or how I could get through this nightmare of a so-called life.

At the urging of close friends, I took a two-month retreat at the Ananda Europa center near Assisi, Italy. Wanting to divert my mind from my problems, I asked to serve in the kitchen, even though I had never entered a kitchen in my sixty years. At home, my wife and our cook took care of the meals.

On my first day I was given a box of carrots to peel. I had no clue where to start. Without making me feel like an idiot, the kitchen staff took me under their wings, helping me lovingly and lightheartedly.

We chanted, we chatted, and we shared our life experiences. The cooks were always smiling, even when under heavy pressure to get out a hundred meals three times a day. Those of us in the service program quickly got into the spirit of doing things with joy. Day by day in their company I felt my burdens lightening and my veggie-cutting skills improving. I felt protected in a bubble of divine friendship.

I began going to the morning meditations every day, sitting from 7 to 8.30. It was a marathon at first – my knees hurt, my back was sore, and my shoulders were frozen. But I kept sitting day after day, opening my eyes from time to time and drawing inspiration from my spiritual brothers and sisters who were able to sit straight for hours without moving.

A day finally arrived when the pain ebbed and time flew – ninety minutes seeming like a half-hour. I was enjoying meditation, and day by day my identification with my problems melted away.

When my retreat stay ended, I was changed. Light had come back to my eyes, joy to my heart, and health to my body. Being with these kind, loving souls had saved my life.
–**Rohit**, *New Delhi*

Who inspires you?

Make a mental list of three people who inspire you, and find ways to spend time with at least one of them, in person or virtually, every single day.

Overcome a bad habit and replace it with a healthy one. One of the best ways to develop willpower is to set yourself a goal of eliminating a health-robbing habit and establishing a good one in its place. You will find an effective method for accomplishing this in Part VII.

Life Force Energization Exercises. We met these powerful exercises in Part IV of Volume One. They are one of the very best tools for reinforcing your willpower daily.

> "Yogoda" System teaches the science ignored by most exercises. It teaches its students the maximum use of conscious Will and Life Energy, in exercising and vitalizing not only muscles but all tissues and cells of the body. It teaches its students to concentrate on their Life Energy and Will, awakening the consciousness of their subtle spiritual nature. It teaches its students that strength comes from within and not from the muscles, and that life does not solely depend on food and exercise but is sustained from within.[18]

You can learn the exercises with the help of a video series that you can watch and download in the Appendices.

SWAMI KRIYANANDA'S SUGGESTIONS FOR DEVELOPING WILLPOWER [19]

Never allow yourself to dwell on the no-saying principle. Learn always to say Yes to life!

Look always for solutions, instead of concentrating too much on your problems.

Look for goodness in people; don't concentrate on their faults.

Train yourself to face life's challenges vigorously, always affirming, "I can!"—even when your mental habits cry out in protest, "Don't be ridiculous: How can you possibly?"

Set yourself specific tasks to accomplish— small ones at first, then increasingly challenging ones. Be sure to see each one through to completion.

Here is a technique that can help you to develop all-conquering willpower.

- Concentrate at the point between the eyebrows.

- Around that point revolve your intention with increasing willpower.

- Affirm, with ever-greater conviction and magnetism, "My will is one with Thy will. United to Thine, my will can move mountains!"

Points to Remember about willpower

- **Willpower = desire + energy → fulfillment.**
- Willpower activates a flow of healing life force. The greater the will, the greater the flow of life force.
- The major enemies that weaken our will are passivity, procrastination, doubts, and bad habits.
- It is of utmost importance that our thoughts and our mental self-image remain positive regardless of our outward circumstances.
- Strengthen your willpower by acting willingly, accepting challenges, and doing something creative every day.
- Willpower is greatly strengthened by developing positive habits.
- The Life Force Energization Exercises are the most efficient way to develop strong willpower.

PART VI CHAPTER FIVE

Visualization

> A well developed...imagination is the spring from which flows the creativity of genius.[1]
> —KRIYANANDA

One of the conscious mind's most effective healing instruments is the power of visualization, also referred to as "imagination." These words are often used interchangeably. Is there a difference between them?

The dictionary defines imagination as the power of forming a mental image of something not present to the senses or never before wholly perceived in reality. The art of visualization uses mental images to stimulate and support the process of turning our ideas into reality. A composer might *imagine* a sequence of notes, and, using them, mentally create a composition. A film director might *envision* a character, endow him with a personality, hear the timbre and cadence of his voice, and use that visualization when casting for the part. Pratically, imagination and visualization go hand in hand.

When we recall events from the past, we retrieve mental images from the subconscious where our memories are stored. Our subconscious memories powerfully influence our lives – haunting us with negative images, or influencing us positively with images of happy times and past victories. Subconscious images influence our decision-making, our relationships, our work – and most definitely, our health.

The subconscious holds our self-images. We see ourselves as young or elderly, dynamic or passive, healthy or ill. Even if the body is ill and weak, it is extremely important that we maintain self-images that reflect our essential nature: filled with vitality, dynamically engaged, hopeful and happy. Holding and affirming these positive self-images opens channels for the healing life force to enter, and attracts opportunities that enable us to fulfill our higher reality.

Elite

Successful athletes practice visualization as a standard element of their training. Superstar gymnast Simone Biles says: "Visualization is a crucial part of my training. I visualize my routines and see myself executing them flawlessly." [2]

> "There is one thing that separates elite athletes from average athletes: Elite athletes utilize the power of **guided imagery or visualization**.... **Visualization in sports** or mental imagery is a way of conditioning for your brain for successful outcomes....[it] actually stimulates the same brain regions as you do when you physically perform that same action.
>
> Competitive swimmer Michael Phelps, the most decorated Olympian of all time, has used visualization techniques as an integral part of his training since he was a teenager. His coach instructed Michael to watch a "mental videotape" of his races every day before he went to sleep and when he woke up in the morning. He would visualize every aspect of swimming a successful race, starting from the blocks and culminating in a celebration after the race was won." [3]

※ Under Par ※

He couldn't be certain any more how long he had been there. In the beginning he had counted the passing days, the weeks, the months. It was years now John had been in the prison cell in Vietnam, a space not even long enough to accommodate his tall body.

Completely isolated, John was alone day and night with only his thoughts for company. To keep himself sane, he imagined the tropical jungle outside the prison – the lush growth, the delicious fruits, the extravagantly colorful birds.

John also passed the time by using his imagination to improve his golf game. Every day, in his mind he played eighteen holes, seeing every stroke perfectly timed and the ball soaring over the fairway past sand and water traps, landing on the green and rolling neatly into the cup. He experimented with different clubs, and when he was released at last, his mental handicap had fallen to an even par.

Soon after returning home, John visited the golf course, hoping to see a familiar face, but found only one person there, a stranger, and after introductions and some small conversation they went out to play a round.

When the stranger asked, "Have you played much golf?" John replied, "Not for some years. I'm afraid I won't give you much competition."

On the first hole, John slammed a 250-yard shot down the center of the fairway. His second stroke brought him close to the green. The third put the ball within a few feet of the cup, and a fourth tap put the ball in the hole for par.

His partner was duly impressed. John put it down to luck, but as he strung together hole after hole of pars or birdies, his companion became irritated, then angry, accusing John of taking him for a ride. Obviously, John was a professional.

When John told him the story of how he had spent his prison years visualizing game after perfect game, the partner was amazed and began cheering him on. When they completed the eighteenth hole, John had shot three under par for the first time in his life. His new friend bought drinks for everyone at the Nineteenth Hole Bar, and they reverently toasted John's heroic service, his stoic survival and his remarkable golf prowess.

The mental images we carry of ourselves and our health exert a profound influence on our wellbeing. In the 13th century, Tibetan monks used visual imagery to cure disease. In the 1970s, oncologist Oscar Carl Simonton, MD [4] and his wife Stephanie Matthews-Simonton developed an innovative form of counseling for cancer patients that used "guided imagery," in addition to other holistic approaches. The patients were guided to visualize, and also draw, their body cells fighting off the cancer. As the therapy progressed, the drawings showed the good cells winning the battle. Their pioneering clinics in Texas and California have had remarkable success, and guided visualization has become a feature of mainstream oncology and pain management.

Visualization can greatly magnify the effects of the healing practices in this book. By cutting positive grooves in the subconscious, visualization becomes a valuable ally in our quest for health.

Visualization powerfully magnifies the healing effects of the Life Force Energization Exercises and the Full Body Recharge – when, for example, we visualize the doorway of the medulla oblongata opening wide and the currents of prana energy streaming into each muscle group.

Affirmations are also greatly enhanced when we hold mental images of ourselves as powerful and healthy while we repeat them with focused attention and willpower: "I am strong! I am well!"*

The same is true also for forming healthy habits. Like athletes who routinely use visualization, we can hasten the victory by holding images of ourselves already in possession of new, healthier habits, and feeling the satisfaction and wellbeing that accompany the new behavior.†

Visualization is useful as well in meditation. When you sit to meditate, see yourself calm and joyful from the start.

> Visualize your consciousness expanding like a blue light, encompassing all space. Imagine the stars and galaxies shining like the lights of a distant city within the infinitude of your being. Meditate on your vastness within. You will find in this visualization an important adjunct to the meditation techniques. It will help to remind you of your inner, divine nature.[5]

While you work toward success, see yourself already successful and prosperous.

> It is best to feel by visualization and by Divine contact in meditation that you are already perfect in health and wisdom and have abundance.[6]

---

* For instruction in the practice of affirmation, see Part VIII.
† Habits are discussed in Part VII.

❋ Yoga in the Kitchen ❋

I wasn't actually unhappy in my work, but in my heart I knew that something more fulfilling awaited me. When I joined a course in yoga for children, I strongly felt that it was my destiny. Even when the people in my environment were decidedly not encouraging, I felt a powerful inner determination that neutralized their negativity.

I began to visualize how I could incorporate a yoga space in my small house. One of the two rooms was a spacious kitchen, and in my mind I created an attractive partition in front of the appliances. In the remaining space, I saw myself doing yoga with my son and his friends.

So clear in my mind was the partition that within a month I had drawn a design, and we created it in a single evening. It showed a flower-filled meadow with a big sun and a colorful Ganesha – the Indian god of good fortune.

On Saturday mornings, the kitchen became a yoga studio for my son and a growing number of his friends. The few friends soon became many, and it was apparent that we needed a house that would accommodate a larger yoga space.

My thoughts had to get bigger. I began to envision a home with a big, bright room filled with young children and teens.

The first houses we looked at weren't suitable, but I continued, undiscouraged, to visualize an ideal house, where I already saw the children playing.

One day, my aunt called out of the blue and told me about a friend who was putting her house up for sale.

The first thing we saw outside the house was a large statue of Ganesha! And on the wall inside there was a small painting of St. Francis. A little farther down the corridor there was a double door that opened onto a large and very bright room.

My heart was pounding as I understood that my thoughts had given birth to this creation. We bought the house, and in that bright room we practice yoga and sing, dance, and enjoy the gift of life.

So much joy, that it had to expand! Some years later, together with a fellow yoga teacher who is a dear friend, we created an association, and in a short time we had found an even larger space where we are able to share with more and more people.

I now know from my own experience that our thoughts create our reality, and that the desire of the heart sets in motion a will that directs subtle energies toward their materialization. The direction of our thoughts and energy is our choice. If the direction is right for us, we are aided and accompanied by a universal force, and events unfold as they should. The power of thoughts and of faith knows no bounds – so let's think big! –**Stefania**, *Sardinia*

Develop your visualization superpower

We all have the ability to visualize. Those who find it easy will have developed it in the past and are merely continuing to practice it in the present. If you have difficulty visualizing, be assured that just as we can develop our physical muscles and the mental muscle of our willpower, we can also grow our ability to visualize.

Visualization doesn't only mean seeing images in your mind. Some people are more prone by nature to visualize a feeling.

For instance, when you try to visualize water, you may see mental images of a lake, ocean, river, waterfall, or refreshing rain. Or you might imagine the touch of water on your skin, hear the sound of waves crashing on a rocky shore, or feel yourself floating weightlessly on gentle waves. Usually, a combination of sensations will make your visualization more effective.

Affirmation

"Today I will develop the power of visualization and the power of hearing. I will concentrate upon one good thing strongly. I know that if I concentrate for long on a certain image, the life force becomes concentrated in the spiritual eye, reproducing an astral motion picture of that image."[7]

Your virtual reality

Mentally create a tree of a type that you are familiar with – a fruit tree will be best for this exercise.

- Close your eyes, relax, and focus your attention gently upward at the point between the eyebrows, the spiritual eye.
- Call to mind a specific tree. Say its name several times aloud.
- In your mind, see the leafless tree in winter. Take time to see it clearly – its branches, its shape, its height, and its surroundings. Feel the cold of winter on your skin. Smell the damp earth and the decaying leaves.
- Now see spring arrive, spreading a carpet of tiny green shoots in the soil, and yellow spring wildflowers. See buds emerging from the tree's smallest branches. Hear the insects, the buzzing of bees. Smell the emerging grass and flowers.

- See the buds opening into leaves, multiplying until the branches are filled and the tree is in its full green spring glory.
- See birds alighting on the branches, and hear them sing.
- See small green fruit beginning to form.
- See the tree loaded with mature fruit, branches bending with their weight.
- See yourself walking to the tree and picking a fruit, smelling it, taking a first bite, and eating it.
- Imagine the taste. feel the texture, and smell the delicious aroma.
- Image your satisfaction as you enjoy the sweetness of the fruit.

When reading, follow the story line with a mental movie. If there are fictional characters, mentally create an image for each of them. As they reappear in the story, make their images more detailed: height, clothes, tone of voice, and so on. As the tale unfolds, mentally watch the characters interact, and notice how their behavior changes as the story progresses. Mentally create a scene for each event in the story.

When listening to a speaker, or a podcast or other event, follow it with a simple mental movie, placing yourself in the movie and imagining how what is being said affects you.

When planning a trip, mentally see yourself buying a ticket, packing specific items in your suitcases, arriving at the airport or station, or getting in your car. See yourself arriving at your destination, and imagine how you feel as you begin your adventure. You might visualize yourself and others engaged in the activities you hope to do there.

When developing a project, try to visualize its completion at the outset, including how it will look and feel when completed, and how *you* will feel when the work is done.

As a way to enter meditation

> Try visualizing your body as a rock, so firm that you can't move it, so heavy that no one else could move it.
>
> Sit perfectly still with a straight spine. After a few minutes you will lose the desire to fidget.
>
> Then visualize your mind, too, as a rock, so immovably fixed that no thought, no emotion can sway it.[8]

When developing your memory

> The art of visualization is very important in developing memory.
>
> A good method of practice is to look steadily at a certain object, or at some scenery, or in a store window, then turn away quickly and see how many of the details you can enumerate.
>
> The deeper your impressions, the more details you will be able to remember.
>
> This is splendid practice for developing memory of important details.[9]

Use visualization in your work. When writing or speaking, use words that evoke images and feelings to paint pictures that will make your presentation more engaging and more effective. If you include stories, examples, anecdotes, metaphors or similar narrative devices in a presentation, choose words that encourage both images and feelings, painting a mental picture that your listeners can easily follow. Therapists, coaches and healers can use guided visualization to enhance the effectiveness of the therapies.

Guided visualizations with Swami Kriyananda*

In *Education for Life,* Kriyananda offers visualizations to nurture children's imagination and their ability to explore rich mental worlds.

> The imagination should be trained also. A well developed and healthy imagination is the spring from which flows the creativity of genius. Visualizations can be offered to children as a means of stimulating their imagination.

---

* In *Meditation for Starters,* Kriyananda offers ten visualizations that can help us make the transition from mental restlessness and worries to states of inner calm. An audio recording is included with the book. Kriyananda made a recording called "Meditations to Awaken Superconsciousness" to stimulate our ability to visualize and lead us into a calm meditative state. www.crystalclarity.com.

For instance, tell them: "Imagine yourself living in a forest. What is the forest like? Are you afraid, or are you happy there? Build yourself a home in the forest. What kind of a home would you like to build? Is it in a clearing, or in the deep woods?

"Think of the forest animals. Are they your friends? Or are you afraid of any of them? If so, why?

"See yourself walking along a forest path. Whom do you meet there? Is it an animal, or a human being? If it's a human being, does that person smile when he or she sees you? Have you done something to make him or her smile? If not, is there something you can do to make this friend smile?

"Imagine a pond in the forest. In the middle of this pond, there is a small island, and on the island a cup rests on a marble pedestal. What does the cup look like? Describe it. Does it contain something good to drink? What is that drink?

"Think of the cup as containing a wonderful, clear amber liquid, bubbling with energy and happiness. Drink it. Suddenly: Look! Everything in the forest is becoming cheerful, peaceful, and beautiful—full of sunshine and hope.

"Call to your friends, whoever they may be: children, grown-ups, or animals. Ask them to come and enjoy this magical drink with you. Now, walk with them through the magical forest.[10]

Visualizations are wonderful ways to let your imagination take you to new places, to show you new dimensions – even to transform your consciousness. Here are two more that you might enjoy.

Life Force / **76**

Balloon of Light

Meditate with closed eyes. Mentally say: "I dissolve my body in darkness." Watch the limitless dark space of Eternity spread above, beneath, in front, behind, ahead, within and without – everywhere. Then, all at once, visualize a sealed rainbow balloon of light surrounding your body. Remember this rubber balloon of light can never burst, no matter how you blow your luminous breath into it. Throw the breath out very slowly and visualize this balloon of light as expanding with your luminous breath until it becomes big enough to contain the star clusters, universes and planetary and solar systems, including your earth and body, and everything.[11]

Tunnel of Golden Light

Concentrate at the point between the eyebrows. Visualize there a tunnel of golden light. Mentally enter that tunnel, and feel yourself surrounded by a glorious sense of happiness and freedom. As you move through the tunnel, feel yourself bathed by the light until all worldly thoughts disappear.

After soaring through the tunnel as long as you feel to so do, visualize before you a curtain of deep violet-blue light. Pass through that curtain into another tunnel of deep, violet-blue light. Feel the light surrounding you. Slowly, the tunnel walls disappear in blue light. Expand your consciousness into that light—into infinite freedom and bliss. Now there is no tunnel. There is only the all-encompassing blueness and bliss of infinity.

At last, visualize before you a silvery-white, five-pointed star of light. Mentally spread out your arms and legs, assuming with your body the shape of that star. Give yourself to it in body, mind, and soul as you surrender every thought, every feeling to absolute, Self-existing Bliss.

Bliss cascades gently over you, like a waterfall of mist, filling your heart with ineffable peace.[12]

Points to Remember about visualizaion

- Visualization is a superpower of the mind. It is an important secret of success.

- Visualization is creating images that will help us reach the goal we visualize.

- Visualization stimulates the same brain areas and muscles that are activated when we perform an action.

- Visualization can include all of the senses to give us a richer experience than if we imagine visual images alone.

- Visualization combined with self-healing techniques enhances their effectiveness by creating deeper memory grooves in the brain.

Thoughts that are energized with deep attention, feeling, and strong visual imagery are embedded in the subconscious, where they form habit patterns. We will now look at the ways the subconscious can support or harm our health.

PART VI CHAPTER SIX

The Subterranean Subconscious

Consciousness, subconsciousness, and superconsciousness... can never be entirely independent of one another, although one state is usually stronger than the others... The subconscious mind is always awake; it works through memory while consciousness predominates.[1]

The conscious mind works with the sense of sight, hearing, smell, taste, and touch during wakefulness, but sleeps at night. The subconscious mind works through memory during wakefulness and through dreams at night. It is awake during the day, working in the conscious mind making records for it, and it is also awake during sleep at night looking after the functions of the heart, lungs, and so forth, of the human engine.[2]

The subconscious mind is the memory mind.... It keeps experiences locked up, ready to be used again upon instant notice. Experiences from the conscious mind enter the subway of consciousness, remain locked up there only to come out again through another opening into the conscious mind.[3]

—YOGANANDA

The principles of psychology were outlined centuries ago by Patanjali, a sage who lived somewhere between the second and fourth centuries C.E. Patanjali said that the attainment of perfect wholeness and happiness comes when we are able to calm the vortices of our emotional reactions: *"Yogas chitta vritti nirodh"* – "Yoga is the neutralization of the vortices of emotional feeling." These emotional reactions are localized in the subconscious.

The subconscious is a primary concern of modern psychology. Both Freud and Jung talked about the "collective unconscious." But while Freud believed that the subconscious is built up from our personal experiences, Jung posited that it is "inherited from the past collective experience of humanity." [4]

Yogananda reconciled this apparent contradiction by observing that both are true. Engrained in the subconscious mind are thoughts that reflect our individual history, but also thoughts that are universal. In his *Autobiography* he writes: **"All thoughts vibrate eternally in the cosmos.... Thoughts are universally and not individually rooted."** [5]

How can thoughts be both personal and universal?

> You are the product of your actions, attitudes, and the things that you've developed during this life and many previous lifetimes. You are the product of all of that, and yet you are none of those things. You aren't jealous and vindictive, or kind and forgiving. Those are qualities that are coming through you, perhaps, because you've opened yourself up to those aspects of a much greater consciousness.[6]

While Freud, Jung, and many of their successors have focused on the negative contents of the subconscious, Yogananda highlights its positive features – for example, its ability to record and store our thought patterns, emotional reactions, and habits. The subconscious is the amanuensis of our past and present lives.

The bridge between the subconscious and superconscious mind

Each of the three dimensions of our consciousness – subconscious, conscious, and superconscious – perceives reality in its own unique fashion. Their perceptions influence our daily decisions. The subconscious is active when we sleep. During waking hours, the conscious mind prevails, although impressions from the subconscious exert a powerful influence on our waking lives.

> Conscious decisions are tainted by influences of which the conscious mind is not even aware. We say we are free to do what we like, but what makes us like to do what we do? It isn't that attractiveness is inherent in those things. Likes and dislikes are subjective. They rise to the conscious level from the subconscious, and keep us bound to the world's delusions whether we consciously agree or not.[7]

It is humbling to realize how many of our perceptions, understandings, feelings, and decisions are influenced, and even dominated, by the subconscious.

> The subconscious mind is much more influential than a quiet voice in the background because it penetrates to all of our conscious activities. To a large extent, the subconscious guides our actions, reactions, and habits. The subconscious is developed over a span of lifetimes through countless thoughts and impressions.[8]

In this chapter we will learn how to master the subconscious realm, looking more deeply at how the subconscious affects our health, how to deal with its negative influences, and how to take control of its abilities and use them for our highest good.

Memory storage

The storage banks of the subconscious are immense – they are filled not only with memories of our present incarnation, but those that extend far back in time through countless previous lives. The subconscious holds the record of all our successes and failures – our acts of kindness and generosity or of aggression and cruelty, our hopes and dreams realized or abandoned, our joys and sorrows, our anxieties and fears, and our fulfillments and disappointments.

As computer information is stored on memory chips, our subconscious habit patterns are stored in the memory "grooves" of the brain.

> **Disease tendencies, habitual failure tendencies, and innate ignorance, are entrenched in brain cells and subconscious mind.**[9]
>
> **Just as a needle, when it strikes the grooves of a record,* plays a certain song, so also, the needle of an evil action, when it touches a grooved evil tendency in the brain, brings forth the corresponding song of evil experience.**
>
> **Every experience, good or bad, if intense, leaves a mental and physical record in the brain. This mental and grooved physical record in the brain can be played at any time by the suitable needle of specific association of ideas.**[10]

The memories stored in the grooves of the brain can be very helpful to us in our quest for greater wisdom and freedom. If we could fully remember the consequences of our actions, we could use that information to help us choose only those thoughts and actions that will bring us greater happiness – and avoid repeating thoughts and actions that will bring us only suffering.

* Yogananda refers to the old 78-rpm vinyl disks used in the first half of the twentieth century for audio recordings.

Positive memory retrieval

Our ability to remember makes learning possible.

The most intelligent animals have impressive memories. The short-term memory of a cat is twenty times longer than that of humans. Dolphins recognize each other immediately, even after twenty years of separation. Chimpanzees have photographic memory – when exposed to an image for a very short time, they remember every detail of the image when exposed to it later. Elephants, whose powers of memory are legendary, can simultaneously keep track of thirty individual elephants in the herd.

One of delusion's most powerful weapons is its ability to make us forget the suffering that followed our past unwholesome thoughts and actions – the stomach ache after a heavy meal, the headache after an ice-cream binge, the remorse after a temper tantrum.

On the positive side, we can also remember the thoughts, actions, and habits that have brought us success and happiness. For example, our memories of the glowing health and joyous high energy we've reaped from eating well and exercising regularly will encourage us to continue these positive habits. Paramhansa Yogananda says that when we sit to meditate, we should recall the feeling of the best meditation we've had, and use that memory as a starting point to explore even deeper experiences.

> **All the experiences that you have are reproduced by your mental subconscious faculty so that you may be able to profit by some of them and discard the rest.**[11]

Even though the tendency of the subconscious mind is to overlay an emotional patina onto every memory, we can train our mind to accurately perceive, store, and recall experiences without emotional bias.

> The subconscious mind .... can be trained so that it will correctly memorize and recall at will all conscious experiences. Memory is the recalling power by which we are saved from being children each day and prevented from having to repeat our experiences.[12]

Habit archives

The subconscious is a two-edged sword. On the one hand, it can remember the consequences of our thoughts and actions and help the conscious mind package them as helpful habits. On the other hand, it can, under the influence of emotion, selectively store the memories of fleeting past pleasures while forgetting their long-term negative consequences.

Marketing experts now use the internet to display enticements on our computer screens that reflect our past preferences, for good or ill – much like the subconscious mind.

The subconscious is a blind repository – it merely stores information and emotions. Thus, it does not create good or bad habits. However, its memory banks are where our habits are nurtured. The conscious mind creates habits through repeated actions, based on subconscious memories of the results of those actions. The conscious mind is where we can decide whether to let our habits dominate us, or to use our discernment, concentration, and willpower to create good habits that will bring us health and wellbeing.

> Good habits and virtues are eternal joy-making qualities. It is lamentable to be compelled to do evil against one's will because of the strength of an evil habit, and then to have to suffer for one's evil actions.[13]

It is so vitally important to understand how we can eliminate habits that destroy our health, and substitute habits that will bring us happiness and success, that we will devote all of Part VII to learning how to develop the habit-creating superpowers of the subconscious mind.

Subconscious distortion of conscious experiences

The subconscious is a fanatical archivist – but not a fastidious one. The memories stored in its archives are in hopeless disarray. When we search our subconscious memories to discover the past causes of our current ills, there is no neat index that will help us find the relevant files.

Although historical references can be useful guides in establishing future directions, history is never unbiased, and the history books, like the memories stored in our subconscious, can be an unreliable guide. When we open the portals of the subconscious to scan our memories, we can never be certain that what we find there will be useful, or even true.

An example of the convoluted behavior of the subconscious mind is the nature of dreams, which the subconscious mind fashions from our myriad past impressions into fantastical and disjointed sequences. Whereas dreams may occasionally be symbolic or cautionary, they are generally produced without the aid of an executive director.

> Dreams...are created by the intelligence of the conscious mind, with the subconscious mind as the director and the visualizing subconscious imagination as the cameraman. The players are the thoughts, feelings, determinations, and desires.
>
> The different dramas of comedies, tragedies, and real facts passing through the conscious mind are photographed by the intelligent subconscious mind. These inner mental films are stored away in the groove-like shelves in the convolutions of the grey matter in the brain.[14]

Somewhat different than the case of the intelligent animals mentioned, human memories are accompanied and distorted by emotions. As "beauty is in the eye of the beholder," so reality depends on which aspect of the mind is observing it.

A mirror can accurately reflect an object if its surface is perfectly smooth and unclouded. We have met the mind's mirror in Chapter One: *manas,* the impartial reflection of whatever is being observed.

That reflection as seen from the perspective of the subconscious mind, however, becomes distorted by the filter of *chitta*, which places an emotional, ego-oriented spin on what it sees.

One of Yogananda's best-known sayings is: **"Circumstances are always neutral. It is how you react to them that makes them seem either happy or sad."**

Whereas the superconscious mind perceives reality without emotional bias, to the subconscious mind our circumstances are never neutral. Our emotional reactions to our experiences are stored together with our memories of the circumstances themselves. Our memories are colored by these emotions, which will surface when we face similar circumstances in the present. Thus we find ourselves reacting to events with the emotions we experienced while facing similar events in the past. It is our emotional reactions that prevent us from experiencing each situation on its own objective, unbiased merits.

As an example of how our memories come with feelings attached, we may vividly remember a disappointing dinner, not for the lousy food, but for our feelings of disappointment and regret. Similarly, we may remember the betrayal of a friendship not for the circumstances that led to it, but as a blanket fear of intimacy.

Unchecked emotional reactions can play a major role in the onset of illness. A habit of reacting with anger, worry, fear, disappointment, a desire for revenge, or helplessness creates imbalances in the flow of energy and hormones in the body, which can, in time, cause severe illness. The well-documented causes of cancer include bereavement, depression, a sense of helplessness and hopelessness, suppressed anger, and major life upheavals.[15]

Life teaches us that it is never constructive to make decisions while we are caught in the whirlpools of emotional reactions. The very structure of the brain dictates that when we are seething with raw emotions, impartial reason and analysis are completely out of reach, as is the superconscious power of wise intuition.

Discover your subconscious reactions

To help us understand our subconscious thought patterns, let us image two hypothetical, "neutral" situations and see how the subconscious mind might react to them. Try to imagine yourself in each of these circumstances, whether or not they are relevant to your current situation, and reflect on how you would respond.

Situation A. Your employer no longer needs your services, and you suddenly find yourself unemployed.

Situation B. A routine health checkup reveals unusual cell growth, and lab testing is scheduled.

In each of the sections that follow, make a mental or written list of how you would react. It takes no small amount of courage to unwrap our habitual emotional reactions and face them squarely, and expose them to the clear light of truth.

Once we are aware of our habitual subconscious reactions, we can gradually develop the ability to override these instinctual patterns by applying the superpowers of concentration, self-control, and intuitive superconscious understanding.

Usually the first subconscious reaction to either Situation A or B would likely be **disbelief and denial**. When faced with an unexpected and undesirable circumstance, the subconscious default pattern is to deny the reality or relevance of the situation. Depending on our own past experiences, typical reactions of this nature may vary from "There must be a mistake!" to "The computer obviously has me mixed up with someone else." or "This has got to be a dream – when will I wake up?"

Take a moment to think how you might react with denial when facing Situation A, then Situation B.

Two close friends of denial are **avoidance** and **escape**. "If I ignore this, it will go away." "After a few drinks, things will look rosier."

If you lost your job or your health, how would you try to avoid or escape the situation?

※

When we realize that there is no easy escape from a difficult situation in our life, the subconscious will often resort to **blame**. The last thing the ego likes is to acknowledge a mistake or a weakness – thus it will generally cast about for someone or something to blame.

Where we direct the blame will depend on our personal subconscious – a spouse, our children, our parents, our childhood circumstances, our colleagues and/or our boss, an unjust God, bad luck, bad karma, or as a last resort, ourselves.

But self-blame is not the same as accepting responsibility. Self-blame is accompanied by **guilt** and **helplessness**, whereas responsibility is accompanied by the desire to understand the error and a strong determination to change and do better.

Take a moment to think about whom you would blame if you were fired from your job, or if you lost your health.

※

ANGER

As the subconscious ego builds momentum, one reaction leading to another, it takes us from blame to **anger.** Anger wants to lash out at those it believes are to blame for their suffering. From righteous indignation – "This is *completely unfair!*" – to thoughts of revenge – "They won't get away with this! I'll sue them!"

In Situation A, then in Situation B, where might you direct your anger? What could be the long-term effects?

While venting anger might at the moment release some internal pressure, it can be psychologically harmful to others, and over time seriously damaging to our mental and physical health.

In the March 1939 issue of *Inner Culture*, Yogananda answered an important question: "What causes anger? How can I conquer it?"

> When a desire of yours is obstructed or contradicted, it usually results in anger... whenever you are angry, you must consider that you are in a slow baking oven. All your nerves and your brain cells and flesh are baking in the fire of anger, which at times has caused even death. Anger carried to extremes is not safe for the body, mind, or soul. Many illnesses are caused by anger, which also brings on old age quickly. The face of an angry man is distorted. Do not desecrate your face and mind, which are made in the image of God....
>
> When wrath comes, you forget your position, and when you forget your position, you do wrong things, and when you do wrong things, you are the tool of ignorance. If something has gone wrong, correct the error. Look at things intelligently and peacefully. The divine law will give you the right understanding." [16]

If you habitually respond with anger, the time to intervene with an antidote is before the emotion can grow powerful enough to overwhelm you.

There are signposts on the road to runaway anger that even a little bit of objective self-observation can help us recognize. For starters, consider any possible physical causes.

We tend to be more susceptible to anger when we are exhausted from too much work and/or too little sleep; and when our lives have become unbalanced – we haven't given sufficient time to exercise, wholesome activities outside of work, and time for relaxation and recreation....

Emotional habits that can make us vulnerable to anger include habitual impatience and annoyance with others, and frustration when things don't go our way, or our expectations are not met. When any of these alarm bells goes off, you can redirect your thoughts and energy in positive channels. In Part VII we will consider how to override negative habits by channeling their energy into more constructive channels.

We can learn valuable lessons about anger by carefully and dispassionately observing the aftermath. Taking time to take stock of the devastating effects, to ourselves and others, will give us powerful motivation to work toward a permanent cure.

It is very important, however, to avoid wallowing in feelings of guilt. Be patient. Give yourself time. Our deep-seated subconscious emotional habits have great power, and we will rarely be able to learn to redirect their energy into positive channels without long practice, even if we are keenly aware and convinced of the need to change.

They will continue to appear, though with decreasing intensity, as we become more clearly aware of them. Be realistic. We should expect that they will re-appear, and that for a time our reactions will remain largely beyond our control. But once we have become aware of them and the gravity of their consequences, we can give our attention to our options for learning how to respond constructively.

Yogananda's antidotes for anger

> When anger attacks you, conquer it. When you are angry, say nothing. Knowing it to be a disease (like a cold, for instance), throw it off by a mental warm bath. Fill your mind, to the exclusion of all else, with thoughts of those with whom you can never be angry, no matter what they do.
>
> When violently angry, douse your head with cold water, or rub the medulla, the temples, the forehead (especially between the eyebrows), and the top of the head with a piece of ice.
>
> Develop metaphysical reason in order to destroy anger. Look upon the anger-rousing agent as a child of God, a little five-year-old baby brother who has unwittingly, perhaps, stabbed you. You cannot wish to stab back this little brother who did not know what he was doing when he injured you...
>
> Mentally destroy anger; do not permit it to poison your peace and disturb your habitual joy-giving serenity. When anger comes, think of love; think that, as you do not want others to be angry with you, you do not wish others to feel your ugly anger.[17]

WORRY

Once our anger has subsided and our situation is still unchanged, the road ahead will often look bleak and hopeless, leading us to indulge in anxiety and worries: "What will become of me and my family?"; "How will we survive if I am unable to find a job?"; "If I die, how will my family get along without me?"

What worries would surface for you were you to find yourself in Situation A and in Situation B?

The subconscious is a worry trap. It hypnotizes us into believing that worrying is a necessary step toward a solution. But worries just feed on themselves, magnifying the situation by imagining endless catastrophic outcomes. Worry steals energy that we could otherwise use to activate the creative conscious mind to find effective solutions.

Yogananda's worry fast [18]

Three times a day, shake off all worries.

- At seven o'clock in the morning say to yourself, "'All my worries of the night are cast out, and from 7 to 8 A.M. I refuse to worry, no matter how troublesome are the duties ahead of me. I am going on a worry fast."
- From 12 to 1 P.M., say, "I am cheerful, I will not worry."
- In the evening, between 6 and 9 P.M.…mentally make a strong resolution and say, "Within these three hours I will not worry, I refuse to get vexed.… No matter how tempting it is to indulge in a worry feast, I will resist the temptation."

Whenever you find yourself indulging in a worry feast, go on a partial or complete worry fast for a day or a week. Whenever you make up your mind not to worry, stick to your resolution. You can stop worrying entirely. You can calmly solve your most difficult problems, putting forth your greatest effort, and at the same time absolutely refuse to worry. Tell your mind, "I can do only my best, no more. I am satisfied and happy that I am doing my best to solve my problem; there is absolutely no reason why I should worry myself to death."

When worries assail us in any situation, the best way out of the trap is to **do** something. Taking even the smallest step toward a solution will put energy in motion that will attract to us even better solutions through the law of magnetism. Swami Kriyananda advises: **"Do what you can do; don't worry about the obstacles that are beyond your strength."** [19]

The following is a personal story about a worrisome situation.

✻ Running Shoes ✻

My husband is a licensed contractor, electrician, plumber, and painter. Soon after we were married, he started a small construction company, hiring qualified friends to join him.

The first houses the company built were beautiful – they were designed with loving attention, with attractive details such as carved beams and stained-glass windows. The houses sold before they were completed, and the company was off to a fine start.

Although I had a full-time day job, I did the company's accounting in the evening. It was simple enough: I paid the bills and balanced the checkbook.

Before leaving for an extended visit with my parents, I put the accounts in order, carefully noting the bank balance and the bills to be paid during my absence. When I returned, the bank balance was dangerously in the red – how could that be! My husband never spent money carelessly – where had the money gone?

Reviewing the bank statement, I discovered that I had made an error in the available balance, making it seem that we had $1000 more than was actually in the account. My husband, confident in my numbers, had gone ahead and paid several additional bills.

Suddenly I was in a tailspin – I imagined the company's checks bouncing all over town, and angry suppliers calling. I visualized liens against the company, foreclosure, bankruptcy – divorce!

As each worry led to a darker eventuality, tears spilled down my face. And then I realized that I had to get a grip on myself and pull out of the spiral.

My husband would arrive in a couple of hours. How would I tell him? I put on my running shoes and set off at a vigorous pace. After five minutes I stopped crying. At ten minutes my breath steadied into a regular flow. At fifteen minutes I began to see the situation in a new light.

Yes, the checks were bouncing, but there was a flow of income, and soon we could issue new checks. The suppliers liked us, and we had always paid on time. I was sure that they were grateful for our business, and that they would understand. Not so bad, after all. Where had the dark thoughts come from?

It was sundown when my husband returned after a long day's work. I greeted him at the door, holding his running shoes. "Let's run – I have something to tell you."

"Can't you just tell me now? I'm tired and hungry?"

Reluctantly, he put on his shoes and we ran out in the twilight. After fifteen minutes I told him the whole story. "Oh, don't worry," he said. "Several clients are making payments next week, and I've been wanting to talk with our suppliers anyway about some new materials. Let's go to town together tomorrow and see if they'll extend us credit for a short while."

And thus was the imagined divorce avoided!

—**Shivani** (*the author*)

Aside from worrying about our personal lives, we might easily be tempted to drown in worries about the dire condition of our world. As I write these words, the world has recently emerged from a major pandemic. A war in eastern Europe is threatening to erupt into a global conflagration. Accelerating climate change is affecting lives and livelihoods everywhere. And inflation is threatening the world economy. These are worry-worthy situations, to be sure!

What positive constructive tools can we avail ourselves of to avoid becoming consumed by anxiety? Yogananda offers the following advice.

> You are not the controller of the destiny of the world. Do not worry uselessly about the terrible things that are happening. You must realize that God never forsakes the righteous and He loves all equally well, and through His love we shall see a new world. He who has given life will again rehabilitate the world in a better way. You must help the world by your constructive thoughts.[20]

The need for mental relaxation

When there is tension in the physical body, we have many options for relaxing our muscles: exercise, sports, yoga, massage, etc. We also have many options for relieving mental tensions and worries.

Reading, especially lighthearted books and stories, can provide a welcome mental vacation from our worries. Swami Kriyananda loved the British humorist P. G. Wodehouse and would often entertain us by reading his short stories. Two other favorites were Saki (H.H. Munro) and Mark Twain. Fortunately, there are kind-hearted humorists in every culture and tongue.

Plays, concerts, museums, and nature walks – these offer us environments where the mind can drop its worries for a time. Rest, recreation, and relaxation are as important for a healthy mind as for the body.

Yogananda's Joy Cure

The negative method for overcoming worry poisoning is worry fasting. There are also positive methods. One infected with the germs of worry must go on a strict mental diet. He must feast frugally, but regularly, on the society of joyful minds. Every day he must associate–if only for a little while–with "joy-infected" minds. There are some people the song of whose laughter nothing can still. Seek them out and feast with them on this most vitalizing food of joy. Continue the laughter diet for a month or two. Feast on laughter in the company of really joyful people. Digest it thoroughly by whole-heartedly masticating laughter with the teeth of your attention. Steadfastly continue your laughter diet once you have begun it, and at the end of a month or two you will see the change–your mind will be filled with sunshine.[21]

FEAR

Worry and fear are almost, but not quite synonymous. They are subconscious reactions, stimulated by circumstances, which, when we imagine the worst, quickly grow out of all proportion to the present reality. While worries can be set aside, fear can send us into a tailspin of anxiety and panic. Fear is dangerous to our health because it keeps the body and mind in a constant state of alarm, exhausting the glands that are meant to produce "fight-or-flight" hormones in response to real emergencies.

> Fear aggravates all our miseries. It intensifies a hundred-fold our physical pain and mental agony.
>
> Fear has a very deleterious effect on the heart, nervous system, and brain. It is destructive to mental initiative, courage, judgment, common sense, and to the will.
>
> Fear develops in an individual a malignant magnetism by which he attracts the very object of which he is afraid, as a magnet attracts a piece of iron or steel.[22]

At the heart of fear is the ego's resistance to change—its distrust of the unexpected, its fear of the unknown. Dominated as it is by the ego, the subconscious mind fears the loss of security of having a steady job. It fears the disturbance to life's usual routines that a sickness portends.

Take a moment now to reflect once again on the fears that might emerge from your subconscious if you were to lose your job or if you were told that you might have a life-threatening disease.

How can we combat our fears? Yogananda advises:

- Kill fear by refusing to be afraid of it.

- Uproot fear from within by forceful concentration on courage – and by shifting your consciousness to the absolute peace within.

- When something is threatening you, do not sit idle — do something about it calmly mustering all the power of your will and judgement.

- When fear comes, tense and relax — exhale several times. Switch on the currents of calmness and serenity. Let your whole mental machinery awaken and actively hum with the vibration of will to do something.[23]

The inevitable and unavoidable change to be confronted is death.* We have experienced death times beyond number, our souls rejoicing in freedom from earthly limitations until our karma calls us to be born into this world again.

> Another form of fear is the fear of death....
> [which is] born of the greatest ignorance, and
> it paralyzes activity, thought, and ambition....
>
> Death should be regarded as a universal experience, a change which everyone passes through. It should be looked upon as good, as a new opportunity, as a rest from the weary struggle on this earth....
>
> **Live today well and the next step
> will take care of itself.**[24]

---

* Overcoming the fear of death is discussed in the Epilogue, Volume Three.

An effective way to deal with our fears, including the fear of death, is to experience that aspect of our Self that is the changeless Spirit. Kriyananda writes:

> The secret of overcoming fear of death
> is to deepen your awareness of that central
> part in your being which never changes,
> but weaves like a thread through life's tapestry
> of apparently unrelated circumstances.
> The consciousness of change is allied to the fear
> of death. But to see changelessness at the heart
> of change is the secret of immortality.[25]

The best way to get in touch with the soul's immortality is by the regular practice of meditation.* When we can enter a state of breathlessness and profound inner stillness—those moments when the inhalation and exhalation become neutralized and the breath becomes suspended—we begin to experience a profound freedom from earthly limitations. The ego calls us back by reminding us to breathe, but with continued daily practice, we can train ourselves to relax and linger in that state of breathless freedom.

> Breathless silence is almost a condition,
> a passport required to enter the spirit world.[26]

An intelligent design

On an even deeper level, fear is based on the false notion that we are nothing but pawns in a game that is controlled by powers outside ourselves. But with long observation, introspection, and increasing self-awareness we find that no matter how baffling our life's experiences may seem, they are not random.

No matter how inconsequential we may appear to be, each of us has a divine destiny to fulfill. Faith begins to override fear as we

---

* Meditation practices are the subject of Part II, Volume One.

gradually perceive that there is a benevolent and intelligent purpose behind our life's experiences, and that each experience is designed to help us develop our inner strength. Then, a deep faith begins to displace our fears.

✵ A DIVINE HAND ✵

I was a single mother with two children. My parents were gone, and when the first wave of the Covid pandemic hit, I had no permanent place to live, no savings, and no work.

Part of me was deeply worried – how could I manage? Yet a separate, wiser part of me knew that it would all work out, and that it was, in some way, part of a plan that was leading me to a new life.

My passion is teaching yoga, but for the moment I was happy to find work in a supermarket, and receive a short-term loan so that I could rent an apartment.

With no material goods as my security, I had only meditation, Kriya Yoga, inner peace, and an abiding conviction. I knew that my Guru would protect and support me.

Every day at the supermarket I transformed each action into a spiritual practice, seeing the good and the God in each person and asking for guidance in the smallest things, while softly chanting and reciting mantras (to the annoyance of my manager).

A month into the job, a man who had found *Autobiography of a Yogi* asked me for private yoga lessons, and paid me so generously that I was able to resolve all my financial difficulties.

That very trying period was revealed to be, indeed, a stepping stone. I now live near Moscow where I have opened a yoga studio. Although the world around me is unstable and the future is uncertain, I know that I need have no fear, for I have experienced a divine hand that is guiding and protecting me. —***Raimira***, *Russia*

How to avoid depression, despair, and helplessness

If we spend too much riding the fear train, we risk crashing into a pit of despair. The thoughts that will take us there include: "There is nothing I can do in this situation."; "My circumstances are bound to go from bad to worse."; "There are no solutions to these problems."; "I don't have the strength or resources to deal with this." and "There is no one who will help me."

Were you to lose your job or be faced with a potentially serious disease, what thought of despair might arise in your mind?

To escape the train, we must vigorously activate our conscious reason, concentration, and willpower long before we reach the final destination, and rise to the challenge of generating a higher level of energy.

❉ Kitchen Cleanup ❉

The dinner was sublime, and the dining room was filled with happy guests who were thoroughly enjoying each other's company. In the kitchen afterward, we encountered a mountain of pots, pans, and dirty dishes, but with three of us assigned to cleanup duty, I was sure there would be no problem.

The shift started at 20.30, and I arrived early to get things organized. I was still alone at 20.30, at 20.40, and by 20.45 I had to accept that the others were not coming.

I couldn't avoid feeling a certain despair. It was the end of a long day, I was tired, and staring at the mountain of dirty dishes just made me more weary. What little energy I had was being silently drained by my sense of irritation, self-pity, and helplessness.

Then I remembered: "I have a choice – I can be here till midnight and suffer, or I can be here till midnight and enjoy myself."

I looked at a photo of Yogananda and said, "If you want me to be here alone, I'll stay here with you by my side. Let's get to work!"

Loudly I affirmed: "Yes!" And in that instant my energy shifted. I felt a surge of joy, and I began to enjoy the play. Barely two minutes passed, when as I washed the glasses someone came in and asked, "Are you here alone?"

"Just me and Yogananda."

"Well, let's make it three."

A few minutes later several others came along, and seeing us surrounded by pots and pans they joined in. We finished the cleanup much earlier than the original crew would have, while having a wonderful time together.

Whenever I remember that evening, I am struck that as soon as my attitude changed, the direction of my energy shifted from despair to a joy that magnetically drew a completely unexpected solution. –**Arudra**, *Ananda Assisi*

This story makes a vital point: the fastest and best way out of subconscious mood traps is to **do something** that will increase and raise the flow of our energy. In Part III we considered that a low or disturbed flow of energy opens us to illness, whereas a powerful harmonious flow of energy encourages health and healing.

Low energy is the precursor of illness. Almost anything we can do to raise our energy and reverse a downward spiral toward stagnation will spare us from wasting priceless time and health on depression, despair, and mental illness.

Something as simple as a shower can change the direction of our energy flow. Low-energy thoughts and feelings create a stagnant energy field around us, which running water helps remove, leaving us invigorated and ready for action.

Daily practice of the Energization Exercises is a health investment against depression and other mental toxins. Regular practice creates a base level of energy that is stronger than many illnesses and mental imbalances. Doing the Energization Exercises or Full Body Recharge after a shower works every time!

Swami Kriyananda's secrets for overcoming depression

- The secret of overcoming depression is **useful activity,** devoted selflessly to helping others.

- The secret of overcoming depression is not to try reasoning your way out of the slump, but vigorously to raise your level of energy from the heart to the brain, then channeling it outward in creative activity, or in useful service to others.

- The secret of overcoming depression is to affirm mentally, "I am not my moods, and I am not subject to the moods of others. I am ruler in my kingdom of thoughts and feelings!" In everything you do, strive to be a cause, not an effect.[27]

An attitude of gratitude

The negative thought patterns in the subconscious mind, once they are activated, dwell not only on fears and worries about our personal fate, but also on the injustices of life, on what we don't have or can't obtain, and on paralyzing **doubts** about ourselves and about God.

Gratitude List

Make a list every day of the things for which we are grateful. Read the list aloud every morning and evening – in the form of a prayer if you are so inclined, or as a simple recitation. As you read each one, visualize yourself enjoying that special gift.

> The secret of overcoming doubt is to concentrate on your reasons for gratitude to life, and not to focus on all those things which seem to you imperfect. Love other people. Love truth. Love! Fill your heart with generous sentiments, and doubts will flee like shadows before the sunrise.[28]

> Do not forget when you meet Beauty,
> beauty of every kind—the gorgeous color
> of the sunset, the music of birds,
> the glistening water, the rustling trees,
> the soft breeze on your face, the warm sun,
> the joy of love and friendship—
> to speak your gratitude to the Father within
> for surrounding you with so much wonder
> and beauty and for opening your eyes
> that you might see and enjoy it.[29]

Subconscious self-identity

At each level of our consciousness – subconscious, conscious, and superconscious – we harbor images of ourselves that have a profound influence on our health and happiness. Swami Kriyananda writes:

> It is common for people to perceive themselves according to their present realities. A person in ill health says, "I am ill." Few say, "I am well; it is my body that is suffering." [30]

The pictures we paint of ourselves, and that we constantly affirm by our thoughts, words, and deeds, become a self-fulfilling prophecy of what we can and cannot achieve. Olympic medalists never dwell on images of themselves as losers, failures, or quitters; they visualize themselves on the highest step of the winners' podium.

We construct our subconscious self-identity from our thoughts and emotions about the memories of our past performance. The memory of a poor performance during a singing or acting audition will support the thought "I am not a good actor or singer" – accompanied by mental images of ourselves failing and feeling downcast about it.

The thoughts of others can also contribute to our self-image. Children who are scolded harshly for their bad school grades and test scores absorb the parent's or teacher's image of themselves. We should be careful about the images and thoughts we project onto others, and that we allow others to impose on us. Parents, teachers, coaches, and counselors have a responsibility to influence those entrusted to them in positive ways.

※ Tall Enough ※

He loved to watch Kareem dunk the basketball. But it was clear that he would never be seven feet tall (2.18 m) like Kareem. Yet a desire to play in the NBA burned in his heart.

He spent most of his time outside of school on the basketball court in his underprivileged Yonkers neighborhood. On weekends he would shoot hoops for ten hours straight or longer. Pudgy and awkward-looking, he wasn't even a starter on his high school team.

By then he had reached his maximum height of five feet eight inches (1.73 meters) and was ridiculed for his size and his absurd dream of playing in the NBA.

Defying the humiliations, he increased his practice and time and played pickup games, honing his best skills – he was remarkably fast, athletic, and a wizard ball handler. He was fearless on offense and defense and was a jaw-droppingly accurate, consistent shooter. Although they called him "Mosquito," his skills and fearlessness earned him respect.

In college at New Mexico State, he helped lead the team to three consecutive appearances in the NCAA regionals. On the court he looked comically small, but in his mind he wasn't too short to get the ball, defend it, and score. Even so, his dream of going pro was scoffingly dismissed because of his size.

After failing to be noticed by the NBA scouts, he kept his dream alive by playing in the Eastern Professional Basketball League, where for four years he was the league's best-ever scorer and a three-time MVP while leading the team to two championships.

An Atlantic Hawks scout wandered into an EPBL championship game, and before the game ended he was on the phone to the Hawks, singing the Mosquito's praises.

The NBA's oldest-ever rookie at twenty-eight, Charlie Criss played seven seasons with the Hawks. Once he had the ball, he was unstoppable. A special favorite of the fans and press, he became an Atlanta legend and an icon in basketball history.

Like his fans, let us remember him for his refusal to harbor negative self-images and his determination to achieve what the whole world considered an impossible dream.

By its very nature subconscious self-perception is retrospective. But while our past actions undoubtedly contribute to our present reality, we should never let them circumscribe the present. Just as the seeming reality of dreams disappears upon wakening, our incomplete subconscious self-image begins to dissolve with the dawning of higher awareness.

In the chapters that follow, we will construct a picture of our true identity that will help us on the road to self-healing and Self-realization. In the superconscious dimension of our consciousness we find a multi-dimensional perception of the Self that includes all of the seemingly separate phases of our evolution.

CHAPTER 6: *Points to Remember*

- The superpower of the subconscious is its ability to store our memories, emotions, and habits.

- Thoughts and actions initiated by the conscious mind are incubated in the subconscious, where they become habits, whether helpful or harmful.

- Our memories are stored in the "grooves" of the brain. Special skills for working with these habit grooves will be revealed in Part VII.

- Much of the information stored in the subconscious is unreliable, as it is colored by our emotional reactions.

- Our subconscious memories interact with the conscious mind, sometimes uninvited, and other times when we deliberately recall them.

- Our conscious decisions are greatly – often entirely – influenced by impressions, emotions, and habits that filter up from the subconscious. These can influence us in both positive and negative ways.

- Among the most health-harming emotions are the "mental toxins" of anger, worry, and fear.

… PART VI   CHAPTER SEVEN

Superconscious Intuition

> The superconsciousness is the pure intuitive, all-seeing, ever-new Blissful consciousness of the Soul.[1] —YOGANANDA
>
> What is the difference between understanding and intuition? Understanding depends upon the senses for knowledge; intuition brings direct perception of truth.[2] —YOGANANDA
>
> There is no logical way to the discovery of elemental laws. There is only the way of intuition, which is helped by a feeling for the order lying behind the appearance. When the solution is simple, God is answering. —ALBERT EINSTEIN

✵ AN INTUITIVE UNDERSTANDING ✵

The members of our family were frantic, running in all directions mentally, physically, and emotionally, without the slightest notion of what to do or where to turn for help.

The palpable stress was far beyond manageable. Within just ten days, our mother had been transformed from an energetic, loving woman in full possession of her life, to suffering slight lapses of memory, followed by aggressive behavior and a violent psychotic episode.

When we called for medical assistance, she was taken to the hospital where she was diagnosed with advanced Alzheimer's. It appeared that she would require full-time care in a specialized facility. The doctors said that our mother would never return to a normal state of mind, and that it would not be helpful to keep her at home, nor would it be easy for the rest of us.

Our father agreed, and while the whole family got busy looking for an affordable facility, I sought answers in my meditations.

Before I joined the search for an appropriate place for our mother to live, I wanted to feel sure that it would be the right choice for her soul. When anxieties and uncertainties threaten to sweep me away, I am in the habit of taking time for a short "meditation snack," to come back to inner calmness and look for intuitive solutions.

Our outward investigations met with innumerable obstacles – the waiting periods were at least a year, and the available care facilities were vastly expensive, far beyond our means, even if there was an opening.

And then quite unexpectedly a social worker called me with good news: there was an opening in an excellent facility just ten kilometers from our home. Logically, it seemed like a good solution, but I wanted to know that it was the *right* one. Much to my family's displeasure, I decided to take a weekend meditation retreat to look for inner guidance.

By Sunday evening when I returned, the storm of emotion in the family had become a hurricane, with everyone saying that we must get mother into the facility as soon as possible. But when I meditated on Monday morning, I felt that I should see our mother first before visiting the care facility.

Mother was perfectly calm and lucid – she recognized me and was fully aware of her surroundings and her situation. She wanted to go home as soon as possible. Our father was relieved, and we made arrangements for her to be dismissed the following day.

It was clear that our mother would need assistance at home – where could we find the right person? I took time

> for another "meditation snack" before meeting a friend for a lunch date. During our conversation she told me about an excellent caretaker who was looking for work.
>
> She turned out to be perfect! There was no need to look further. My mother is very happy with this kind woman from Sri Lanka whose smile and shining eyes remind us that when we put our lives in God's hands, He will take care of every detail. *–Silvia, Cortona*

We come at last to the level of consciousness that has a 360-degree perspective on us and the trajectory of our lives, and from which we can draw true connections, conclusions, and solutions.

When we learn to take control of the subconscious mind, we can use it to develop good health habits. When we take the reins of the conscious mind, we can use its superpowers of concentration, willpower, and visualization to ensure our wellbeing.

Now we will discover how we can pierce the veil between the dimensions of the conscious and superconscious and drink from the wellsprings of a higher intuition.

> Intuition does not depend upon any outside data whatsoever....Intuition is that directly perceiving faculty of the soul which at once knows the truth about anything. Unless you have the power of intuition, you cannot possibly know Truth. It is the knowing power of the soul without the help of the senses or the mind. Intuition can give you knowledge about things which your senses and understanding can never give.[3]

Intuition is not, as many believe, the sole purview of women and psychics – the guidance and insights of a higher intuition are available to everyone.

Surely you have had intuitive feelings at some point in your life. You have met someone for the first time and been sure that you have "known" them in some unremembered past. You have visited a place and had a powerful feeling that you should or should not stay there. You have looked for a new place to live, and you've instantly accepted or declined an offer, based on a strong inner assurance. You have interviewed a job-seeker and felt that they were the perfect fit – or that despite their excellent credentials they were entirely the wrong candidate.

Scientists, inventors, artists, and musicians all use methods for achieving a superconscious state of inner mental clarity and receptivity.

Thomas Edison understood that this state is often easiest to access just before we fall asleep, when the mind passes from conscious awareness into subconsciousness. Edison would rest from his labors by taking a nap in a rocking chair in his laboratory, with a metal pail next to the chair. He would hold a rock in his hand that would fall into the pail when he began to enter the subconscious. The sound would bring him back to consciousness, and in the twilight state before he was fully awake he would find solutions and inspirations for his inventions.

> "The major role of intuition is to provide a conceptual foundation that suggests the directions which new research should take. ...The role of intuition in research is to provide the "educated guess," which may prove to be true or false; but in either case, progress cannot be made without it and even a false guess may lead to progress. Thus intuition also plays a major role in the evolution of mathematical concepts." [4]

We use intuition to discover and logic to prove. [5]
—HENRI POINCARÉ

Sometimes our intuitions are born of long experience. Doctors often know what is wrong with a patient before receiving their test results. Sports coaches may be able to spot champions before they even begin training.

But valid intuitions are available even without prior experience. Kriyananda reports that Yogananda "could converse easily with people of specialized knowledge, such as physicians, using their own terminology as though he'd been to medical school himself." [6]

> Intuition is the innate ability in everyone to
> perceive truth directly—not by reason,
> logic, or analysis, but by a simple knowing from
> within. That is the very meaning of the word
> "intuition": to know, or understand from within—
> from one's own self, and from the heart
> of whatever one is trying to understand.
> Intuition is the inner ability to see behind the
> outer forms of things to their inner essence.[7]

Characteristics of superconsciousness

The conscious mind requires hard facts and numbers before it can fully understand, but the superconscious recognizes the essence **immediately** and **directly**, without needing corroborating evidence.

Where the conscious mind delights in compartmentalizing and analyzing, the superconscious sees how the elements are part of a **unified** whole, and how each is connected with the others.

> It is from the point of view of Intuition that every
> fact of the world finds meaning in its totality.[8]

> From a superconscious perspective, all life is a unity.
> From a rational perspective, life is a disunity—
> a bewildering jigsaw puzzle, often, with many
> pieces that never seem to belong together....
> To superconsciousness, everything is related.
> Not relative, merely: related....
>
> It is simply that this is how the superconscious
> works: It ties things together. It dissolves
> difficulties. It offers practical solutions, where
> the rational mind sees nothing but problems.[9]

To the subconscious, everything is personal – it is always "all about me." The superconscious sees life instead from a **universal, impersonal** perspective. We are responsible for the subconscious mind that we have fashioned from the memories of our personal past. Likewise, the conscious mind is created from our effort to develop its powers. But at the superconscious level our individual history interacts with the universal storehouse of wisdom, and with truths that are valid for everyone, in all places and times.

> The conscious mind, indeed, can do no other than *learn* new truths: It cannot recognize them. Recognition of truths that are not revealed to the mind by the senses is specifically the function of intuition.
>
> Within that stillness lie soul-perceptions that have been experienced since time immemorial by the great mystics of all religions: divine love, bliss, wisdom, light, cosmic sound, and an extraordinarily heightened awareness known as ecstasy. Great saints everywhere have attained these states, regardless of their own systems of belief. St. Teresa of Avila said that, in a state of ecstasy, the soul recognizes in a flash truths which reason may require many years to learn. [10]

When we are stumped by a difficult situation, we may throw up our hands and exclaim, "But it's too complicated!" The conscious mind loves complexity, enjoying the act of weaving elaborate threads of reason and logic. The weakness of the conscious mind is that it can trap us in fascinating details without taking us forward.

Superconscious revelations, on the other hand, are always **simple** and clear. The superconscious is like a gardener who prunes the trees in the orchard to their original shape after a summer of exuberant growth.

True superconscious experiences are not merely interesting, they are **transformative**. In subtle, often inexplicable ways, they change us. The great scientist Nikola Tesla, who was far ahead of his time, had a superconscious experience that would change the course of history.

While living in Budapest, Tesla struggled to devise a system for generating electricity using rotating magnetic fields. He was so intent on his pursuit that he became physically and mentally exhausted. During a relaxing walk in a park with a friend, he recited a favorite passage from Goethe's *Faust* and suddenly had a superconscious experience:

> "The idea came like a flash of lightning and in an instant the truth was revealed. I drew with a stick on the sand the diagrams shown six years later in my address before the American Institute of Electrical Engineers, and my companion understood them perfectly. The images I saw were wonderfully sharp and clear and had the solidity of metal and stone, so much so that I told him: 'See my motor here; watch me reverse it.' I cannot begin to describe my emotions. Pygmalion seeing his statue come to life could not have been more deeply moved." [11]

How to develop intuition

The subconscious is agitated by emotion. The conscious mind is busy with restless distractions. The superconscious is accompanied by deep calmness. It is out of the calm stillness of the superconscious that wise intuitive insights are born.

> It is not easy to separate emotion from calm, intuitive feeling. But the emotions, because they fluctuate constantly, can never offer a clear reflection of the realities around them, any more than the rippled surface of a lake clearly reflects the moon. Only stillness within can provide that calm certainty which is the hallmark of intuition... Intuition manifests when the emotions are calm, and when the intellect passes beyond the fluctuations of reason to a state of stillness, perfectly focused.[12]

The way to achieve this state of inner stillness, where no thoughts and emotions can intervene, is with proven meditation techniques that, with practice, still the restless mind and open our awareness to the superconscious world.

> Pure reason and calm feeling lead to intuition. Distorted, skeptical reason and emotional feeling over-cloud intuition. Therefore, the first requisite in developing intuition is to *calmly reason* and *calmly feel* everything. Never be skeptical; never be excited or emotional.[13]

YOGANANDA'S TECHNIQUE
for intuitive problem solving

- First go into deep meditation or silence.
- Don't think of your problem during meditation.
- Meditate until you feel that a sense of calmness fills the inner recesses of your body and your breath becomes calm and quiet.
- Then concentrate simultaneously at the point between the eyebrows (Christ Center) and the heart.
- Then ask God to direct your Intuition, so that you may know what you should do about your problem.[14]

Inner silence has been valued by inventors, statesmen, and the spiritually enlightened.

> Be alone, that is the secret of invention; be alone, that is when ideas are born.... Our senses enable us to perceive only a minute portion of the outside world. —NIKOLA TESLA

> Nowhere can man find a quieter or more untroubled retreat than his own soul. —MARCUS AURELIUS

> The quieter you become, the more you are able to hear. —RUMI

Life Force

It can be difficult to know the ultimate cause of illness, since its roots may be buried in the distant past. And even if we identify the mistakes that led to our present karmic circumstances, there is no guarantee that knowing about it will lead to a healing.

In Part II we saw how the powerful meditation practice of Kriya Yoga can eradicate karma without a need to bring its causes to our conscious awareness. Working regularly with Kriya or similar techniques will over time ameliorate and eventually remove the karmic causes of disease.

In the meantime, the following methods will help us consult the higher intuitive guidance of the superconscious which can reveal the physical and mental causes of illness.

Intuitive listening

Intuitive listening is a superpower of the superconscious mind. When something is out of balance, the universe wants to remedy it, and actively sends guidance to those who are open. By its nature, inner guidance is subtle, and needs to be sought sincerely and sensitively: intuitively.

Having asked for guidance, we need to be confident that it will come, and be sensitively vigilant and receptive to recognize it when it appears. Those who are receptive, and who hold themselves in readiness, watching and listening, will be led, as if on a treasure hunt, step by step, clue by clue, to the solution. As Jesus said: "Who hath ears to hear, let him hear." (MATTHEW 13:9)

> The voice of intuition is usually very quiet and calm, so it's often easy to ignore or shout down. Listen for the merest whisper and be prepared to follow it, because often it's the quietest voice of all that's most likely to be right...Intuition is a constantly evolving, fluid state of awareness that's always adapting to meet our present needs. It's a subtle flow that needs to be followed in the manner of a surfer riding a wave. Don't think of tuning in to intuition as receiving answers from some prophetic voice from on high, but rather as listening sensitively to the whispers of your own higher self.[15]

Recently, when severe shoulder and arm pain nearly prevented me from writing, I began to listen more carefully to the messages that seemed to be arriving from the superconscious.

A friend suggested mud treatments, and when I asked my family physician's permission for the therapy, he insisted on a sonogram. It showed several areas of inflammation in the shoulder, for which he suggested physical therapy.

The therapist decided that the primary inflammation was in a nerve that runs from the neck through the shoulder to the arm. Now, with therapy and special exercises, I am grateful to be pain-free.

It was an interesting treasure hunt, with one clue leading to the next, and finally to a solution. Although I knew that the first clue (mud therapy) wasn't practical at the time, my many experiences with intuitive listening told me to keep following the trail, because I was aware that the inner guidance often comes in this way, one step at a time.*

Hallmarks of intuition

It usually takes time and repeated practice before we are able to feel completely comfortable with the methods for developing our intuition. When you feel a clear inner guidance for the first time, you may question whether it is from the wisdom of the soul, or from your own ego-born desires. How can you know the difference?

> A real intuition can never be wrong. It does not consist in believing a thing firmly or doggedly, but in knowing it directly and unmistakenly. An intuition does not contradict, but is always supported by right sense perception, reason and inference. All things known by intuition are invariably true both materially and intellectually, but the opposite is not always true.[16]

* Guidelines for receiving inner guidance are the subject of Chapter Four in Part IX.

To recognize the kind of feeling that indicates true guidance, look for three qualities: **calmness**, **clarity**, and **joy**.

1. Intuition is always based in a deep sense of **calmness** and detachment...(I)f the guidance you've received makes you feel excited or restless...then it's safe to assume that you're just going along with your own desires. (A)ssociate true guidance with a sense of calm acceptance.

2. The second thing to associate with true intuition is a sense of **clarity**. If you're visualizing different alternatives, or if guidance comes to you in a dream, it's important to distinguish between subconscious and superconscious influences. Subconscious images tend to have a certain obscurity or cloudiness to them, and the colors appear dim or muddy. These signs indicate projections of the subconscious mind and shouldn't be trusted. In superconscious experiences, the colors will be bright, pure, and brilliant, and the images filled with clarity or radiance. The clarity of colors and images are strong signs that you've tuned in to true intuition.

3. Finally, look for a sense of inner **joy**. The basis of this kind of joy should be calmness and deep impartiality. If it makes you feel emotionally excited, then it probably only reflects the temporary happiness that comes when our desires are fulfilled. True guidance should have a joy that takes you inside rather than outside of yourself. Like a current of energy, this kind of joy should take your consciousness inward and upward... with a sense of soaring freedom.[17]

How to test your intuitions

It is important to test intuitive inspiration and solutions with the conscious mind—the organizer and administrator in the family of consciousness—to see how they play out on the stage of our life, taking one step at a time and evaluating the results.

- In developing your ability to recognize intuition, it's important to test your guidance over a period of time. Unless you have no choice, don't make big decisions on the strength of intuition. It's better to begin with small decisions, and continually test your ability. You'll begin noticing that when a certain feeling comes, and you follow it, things work out well. Then there's a different feeling, less calm or clear... Gradually you'll come to understand the difference from your own experience.

- Another way to recognize intuition is to act it out and watch your reactions as you go. If you're doing the right thing, your inner feeling will gradually come stronger and clearer as you act. If you have no guidance at all, sometimes it is better just to start anyway... You'll find by doing a little, the energy starts to flow (and) the guidance gradually comes into focus.

- There's another method that has also worked for me over the years. If you're unsure of your guidance, try inwardly saying no to it and pushing it away. If the intuition continues to come back to you with strong energy, then it's probably more than just your own thoughts at work.[18]

Superconscious dreams

Our dreams are generally fashioned by the subconscious from the vast array of our experiences, and from its emotional reactions to those experiences. The subconscious can fashion fantastical narratives and images that have little relation to reality. But the intuitions, understanding, guidance, and healing that come through superconscious dreams are of another order.

> **Dreams are produced by the Life Energy passing through the film of experiences preserved in the sub-conscious mind.... The subconscious mind usually produces false dreams. The superconscious mind produces true dreams.**[19]

❊ Healed in a Dream ❊

I had lived in the Ananda Assisi community for barely two months, when I found myself in the hospital, close to death.

I had a constantly high fever, I was in the bathroom day and night with diarrhea, I couldn't digest anything, and my weight had plummeted to only thirty kilos (66 pounds).

After weeks of testing, the doctors were still confounded. They had no diagnosis, and nothing to offer other than medication to placate the diarrhea.

A young doctor came to my room one day. He said that he had recently graduated from medical school. After examining my chart, he had an intuition that I was suffering from Crohn's disease, an autoimmune inflammation of the entire intestinal tract from stomach to anus, accompanied by the symptoms I was experiencing, and fatal if untreated.

He referred me to a specialist at another hospital, where I began treatment.

Before beginning the treatment protocols, I had a dream in which I saw Paramhansa Yogananda, an orange shawl around his shoulders, seated in an armchair. I went to him and knelt, and when I kissed his feet I noticed that he had the same spots on them that I had. He lifted his pants leg, and I saw the same swelling of the ankles that I was experiencing. I thought, since he has this illness, perhaps it is not so bad. Looking into his eyes, I knew in that moment that I was healed, and that he had taken onto himself the karma of my disease.

Crohn's disease is difficult to eradicate completely, and often reappears. But in the past thirty years it has never bothered me again. I understand now that whether a realized master is living in a physical body, or if he has left this earth, he retains the compassion and the power to heal us, even in our dreams. —**Rasamayi**, *Ananda Assisi*

Superconscious Living

Based on Yogananda's teachings regarding superconscious awareness, Swami Kriyananda developed a system of "superconscious living."

> To live superconsciously is to maximize our abilities in every department of life. For the rational mind, with its focus on differences, is essentially problem-oriented. The superconscious, with its broader, more unitive view, is solution-oriented.[20]

> Learn to be solution-oriented, rather than problem-oriented. Realize that, for every problem that presents itself in your life, there has to be an <u>innate</u> solution. For all things are subject to the Law of Oneness. Learn to view life not so much analytically as from a vision of its underlying oneness.[21]

Superconscious thinking

> You don't have to be in superconsciousness to *think* superconsciously. All you have to do is train your mind to adjust your thinking to superconscious modes of perception. Think more unitively, less analytically. Concentrate on finding the relationships between things; don't dwell at length on the differences. See other people, not as separate from you, but as part of your own greater reality. Look on them as friends, even if they appear outwardly to be strangers.[22]

Superconscious surrender

> Superconscious living means to trust one's life to the flow of a higher wisdom. Superconsciousness arranges things in ways that we might never imagine.[23]

Superconscious joy

> To live superconsciously means to live with meditation-born awareness. Be guided more consciously by your inner joy. For when you are guided superconsciously, you will feel joy in everything you do. You will reach the point of understanding that, if that quiet joy is missing, whatever you contemplate doing were better left undone.[24]

CHAPTER 7: Points to Remember

- The superpower of the superconscious mind is intuition.
- Intuition is the ability to perceive truth directly, without recourse to sensory input or logical reasoning.
- Intuition is useful in all areas of inquiry – scientific, artistic, spiritual – and especially for understanding and dealing effectively with health issues.
- Intuition blossoms when the rational mind is still and the emotions are calm.
- Refer your intuitions to the conscious mind to activate and test them.
- False intuitions will become apparent as you follow them slowly, one small step at a time.

NOTES | PART SIX

Title Page
1 Yogananda, *Scientific Healing Affirmations*, 12.
2 Yogananda, "The Healing Power of Thought," *Inner Culture*, July 1934.

Chapter One
1 Yogananda, "Is God a Magician?" *Inner Culture*, April 1944.
2 Kehoe, John, "Are Thoughts Energy? How to Use Them," https://www.learnmindpower.com/are-thoughts-energy/#.
3 Haanel, Charles Francis, "The Master Key System," Chapter 8, part 18, New Thought Library, http://newthoughtlibrary.com/haanel-charles/Master-Key-System/audioEbook/master-key-systemRAW.pdf.
4 Yogananda, "Second Coming of Christ," *Inner Culture*, December 1937.
5 Yogananda, December 1937.
6 Yogananda, December 1937.
7 "It is a misnomer, in discussing the subconscious, to label it (as many do) the 'unconscious.' There is nothing unconscious about it. Indeed, there is nothing unconscious about anything. Not even the rocks are totally unconscious. There is only that aspect of consciousness of which we are not dynamically aware, in the conscious mind. In a country, this aspect would represent that segment of society which aristocrats used snobbishly to write off as the 'great unwashed.' It is the unprocessed residue of thoughts, actions, and memories that are ever present, but more or less unnoticed. They greatly influence the conscious mind, which doesn't often realize how ungoverned by free will its decisions really are."
– Kriyananda, *Awaken to Superconsciousness*, 66-67.
8 Kriyananda, *Meditation for Starters*, 21-22.

Chapter Two
1 Yogananda, "How Jesus Healed," *Inner Culture*, September 1938.
2 Yogananda, *Super-Advanced Course No. 1*, Lesson 5.
3 Yogananda, "The Healing Power of Thought," *Inner Culture*, July 1934.
4 Maloney, Bree, "The Effects of Negativity," Marque Medical, ue Meq https://marquemedical.com/effects-of-negativity/#.
5 Kriyananda, *Art and Science of Raja Yoga*, 221.
6 Navarro, Adriana, "Study Links Temperatures with Prevalence of Hate Tweets," UPI, September 16, 2022, https://www.upi.com/Science_News/2022/09/16/study-heat-hate-tweets/3581663338922/.
7 Yogananda, "Influence of Environment," *Inner Culture*, October 1938.
8 Lindberg, Sara, "Is Watching the News Bad for Mental Health?," Very Well Mind, May 18, 2020, https://www.verywellmind.com/is-watching-the-news-bad-for-mental-health-4802320.

Chapter Three
1 Yogananda, *Praecepa Lessons*, Vol. 1:16.
2 Kriyananda, *Art as a Hidden Message*, 98.
3 Yogananda, "Second Coming of Christ," *Inner Culture*, July-September 1942.
4 Yogananda, *Praecepta Lessons*, Vol. 1:16.
5 Yogananda, "The Surest Way to Prosperity," *East-West*, October 1932.
6 Kriyananda, "Concentration," *Affirmations for Self-Healing*, 81.
7 Yogananda, "Developing Memory," *Inner Culture* magazine, April 1939.

8 This advice is compiled from the *Yogoda Course*, Lesson 7 and the article "Developing and Improving Memory," *Inner Culture*, April and October 1939.
9 Epinephrine, released into blood from the adrenal medulla in response to arousing experiences, is a potent enhancer of learning and memory processing. –Gold, Paul E., "Regulation of Memory," National Library of Medicine, January 7, 2014, https://www.ncbi.nlm.nih.gov/pmc/articles/PMC4039576/#.
10 Yogananda, Praecepta Lessons, Vol. 1:16.

Chapter Four

1 Yogananda, *Super Advanced Course No. 1*, Lesson 8.
2 Yogananda, "Yogoda: Its Fundamentals," 1923.
3 Kriyananda, "Success," *Affirmations for Self-Healing*, 81.
4 Kriyananda, *The Hindu Way of Awakening*, 110-111.
5 Kriyananda, *Conversations with Yogananda* No. 216.
6 Yogananda, *The Rubaiyat of Omar Khayyam Explained*, quatrain 31.
7 Yogananda, *Advanced New Super Cosmic Science Course*, Lesson 1.
8 Paramhansa Yogananda, "Vibratory Healing," *Inner Culture* magazine, September 1936.
9 Kriyananda, *Rays of the Same Light*, Week 40, Bible, Vol. 3, 71.
10 Kriyananda, "Willingness," *Affirmations for Self-Healing*, 50.
11 *The Noble New*
Sing songs that none have sung,
Think thoughts that in brain have never rung,
Walk in paths that none have trod,
Weep tears as none have shed for Lord,
Love all with love that none have felt, and brave
The battle of life with strength unchained,
Give peace to all to whom none other gave,
Claim him your own who is e'er disclaimed
–Yogananda, *Songs of the Soul*, 51.
12 Yogananda, "Meditations and Affirmations," October-December 1941.
13 Kriyananda, *God Is for Everyone*, 80.
14 Yogananda, "The Dynamic Power of Will," *The Attributes of Success*.
15 Kriyananda, *Conversations with Yogananda* No. 421.
16 Kriyananda, *The Hindu Way of Awakening*, 215.
17 Yogananda, "A Message to All Yogoda Students," *East-West*, April 1932.
18 Yogananda, *Yogoda Course*, Lesson 1.
19 Kriyananda, *Rays of the Same Light*: Vol. 3: 71-72.

Chapter Five

1 Kriyananda, *Education for Life*, 147.
2 "Simone Biles Quotes," Mind Training, https://mindtraining.net/motivational-quotes/simone-biles.php.
3 Cohn, Patrick, "Sports Visualization: The Secret Weapon of Athletes," Peak Performance Sports, https://www.peaksports.com/sports-psychology-blog/sports-visualization-athletes/. Also see: Clarey, Christopher, "Olympians Use Imagery as Mental Training," New York Times, February 22, 2014, https://www.nytimes.com/2014/02/23/sports/olympics/olympians-use-imagery-as-mental-training.html.
How to use sports visualization for successful performance:
1. Visualize the outcome you want. When you mentally rehearse your performance in your head, make sure that you are seeing the event as you

want it to unfold. If your mental images turn negative, stop the mental tape, rewind, and restart. Then again visualize the performance you want to see.
2. Use all of your senses from your personal perspective. Visualize your sports performance in detail. What would you see, hear, feel, smell, and taste? Feel how your body would feel as you go through the motions of your performance. Try adding physical movements that coincide with the visual images. Feel the excitement of fulfilling your performance goals.
3. Practice often. Mental rehearsal is a skill that improves with repetition. Practice your visualization or imagery daily.

4 Dr. Simonton's books, *Getting Well Again* and *The Healing Journey* are available from Amazon.
5 Yogananda, *The Essence of Self-Realization* 18:17.
6 Yogananda, "Second Coming of Christ," *East-West*, August 1932.
7 Yogananda, "Meditations and Affirmations," *Inner Culture*, July-September 1941.
8 Kriyananda, "Capricorn," *Your Sun Sign as a Spiritual Guide*, 134-135.
9 Yogananda, "Improving Memory," *Inner Culture*, October 1939.
10 Kriyananda, *Education for Life*, 147-148.
11 Yogananda, *Advanced Super Cosmic Science Course*, Lesson 6.
12 Kriyananda, *Awaken to Superconsciousness*, 137.

Chapter Six

1 Yogananda, *Super-Advanced Course No. 1*, Lesson 3.
2 Yogananda, *New Super Cosmic Science Course*, Lesson 3.
3 Yogananda, "Improving Memory," *Inner Culture*, October 1939.
4 Fritzer, Lisa, "Carl Jung's Collective Unconscious Theory: What It Suggests About the Mind," VeryWell Mind, https://www.verywellmind.com/what-is-the-collective-unconscious-2671571#.
5 Yogananda, *Autobiography of a Yogi*, 154.
6 Kriyananda, *The Light of Superconsciousness*, 29.
7 Kriyananda, *Awaken to Superconsciousness*, 68.
8 Kriyananda, from an undated talk, "The Art of Superconscious Living."
9 Yogananda, "Intuitional Whispers," *Interpretation of the Bhagavad Gita*, *East-West*, October 1932.
10 Yogananda, "Second Coming of Christ," *Inner Culture*, December 1936.
11 Yogananda, "Improving Memory," *Inner Culture*, October 1939.
12 Yogananda, "Developing Memory," *Inner Culture*, April 1939.
13 Yogananda, "The Power of Habit," *East-West*, August 1933.
14 Yogananda, *New Super Cosmic Science Course*, Lesson 3. You will find this entire lesson in the Appendices for Part VI.
15 Fox, Bernard H., "The Role of Psychological Factors in Cancer Incidence and Prognosis," Cancer Network, March 1, 1995, https://www.cancernetwork.com/view/role-psychological-factors-cancer-incidence-and-prognosis.
16 Yogananda, "Questions and Answers: Anger," *Inner Culture*, March 1939.
17 Yogananda, *Super-Advanced Course No. 1*, Lesson 9.
18 Yogananda, Lesson 5.
19 Kriyananda, *A Place Called Ananda*, 150.
20 Yogananada, "Can Faith Alone Save Us?" *Inner Culture*, January 1941.
21 Yogananda, *Super-Advanced Course No. 1*, Lesson 5.
22 Yogananda, Lesson 9. The complete article is in the Appendices.
23 Yogananda, Lesson 9.
24 Yogananda, "Super-Method of Overcoming Nervousness," *East-West*, Novem-

ber 1932.
25 Kriyananda, *Secrets of Emotional Healing*, 31.
26 Yogananda, *Advanced New Super Cosmic Science Course*, Lesson 4.
27 Kriyananda, *Secrets of Emotional Healing*, 3-5.
28 Kriyananda, *Secrets of Overcoming Negative Emotions*, 17.
29 Yogananda, "Meditations & Affirmations," *East-West*, October 1933.
30 Kriyananda, *Rays of the One Light*, Week 12, 43.

Chapter Seven

1 Yogananda, *Praecepta Lessons*, Vol. 2:48.
2 Yogananda, *Super Advanced Course No. 1*, Lesson 1.
3 Yogananda, "Intuition," *Inner Culture*, December 1939.
4 Wilder, R. L., "The Role of Intuition," Science Vol. 156, No. 3775, May 5, 1967, https://www.science.org/doi/10.1126/science.156.3775.605#.
5 Poincaré, Henri, *Science and Method*. Jules Henri Poincaré was a nineteenth-century French mathematician, theoretical physicist, engineer, and philosopher of science. He laid the foundation for the modern chaos theory.
6 Kriyananda, *Awaken to Superconsciousness*, 104.
7 Kriyananda, *Intuition for Starters*, 15.
8 Yogananda, *The Science of Religion*, Chapter Three.
9 Kriyananda, *Awaken to Superconsciousness*, 243, 248.
10 Kriyananda, *Rays of the Same Light*, Week 11, Bible.
11 Rotating Field Revelation – Tesla Science Center at Wardenclyffe, **https://teslasciencecenter.org/pivotalmoments/alternating-current/**.
12 Kriyananda, *Self-Expansion through Marriage*, 60.
13 Yogananda, *Advanced New Super Cosmic Science Course*, Lesson 2.
14 Yogananda, Lesson 2.
15 Kriyananda, *Intuition for Starters*, 54, 63-64.
16 Yogananda, *Advanced Course on Practical Metaphysics*, Lesson 3.
17 Kriyananda, *Intuition for Starters*, 48-50.
18 Kriyananda, 50-51.
19 Yogananda, *Yogoda Course*, Lesson 11.
20 Kriyananda, *Awaken to Superconsciousness*, 245.
21 Kriyananda, "Meditation for Starters."
22 Kriyananda, *Intuition for Starters*, 102.
23 Kriyananda, *Awaken to Superconsciousness*, 245.
24 Kriyananda, *Meditation for Starters*, 90-94.

PART VII
HABITS

The power of habit is all supreme ....
Habits are automatic mental machines installed
by man to exercise economy in the use of initial
will power and effort required in performing actions.
Habits make the performance of actions easier.[1]

—Yogananda

Every individual is a combination of what he does
with free choice and what he does under the influence
of past tendencies and past habits .... Most people act
according to the influence of their environment, hered-
ity, and acquired habits in the present or past lives ....
Past tendencies usually appear as psychological habits
modifying, controlling and prejudicing the free choice
in man. The tendencies of earliest life in
man are due to his actions in past lives.[2]

—Yogananda

A Constellation of Addictions

They say some people are born addicts. Certainly was true in my case! By the time I was a teenager, I was smoking tobacco and marijuana and had flirted with LSD and heroin. The flirtation soon led me to bad company and eventual heroin addiction.

Whenever I stayed in a drug abuse community, I would improve. The protected environment and supportive professionals helped me overcome the habit; but when I'd leave the community I would regress. When heroin no longer gave me the satisfaction I craved, I tried cocaine, which brought new addictive behaviors such as gambling, alcoholism, and sex indulgence.

And then a slight stroke forced me to decide if I wanted to live or die. I discovered that I had a deep will to live, and I began offering fervent prayers for guidance.

I then found a spiritual community called Ananda whose residents and teachers were kind, accepting, and ever ready to help. I learned to meditate, and when I went home I stayed in touch with my new friends who encouraged and helped me through every setback. Meanwhile, the more I meditated, the better I felt.

I very much wanted to learn the Kriya technique – a desire that helped me reduce and eventually give up my drug use and other harmful behaviors. My soul rejoiced when I was accepted for Kriya initiation – and so did my new spiritual friends. Now, they are my family, and knowing that I'm not alone gives me the courage to carry on.

My morning and evening meditations give me more pleasure than drugs were ever able to. I work with handicapped children in a public school, and in my free time I volunteer with local social service organizations. My life is filled with challenges, but Kriya gives me the inner strength to face them. *–Anonymous*

PART VII   CHAPTER ONE

Habits

> Friendly habits are very helpful in performing difficult good deeds easily. Evil habits, however sympathetic, are deadly, inasmuch as they are die-hards and do not stop disturbing the Mansion of Life even when they strongly will to do so.... It is lamentable to be compelled to do evil against one's will because of the strength of an evil habit, and then to have to suffer for one's evil actions.[1] —YOGANANDA
>
> Habit is also, however, an unthinking and undiscriminating servant. If we repeat a wrong action often enough, our subconscious will direct us to keep on repeating it, even without our conscious awareness of its power to influence us.[2] —KRIYANANDA

We often pride ourselves on being independent thinkers, on having our own creative inspirations and using our own free will to make decisions. While our proud independence is occasionally true, for the most part our lives are ruled by habits. As Yogananda says:

> "It is not your passing thoughts or brilliant ideas as much as your every day plain habits that control your life." [3]

It isn't our reason or will that is in the driver's seat for most of our lives. Far more often, our behavior is shaped by our habits. What a humbling idea this is! As we develop physical, mental, and emotional habits, we turn over control to those habit mechanisms.

In *Gitanjali*, a collection of poetry by Nobel Laureate Rabindranath Tagore,* he writes:

> When it was day they came into my house and said, 'We shall only take the smallest room here.'
>
> They said, 'We shall help you in the worship of your God and humbly accept only our own share in his grace'; and then they took their seat in a corner and they sat quiet and meek.
>
> But in the darkness of night I find they break into my sacred shrine, strong and turbulent, and snatch with unholy greed the offerings from God's altar.

In the poem we see how the conscious mind, in the full daylight of reason, invites habits into its home, happy that it will require little effort to host them, and that they will free its attention for other matters. As the habits build a nest in the recesses of our subconscious mind, they seem so harmless, even helpful – yet they quietly gain power over us, until most of our actions are under their control.

A time-saving mechanism

Habits are labor-saving devices, initiated by the conscious mind, then stored as grooves in the rapid-access files of our subconscious.

> Habit formation is a device given us for the easy performance of certain actions. Habits are mental mechanisms which enable us to act automatically, leaving our consciousness free for other duties. A habit is formed by several attentive repetitions of an action.[4]

---

* Rabindranath Tagore, from an illustrious Bengali dynasty of artists, musicians and poets, wrote *Gitanjali*, a collection of poems, in his native language. He himself translated it into English and was awarded the Nobel Prize in Literature for it in 1913. The poem cited is number 33.

As children, how many times did we try to tie our shoelaces before we succeeded? How much intense concentration, with furrowed brow and deliberate, careful movements, was required? The frustration of repeated failure – and the joy of the bow staying firmly tied as we skipped away in shoes that we had tied all by ourselves! Once firmly established, the act became a habit – automatic, and no longer requiring our full attention and a deliberate effort of our will.

The subconscious mind stores countless memories that it can then access to create patterns of thought and behavior. This ability is extremely helpful when we are learning new physical movements that require lots of careful repetition until the actions become an effortless habit – for example, learning to walk, drive a car, play a sport, cut vegetables, or type with all ten fingers.

The subconscious mind also holds emotion-charged memories of the manner in which we have reacted to perceived threats, responded to criticism, or faced disappointment. These subconscious influences prompt us to act in similar, familiar and predictable ways. Our emotional intelligence is formed by the subconscious mind.

When we create a constructive habit pattern, it becomes a reliable support for our well-being, like a lovingly cultivated garden that, in time, will bear good fruits. But when an unwholesome habit takes charge, it becomes a pernicious weed in the garden of our life, strangling our willpower and rendering it impotent. Some habits give us self-mastery, while others make us slaves. It is the interplay of our good and bad habits that largely determines the condition of our physical, mental, financial, and spiritual health.

Karma

In many respects, habits are similar to karma. Karma means simply "action," from the Sanskrit verb "*kri,*" "to do or to act." Yogananda writes:

> The law of karma governs all habits of life ...[5]
> [It] is the law of action based upon the law
> of cause and effect. Every act, good or bad,
> has a specific effect upon your life.
> The effects of actions in this life remain
> lodged in the subconscious, and those brought
> over from past existences are hidden in the
> superconsciousness, ready like seeds to germinate
> under the influence of a suitable environment.
> Karma teaches that as one sows,
> so must he inevitably reap.[6]

Actions that are motivated by the ego initiate a flow of energy that returns inexorably to the actor.

> Because our every deed and desire is
> tied to ego-consciousness, the energy they
> generate rotates, like a vortex, around
> the thought, "I am: I want; I am the doer;
> I am the owner; I'm the one who is affected."
> This vortex of energy settles in the spine
> at its own level of "specific gravity,"
> according to whether it is grossly materialistic,
> or generous, or spiritually elevating.
> As the opportunity arises for fulfilling
> a desire, or for the boomerang completion
> of a deed, the energy in that vortex
> is released, and attracts to the ego
> its own natural consequences.[7]

While each single action will have some karmic consequences, repeated actions create deeper grooves in the subconscious and superconscious mind.

> Each physical activity or bodily sensation
> of disease or health, etc., cuts grooves on
> the brain-cells, which further automatically
> awaken certain habits of disease or health.
> The sub-conscious habit of disease or
> health consciousness exerts a strong influence
> on the continuity of chronic disease.[8]

As Yogananda suggests, the grooves of old habits are activated automatically in response to appropriate circumstances in our lives. Thus, we are never truly free to act as we choose – we are victims of the habits we've created. A relaxing cigarette after a meal, repeated endlessly, becomes a habitual response, and an eventual addiction.

When the soul leaves the physical body at death, it carries with it all of the records we have engraved in the subconscious and super-conscious dimensions of the mind. The conscious mind, which is dependent on external physical stimuli, is dissolved once the physical body is dissolved. The habit grooves, being independent of the physical body, survive the period between births, to return in seed form when we are reborn. In Sanskrit, these seeds are called *"samskars."*

> These samskars—the "seeds" of karma,
> as they are called—are the result of
> repeated actions (karmas) of the past—
> not only of this life, but of many
> past incarnations. Each samskar constitutes
> a subtle vortex of energy. There are
> countless such vortices in the spine.[9]

Yogananda refers to these samskar seeds as our "pre-natal karma," and to the seeds created by our current habits as our "post-natal karma." Only a very few pre-natal samskars will sprout in any single lifetime. When activated, the samskars express as *vasanas:* mental inclinations, desires, feelings, tendencies, and proclivities.

> **Man thinks he is free to do just as he likes; he little realizes to how great an extent his very likes are already decided for him by the tendencies (samskars) and impressions (vasanas) that he has built up in the past.**[10]

Parents of multiple children quickly become aware how each child, even from birth, exhibits markedly individual characteristics. One child may be peaceful, smiling, and happy to be held, while another may be restless and demanding. One child becomes fascinated by mechanical toys, while the other loves to play with coloring books.

The "nature vs. nurture" debate would be more comprehensive – and accurate – if it took into account not only our physical genetic heredity, inherited from our parents, but also our karmic inheritance. How else to account for the tendencies and talents that blossom in children at a very young age? Musical prodigy Alma Deutscher composed her first piano sonata at age six, her first violin concerto at age nine, and a full-length opera, *Cinderella*, at ten, that premiered in Vienna in 2016 under conductor Zubin Mehta. Serena Williams began playing tennis at four. Nadia Comăneci and Simone Biles started their gymnastics training in kindergarten. Negative tendencies can also sprout at a young age – Carroll Cole committed the first of his fifteen murders at age eight.

> **Everything is preordained not by some cosmic destiny, but by your own past actions. What you've done in the past makes you what you are today.**[11]

Sometimes our subconscious memories – our *vasanas* – remain dormant until late in life. Grandma Moses spent most of her life working on a farm, and only began painting after she retired in her late seventies. Guitarist James Louis Carter Ford released his first album at age seventy-seven.

Life Force / **134**

What about free will?

Free will is a two-edged sword. On the one hand, free will allows us to decide for ourselves how we will use our powers. On the other hand, we must live with the consequences of how we've used our free will.

> We are endowed with free will and act as we like, thus accumulating good or bad seeds of actions which govern all our future lives. Having free will, we are the architects of our own destiny." [12]

> One may play with worldly desires as long as he likes, returning here even millions of times, if he so chooses. Eternally, the choice is man's. [13]

In other words, when we use our free will to create new habits, we turn over a significant portion of our freedom to those habits, for good or ill.

> Ignorant people use their free will to allow themselves to be controlled and misguided by their whims, moods, prenatal habits, and instincts. [14]

> True freedom consists in doing things - eating, reading, helping, etc. - in accordance to right judgment and choice of will; not in being compelled by habits. Eat what you should eat and not necessarily what you are used to. Do what you ought, not what your habits dictate. [15]

By wisely applying the techniques in this Part, we can both free our will from the clutches of the past, and use it consciously to create healthy habits.

To do all things, guided by wisdom, is freedom. You can only change your karma if you are guided by wisdom and use will power. If you guide your actions by will power and wisdom, the power of your past wrong actions will grow weaker and your habits of good actions will grow stronger.[16]

The power of a strong will, guided by divine wisdom, is unlimited. To its possessor nothing is impossible.[17]

PART VII   CHAPTER TWO

How Habits Are Created

> Thoughts and actions, frequently repeated, form habit patterns in the subconscious mind. Habits can be positive as well as negative. Positively, they free the conscious mind to concentrate on other things.... However....if we repeat a wrong action often enough, our subconscious will direct us to keep on repeating it, even without our conscious awareness of its power to influence us.[1]

We've created some of our habits consciously and deliberately, but other habits are created over time, without our full awareness and conscious will. None of us sets out to become addicted to alcohol or tobacco, yet our enjoyment of feeling mentally and emotionally relaxed after a drink or a cigarette, over time may exert a power of attraction greater than our will to resist.

A pre-natal tendency of enjoying alcohol that we've indulged in past lives will create an attraction to alcohol in this life that can easily become a craving, then a habit, then an addiction. The pre-natal karma can be so strong that a person becomes addicted after taking a single drink. Even so, there are people who drink regularly but never become addicted, at least not yet. Less-developed habits carried over from past lives can become addictions through repeated indulgence.

All habits begin with a desire – a wish to get "something more." Without desire, there is no will to act.

Here is an example of how we can create a good habit of regular exercise. It often starts with a desire to enjoy a greater sense of well-being by developing a strong, fit body that is bursting with energy. To be successful in our fitness program, we will need to empower our desire with positive mental images and feelings: "In my mind

I see myself wearing attractive sports gear, with well-toned muscles, enjoying boundless energy and having a strong, flexible body that is ready to obey my commands, so that I can affirm to myself and to the world: "I am strong! I am healthy!"

With the desire, image, and affirmation strongly in mind, the next step is to make a **plan of action**.

- Acquire the right clothes, shoes, and equipment.
- Join a gym or fitness club, and consult a fitness trainer.
- Set aside time daily to exercise and shower afterward.
- Make sure your exercise gear and equipment are always conveniently close at hand, perhaps by having separate sets of gear at home and work.
- Adopt an appropriate diet.
- Study fitness books, articles, videos, and other materials.
- Seek out others who share your fitness passion.
- Refine and streamline your routine.

It will take time, effort, and determination to bring all of these factors into focus. At some point, the routine will begin to flow more easily, as it becomes part of our daily life. There are bound to be setbacks, and our routine may be interrupted by life events and other commitments, but if the satisfaction we are receiving from the new habit is strong, we will adapt to the interruptions and overcome the setbacks.

The key ingredients for consciously creating a new habit

1. **Desire:** a clear idea of the satisfactions you wish to enjoy
2. **An affirmation and a mental image** of yourself having achieved your goal
3. **Determination**, a firm decision on the part of your free will to do whatever is needed
4. **Preparation** of everything you'll need to realize your determination

5. **A plan** of specific actions to achieve your goal
6. **Repeating** the affirmation and actions with concentration
7. **Spending time** with people and in environments that are strong in the behaviors and accomplishments you desire.
8. **Evaluating the results** of your actions and refining your routine as needed
9. **Recognizing the satisfactions** and renewing your determination to continue and succeed

Healthy physical habits

In Part V we pondered the positive effects of healthy eating habits, exercise, and actions that cleanse toxins from our system. Consciously creating and maintaining good habits in these three areas can take us a long way toward lasting physical vitality and freedom from disease.

Mental health

Mental health depends in large part on establishing and maintaining good habits that strengthen the mind's powers of concentration, memory, will, and visualization. Just as a well-exercised body is a joy to live in, a well-focused mind is exhilarating at its own level. The focused mind is able to penetrate the unknown, find practical solutions to complex problems, and forge pathways to health and success.

Two of the most important mental attitudes that open doors for a greater flow of life force are ***positivity and optimism***. When our mind is in the habit of viewing ourselves, others, and the situations in our lives in a positive light, we are able to see fresh opportunities and potentials that would otherwise not be apparent. Even in cases of serious disease, an optimistic outlook enhances the chances of cure and recovery.

In the endnotes you'll find references to studies at Harvard Medical School on the links between health and optimism.[2]

Other mental attitudes that open doors for a flow of life force include patience, acceptance of ourselves and others and the situations with which our lives present us, faith, generosity, and kindness. In the next chapter you'll have a chance to think about which of these habits you already possess, and which you might like to develop.

> **TRY THIS**
>
> ## MY FAVORITE FRIENDLY HABIT
>
> In this exercise, you'll have an opportunity to think about and deepen your understanding of one of your friendly habits.
>
> Choose any positive habit that is beneficial for your physical, mental, emotional, and/or spiritual health. It could be related to meditation or other spiritual practices; to physical fitness, personal hygiene, a dietary regime or specific foods you habitually consume; to your approach to your work, your communication skills, a relationship; or to something else entirely.
>
> You can download the exercise from the Appendices to this chapter if you'd like to work on it digitally or print it.
>
> - Describe the habit in a short phrase.
> - What are the satisfactions or benefits you receive from the habit?
> - What thoughts activate the habit pattern?
> - Describe the sequence of actions involved in executing the habit.
> - Which people support you in this habitual behavior?
> - Which other support structures help you stay motivated?
> - How do you feel during and after you engage in the habit?

In the following chapters you'll find more exercises to help you recognize your habit friends and enemies.

Unhealthy habits

Bad habits engage our attention and energy in activities that are detrimental to our physical, mental, emotional, and financial health – such as wrong diet and habitual over-eating, lack of exercise, laziness, and procrastination, judgementalism, lack of personal and environmental cleanliness, over-spending, and greed.

Pervasive habits such as ***negativity*** and ***pessimism*** make it impossible to activate the flow of life force. Pessimism is a generic mental attitude that in turn underlies other negative tendencies such as unwillingness; moodiness; doubt; guilt; insecurity; discouragement; and poor self-esteem.

If you are someone who tends to view things pessimistically, you may have developed this outlook when a life situation required that you critically analyze the people and situations involved. Yet long after that life situation ended, you may still continue viewing everything and everyone with a doubting and pessimistic mindset.

Negativity can be a deeply engrained mental habit – an outlook that assumes bad will and bad intentions on the part of everyone. It nourishes suspicion and nervousness, seeing enemies everywhere. Taken to the extreme, it can lead to paranoia.

More serious are the habits we develop in order to satisfy a mental or emotional craving, such as the desire for pleasure or thrills, to possess things and have power over others, to escape from physical pain or mental suffering, or to protect ourselves from disappointment. These habits can lead to substance or behavioral addictions, as discussed below.

In Part IV we discussed emotional habits that entrap our willpower and instigate hormonal imbalances, the most debilitating being anger, worry, and fear, any of which can lead to panic attacks.

Cravings

Cravings, often indulged, can lead to habits that result in disease. For example, an uncontrolled craving for sugar and sweets can lead to weight gain, which in turn can lead to diabetes. A craving for excitement can lead to behavioral and substance addictions.

Addictions

An unhealthy habit becomes an addiction when the behavior interferes with our daily life, creates addiction-related neurological changes in the brain, including psychological and physiological dependency, and causes harm to ourselves and others. Whereas a bad habit is a willpower thief, an addiction is a self-created monster that has frighteningly taken over our lives. Like a driverless car without manual override, we are completely at its mercy.

Substance addictions – whether to medicines such as painkillers and sleeping pills, or to anti-anxiety medications, anti-depressants, energy boosters, mind-altering drugs, alcohol, or tobacco – effectively paralyze our will and reason and become our masters. Patients who have had a lung transplant have been known to ask for a cigarette as soon as they recovered from anesthesia. To paraphrase Mark Twain: "It's easy to quit smoking, I've done it many times." Once there are neurological alterations and chemical dependency, professional help may be required to overcome the habit completely.

Behavioral addictions can be difficult to overcome because they, too, alter the brain, especially through the production of dopamine, the "pleasure hormone," so called because the body releases it when we do things that make us feel good. Behavioral addictions can include gambling and gaming, sex, internet and social media, eating and eating disorders, even shopping and thrill seeking.

At all costs, we want to be aware of our habit-tendencies so that we can regain control before they morph into full-blown addictions that can destroy our lives.

Bad habits can be redirected

Yogananda offers a way to reclaim our freedom from habits and even serious addictions.

> The inveterate smoker, the drunkard, the opium addict, the palate slave, the sex addict, the servants of anger, jealousy – all feel that they are eternally damned because they act evilly against their desire to be good. However, there is no evil habit, however strong, that cannot be broken by good company, meditation, and continuous effort to adopt the antidote of a good habit to counteract the evil habit.[3]

In the next chapter you'll find help and inspiration for taking stock of the habits that are either promoting or hindering your health. In Chapter Five, you will find suggestions for redirecting the hypnotic power of bad habits into more positive, fulfilling channels.

CHAPTER 2: *Points to Remember*

- Our health and behavior are determined by our habits.
- Habit mechanisms are a useful device that can save us time and energy. With full awareness and proper management, habits can be our friends.
- Unmanaged bad habits can paralyze our will and have serious debilitating effects on our health.
- Habit patterns, whether created intentionally or unintentionally, create karma – they have consequences.
- The patterns that we've carried over with us from our past lives are our "pre-natal karma." They exist as samskars – tendencies that are engraved in the subconscious and superconscious dimensions of the mind.
- The habits that we consciously or unconsciously create in this life are our "post-natal karma."
- Habits are created by a determination to satisfy a desire, and by repeated thoughts and actions directed toward fulfilling the desire.
- Bad habits can be eliminated and replaced with good habits, with patience and a plan.

PART VII   CHAPTER THREE

Discovering your habit allies and enemies

> Very seldom have you realized that the health, success, and wisdom outlook of your life entirely depends upon the issue of the battle between your good and bad habits.[1] —YOGANANDA
>
> Good habits are your best helpers; preserve their force by stimulating them with good actions. Bad habits are your worst enemies; against your will they make you do things which hurt you most. They are detrimental to your physical, social, mental, moral and spiritual happiness.[2] —YOGANANDA
>
> Most people don't know the consequences of acting under the influence of bad habits until they suffer excruciating bodily pain or undergo heart-breaking sorrow. It is pain and sorrow which start the Ego to inquire about the invisible battle between free-will-initiated, wisdom-guided post-natal actions, and pre-natal karmic habits.[3] —YOGANANDA

I imagine that most of us are annoyed by the long, detailed questionnaires we're asked to fill out when we visit a doctor for the first time. They pry into our own past and the lives of our relatives, even before they ask us to describe our symptoms.

Who can know better than ourselves what is ailing us? While we cannot remember everything from our past, and certainly not from our previous lives – with a little patience, self-honesty, and courage we can come to know which of our habitual activities and mental attitudes are affecting our health.

There's no getting around it, our health is determined by the interplay between our good and bad habits. Think of your health as a battle (which is often how it feels). A good general will prepare for battle by determining the strengths and weaknesses of both sides. In all situations, awareness is the first and most important step toward improvement.

In this chapter, we will do precisely that: we will see, on the one hand, which tendencies and habits we can rely on to help us maintain and improve our health. On the other hand, we'll look at any health-destroying habits that are arrayed in battle against us.

The following exercise will help you see your behavior patterns more clearly. (You'll also find this exercise in the Appendices, where you can work on it directly.) After completing the exercise you will, in the next chapter, choose one of your bad habits to eliminate, and a good habit to create to replace it.

Behavior analysis

Guidelines. Place a check mark (✓) next to the behaviors that describe you. Place a star (☆) next to any behaviors that have become good or bad habits.

PHYSICAL HEALTH

~ Allies ~

- A good balanced diet
- Eating in a calm environment
- Eating proper amounts
- Regular fasting
- Regular physical exercise
- Dedicating a day each week for rest and inspiration
- Adequate water/liquid intake
- Good daily personal hygiene
- Daily relaxation periods
- Recreation activities/hobbies
- Good posture
  - When walking
  - When sitting at work
  - When eating
  - When driving
  - When riding in a car or other transport
- Sleep routine
  - Same hours daily
  - Proper mattress and pillow
  - Good ventilation, fresh air
- *Add your own:*

~ Enemies ~

- Eating unhealthy snacks
- Excess consumption of sugars
- Excess consumption of salt
- Overeating
- Eating late at night
- Eating while watching the internet/news/social media
- Eating while driving
- Lack of adequate physical exercise
- Lack of enough liquids
- Doing work or watching videos, internet, social media while in bed
- *Add your own:*

~ Substance Addictions ~

- Tobacco
- Alcohol
- Caffeine
- Chocolate
- Sugary sodas, power drinks
- Mind-altering drugs
- Pain medication
- Sleep medication
- Other prescription drugs
- *Add your own:*

MENTAL AND EMOTIONAL HEALTH

~ Attitude allies ~

- Optimistic
- Kind
- Generous
- Calm
- Accepting
- Patient
- Content
- Friendly
- Enthusiastic
- Willing
- Trusting
- Serviceful
- Grateful
- Receptive
- *Add your own:*

~ Attitude enemies ~

- Choleric (bad temper, grouchy)
- Complaining
- Prone to guilt
- Blaming others
- Resentful
- Impatient
- Reluctant, unwilling
- Suspicious
- Doubting
- Fearful
- Anxious
- Discontented
- *Add your own:*

~ Behavioral addictions ~

- Gambling
- Sex
- Video games
- Internet
- Social media
- Shopping
- Risk-taking
- Procrastination
- Excess sleep

AT WORK

~ Allies ~

- Concentrating on the task at hand
- Giving each task 100% attention and energy
- Removing distractions before starting
- Bringing tasks to completion
- Having a clean, well-organized work space
- Having comfortable and ergonomic equipment
- Insuring proper lighting and air circulation
- Being enthusiastic for each task
- Committing to projects and to the team
- Dealing with problems and obstacles energetically and creatively
- Prioritizing daily tasks
- Including physical movement and mental relaxation throughout the work day
- *Add your own:*

~ Enemies ~

- Having a cluttered work space
- Multi-tasking and losing focus
- Procrastination: putting off unpleasant tasks
- Getting easily distracted
- Keeping social and news channels open during work
- Responding to non-work-related messages throughout the day
- Answering unrelated phone calls during work
- Doing tasks with a minimum of energy
- Leaving a project, communication network, or team when faced with difficulties or opposition
- *Add your own:*

HUMAN RELATIONSHIPS
Home, Work, Friends

~ Allies ~

- Truthful
- Respectful
- Generous
- Accepting
- Forgiving
- Flexible
- Communicative
- Loving
- Empathetic
- Patient
- Collaborative
- *Add your own:*

~ Enemies ~

- Judgmental/critical of others
- Jealous
- Possessive
- Disrespectful
- Suspicious
- Closed, non-communicative
- Mentally rigid
- Competitive
- Argumentative
- *Add your own:*

RELATIONSHIP WITH MONEY

~ Allies ~

- Earn honestly
- Spend within means
- Generous
- Unattached
- Invest wisely
- Charitable to individuals
- Help causes
- Maintain accurate records
- *Add your own:*

~ Enemies ~

- Dishonest
- Spend more than I earn
- Ungenerous
- Miserly
- Spend unnecessarily
- Anxious
- Attached
- Careless with money
- *Add your own:*

SPIRITUAL PRACTICES

~ Allies ~

- Regular practice
- Practice with devotion
- Practice with concentration
- Practice with enthusiasm
- Participate in group meditations, in person and/or online
- Watch spiritual programs online
- Watch/listen to spiritual talks
- *Add your own:*

~ Enemies ~

- Irregular practice
- Distracted during practice
- Sleepy during practice
- Lackluster practice
- Careless practice
- Mechanical practice
- Put off meditation
- *Add your own:*

PART VII   CHAPTER FOUR

Eliminating Bad Habits

> Bad habits are your worst enemies; against your will they make you do things which hurt you most. They are detrimental to your physical, social, mental, moral and spiritual happiness. Starve bad habits by refusing to give them any further food of bad actions."[1] –YOGANANDA
>
> You are the maker of your habits and you must undo them by regular effort... Try from today to overcome the hidden enemy habits within you... and be free to act from reason alone. Your habits are not you. Be yourself, and you will remember the lost image of God within you...Do not despair about your undesirable habits, simply stop feeding them by repetition." [2] –YOGANANDA
>
> If you have a habit–mental, physical, or spiritual– that impedes your progress, rid yourself of it now; do not put it off.[3] –YOGANANDA

I love to weed my flower garden – it provides me with healthy exercise and teaches me how to deal with my habits. A weed may look sweet and innocent, but even the scraggliest has a robust root system, and hacking off its head won't put an end to it. The roots will keep it alive, ready to emerge with the next rain. The only way to get rid of it permanently is to dig out the roots, which is a lot harder.

Admittedly, eliminating bad habits and developing new ones in their place will always take considerable effort and time. We've acquired so many unhealthy habits over countless lives – is there any end in sight? We'll have to fight these battles not only to reclaim our health, but to reestablish the nobility of our soul and the freedom of will with which we were created. As Sri Krishna tells his beloved disciple Arjuna in the Bhagavad Gita: "You are a great warrior, stand up and fight."

Think of a bad habit that you've succeeded in overcoming. Remember how you felt when you conquered it, and the impact the victory has had on your life. Many people have overcome their addiction to smoking. They all report a remarkable improvement in their overall health, particularly their breathing, with fewer colds and ear infections, improved appetite, more acute smell and taste, better skin tone, and a more comfortable ability to engage in physical activity and sports.

Every week without nicotine brings well-documented changes: [4]

- Within 20 minutes of quitting, your blood pressure and heart rate drop to normal.
- Within 12 hours of quitting, your blood carbon monoxide level drops to normal.
- Within 2 weeks to 3 months of quitting, your circulation improves and your lung function increases.
- Within 1 to 9 months of quitting, coughing and shortness of breath decrease. Your airways are better able to clear the lungs, and there's a reduced risk of infection.
- Within a year of quitting, your risk of coronary heart disease is half that of someone who is still smoking, and your heart attack risk has fallen dramatically.

The U.S. Centers for Disease Control and Prevention report that quitting smoking reduces the risk of twelve cancers, including lung, colon, liver, and leukemia.[5]

The psychological benefits of overcoming a bad habit are no less spectacular: increased self-confidence and self-esteem, and a lasting joy in being a victor and no longer a victim. The experience of vanquishing a negative habit gives us a tremendous psychological boost that can help us climb the steps to other victories. The energy that was trapped in a bad habit is now available for new and healthier undertakings.

Choose three unhealthy habits

From the **Behavior Analysis** exercise in the last chapter, choose three bad habits you'd like to eliminate. When you are in a calm frame of mind, ideally after meditating, ask your higher, intuitive Self which habits are appropriate for you to confront at this point in time.

This is an important step, since enlisting a higher power will help you enormously in your efforts to succeed. In a future chapter, we'll look more deeply at ways to enlist the superconscious mind to help us in our efforts to overcome negative habits.

Here are some suggestions for choosing which habit you'd like to overcome:

1. To start, choose a habit that you're fairly sure you can overcome in the short term – say, over a period of about six months. It might not be the habit that's the most detrimental to your health – but a victory here will give you energy and confidence to tackle harder ones. Choose a small habit you might have been thinking about changing, like eliminating dairy or wheat products, coffee, or snacking between meals. If it's too much, leave it for the next level and choose something less intimidating. It could be leaving the dishes to be washed later or by someone else, or the mental habit of criticizing a certain person at home or work.

2. With a victory under your belt, choose a habit that is affecting your health more seriously, and that may require more effort and time to overcome, such as eliminating caffeine, processed sugars, tobacco, or other addictive substances. You could choose a mindset or attitude you'd like to be rid of, such as complaining when events aren't to your liking, or putting off doing certain tasks.

3. The third habit should be one that is seriously detrimental to your health, and that has become thoroughly ingrained, possibly to the point of addiction.

How long does it take to overcome a bad habit?

There are many factors that can influence how long it takes to eliminate an unwelcome habit from your life – including how long the habit has been entrenched, the extent to which it has imprisoned your will, and how much satisfaction or relief you experience from indulging in it. Most of all, it will depend on the depth of your determination to eliminate it, and the amount of consistent, focused attention you can muster to get rid of it.

> People wish to get rid of the germs of bad habits, but seldom actually adopt suitable measures for eliminating or destroying them, and few persist in their use of such mental hygienic measures. They forget that the powerful grip of a habit took a long time to tighten, gradually and by constant repetition. To undo it or loosen its hold also requires time.[6]

Parallel strategies

Yogananda proposes that to overcome a harmful habit we engage in a two-pronged approach. First, we should ***"starve bad habits by refusing to give them any further food of bad actions."*** [7]

Before we can begin to starve a bad habit effectively, we will need to have an understanding of how the habit operates. Exposing its false promises, and the mechanisms, environments, and support systems that sustain it, will put us in a much better position to eliminate it.

Drawing on Yogananda's writings, I've developed a process that makes it much easier to "unmask and disarm" a habit by bringing the skeletons out of the closet and into the clear light of day. **You can find this exercise in the Appendices** where you can complete it on your computer or a printed copy. As you go through the exercise point by point, you may feel a resistance on the part of the old habit soldiers who want to keep themselves hidden, undercover, and unknown. It generally takes going through the exercise several times to discover the habit's subtle lies.

Exposing an unhealthy habit

- **The habit I am determined to eliminate.** Maya (the power of delusion) thrives in darkness. If we can lure a bad habit from its lair and describe it in crystal-clear words, pronouncing them aloud and writing them down, it will help bring the habit out of the fog of the subconscious mind onto the field of the conscious clarity where we can weaken its power over us.
- **The reasons I started this habit.** Try to remember the time in your life before the habit took hold, and ask yourself why you started down this road. There may be many reasons, and they may be intertwined with various aspects of your life. As the exercise proceeds, you may find that you can remember your first expectations more clearly.
- **The satisfactions I used to receive.** For a tendency or a routine to become a habit, there had to be rewards that invited you to continue. What were those rewards?
- **The satisfactions or advantages it offers you now.** Over time, the rewards may have become less attractive and satisfying. What satisfactions are you receiving from the habit today?
- **The unhealthy side-effects.** You've identified this behavior as a bad habit – what harmful effects are you currently experiencing?
- **The thought or thoughts that trigger the habit.** Every action begins with a thought. The thought "I'm hungry" triggers a chain of actions that will result in eating. Devouring a chocolate bar might be a habit pattern that began with the thought "I've worked hard this morning – I deserve a treat." Or "My energy is flagging and my brain is pooped, I need chocolate." What thoughts are sure to set your chosen habitual behavior in motion?
- **The chain of specific thoughts and actions that led to the habit's formation.** Habits are formed by repeated actions. You've likely formed a routine or ritual connected to the habit. In your mind's eye, see yourself engaged in the habit, and write down your process.

The process always starts with a thought. The thought-trigger for coffee drinking might be "I need an energy boost – time for coffee!" If you're driving to work or to an appointment, the ritual behavior might look like this: you think of a favorite coffee shop nearby, find a parking space, place your order, do something while you wait, add the usual amount of sweetener, take a few sips, head back to the car, and continue on your way.

If you're at home, or have access to coffee at your workplace, there may be other specific rituals and repeated actions.

Write down the sequence of thoughts and actions that lead you to act out the habit you've chosen.

- **The environment and circumstances where the habit manifests.** An alcoholic seeks bars, restaurants, and events where liquor is served. The coffee drinker knows where the best coffee is sold. The chocolate lover will visit websites, bakeries, sweet shops, and events where chocolate is sold, discussed, and consumed, and perhaps watch the film *Chocolat* from time to time.

  What kinds of environments and situations stimulate and nourish your habit?

- **The people and support structures that encourage or enable me to indulge in the habit.** We are attracted to, and attract to ourselves, people and groups that engage in the activities we treasure. Among your friends and relatives, there may be some "enablers" who'll be ready to support you in the habit. There may be clubs, chat groups, and social media where you feel comfortable and accepted by fellow indulgers. Describe the support system you've developed that encourages and feeds the habit.

- **How do you feel when the habit overtakes you?** Do you feel relieved by the satisfaction the habit provides? Have you noticed and felt concerned about the ill effects it has on your health, your work, and your family life? Do you feel frustrated or guilty, or both? Try to describe your feelings and emotions when you find yourself trapped in the habitual behavior.

- **Why do you want to eliminate the habit?** Write down the key reasons you want to eliminate the habit.

- **What actions are you willing to avoid?** There are two ways to get rid of weeds in your garden: remove them altogether including the roots, or stop giving them nourishment. In a future chapter, we'll look at ways to remove the roots of bad habits by superconscious means. For now, just know that starving a habit is the key, and the essence of every successful approach.

> If a bad habit bothers you, do two things.
> Negatively, try to avoid it in everything
> that occasioned it or stimulated it, without
> concentrating on it in the zeal to avoid it.
> Then positively try to divert your mind to some
> good habit, and keep it furiously engaged in
> culturing it, until it becomes a part of yourself. [8]

We've mentioned willpower often – but there's another side of the coin. Yogananda called it "won't power." To eliminate a habit, we need to develop the power to resist – to simply and forcefully say "No!"

When I was eliminating sweets from my diet, there were several things I had to resist. One was socializing after meals. The longer I stayed, the more likely I would succumb to dessert. I would excuse myself gracefully, but there were leftover desserts at breakfast the next day, and sometimes at lunch. I had to pass the table on my way to and from meals, and each time I would say aloud: "NO, THANK YOU!" Eventually I discovered a side door from the dining room I could take to avoid the sweets.

List here the actions you need to eliminate. If you're struggling with a substance addiction, professional help may be advisable, supplemented by your own efforts to strengthen your willpower and create a healthy lifestyle.

What environments and people are you willing to avoid? While developing a new habit, you'll likely be attracted to new friends and environments, so you won't feel alone and empty for having lost the old places and pals. Yogananda's very helpful saying bears repeating: *"Environment is stronger than willpower."*

> In preventing the nourishment of bad habits,
> one must get away from evil surroundings,
> and above all, one must never bring evil
> thoughts into the mind. The latter causes
> the former and is more dangerous. [9]

CHAPTER 4: Points to Remember

- Bad habits are your greatest enemies. They will follow you from one lifetime to the next until you can finally succeed in overcoming them.
- You can unmask and deflate the power of a bad habit by recognizing its false promises and harmful effects.
- Starve a bad habit by refusing to feed it any longer with bad actions.
- Remove yourself from the environments and people that encourage the bad habit.
- "It is very consoling to know that no matter how strong the powers of evil habit and material desire are, at any moment in life, there are the soldiers of good habits of this life and of past incarnations ready to give battle." [10]

A Whisper from Eternity

Teach me, O Spirit, to distinguish between the soul's lasting happiness and the temporary pleasures of the senses: touch, taste, smell, sight and hearing.

Strengthen my will-power; teach me not to be enslaved by bad habits.

Teach me to be guided by good habits, formed through good company and meditation.

Teach me, above all, to be guided by wisdom; teach me to stay away from evil, by right judgment and discrimination.

Teach me to adopt willingly the good, being guided by my free choice, and not compelled to evil by hardened habits. [11]

PART VII CHAPTER FIVE

Habit Exchange

> A strong bad habit can be displaced by a strong good habit, which can be created by the repetition of good actions."[1] —YOGANANDA
>
> Habits can be overcome in a day. They are nothing but concentration of the mind. You are concentrating one way. Concentrate another way, and that undesirable habit will cease to exist![2] —KRIYANANDA
>
> Bad habits cannot be destroyed by mere willingness to eradicate them, but only by adopting the antidote of good habits.[3] —YOGANANDA
>
> There is no evil habit, however strong, that cannot be broken by good company, meditation, and continuous effort to adopt the antidote of a good habit to counteract the evil habit.[4] —YOGANANDA
>
> Powerful bad habits can be displaced by opposite good habits if the latter are patiently cultured. First crowd out all bad habits by good habits in everything, then culture the consciousness of being free from all habits...[5] —YOGANANDA

We can apply the willpower we've developed in the struggle to eliminate bad habits to create good, healthy habits in their place. We can channel the energy we formerly invested in the old habits in more positive directions.

Let's review the factors needed to create a good habit

- **Desire:** a clear mental idea, image, and feeling of the satisfaction you want to attain
- **A strong mental image** and affirmation of yourself having achieved the goal
- **Determination**, a firm decision by your own free will to do whatever is needed
- **Preparation** of everything you'll need to realize your determination
- **A focused plan** of all the specific sequential actions that will take you to your goal
- **Repeating the affirmation** and actions with deep concentration
- **Being in environments** and with people who are strong in the desirable behaviors
- **Evaluating the results** of your actions and refining your routines as needed
- **Acknowledging the rewards** and renewing your determination to continue and succeed

Based on your results in the last two exercises (Behavior Analysis and Exposing an Unhealthy Habit), you can choose the good habit you want to create to replace or positively re-direct the energy and willpower trapped in the bad one.

Ask your higher, intuitive Self to help you create the new habit – just as you did when choosing a negative habit to eliminate.

 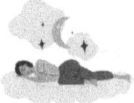    

One possibility is to choose a good habit that is the opposite of the old one. For example, if the habit you want to overcome is being overly critical and judgmental of others, you might choose to create a habit of offering your understanding and support, starting with a person you've formerly judged. If the undesired habit is procrastinating, the new one might be a "Do It Now" approach to your life: immediately performing essential tasks, or at least immediately setting out in the right direction.

In the following story, Alessandra recalls how she replaced a bad habit with its opposite.

❋ Awake and ready! ❋

They say that dawn, just before the sun rises, is an ideal time to meditate. My usual wake-up time was 7:30, and if I wanted to meditate before going to work, I needed to convince myself to get up earlier. I noticed that when I succeeded in meditating in the early morning, I felt better throughout the day, and things seemed to go more smoothly.

The 7:30 habit was fairly deep-rooted, so I needed a strategy. The first thing I did was to put a recording of Yogananda on my phone and set the alarm for ten minutes earlier in the morning – so the Guru's thunderous voice would shake me from my slumber. On my nightstand I put a photo of Sri Yukteswar whose firm gaze ensured that I wouldn't go back to sleep.

I moved the alarm ten minutes earlier each day, and in less than two weeks I was waking up at 6 a.m. Since I achieved that goal, I wake up automatically now every morning at 6 a.m. without effort. This victory strengthened my willpower and gave me confidence to make other positive changes in my life. –*Alessandra*, *Siena, Italy*

At the other end of the sleep spectrum, Loredana made a significant change.

❊ Night Owl No Longer ❊

Since I was a child, I've always had a habit of going to bed very late. Studying, working, and writing were my late-night activities. About five years ago, when a period of intense stress began, my late-night habit led to severe insomnia. For about a year I hardly slept, often spending the entire night wide awake, my mind spinning with a thousand thoughts.

In keeping with Paramhansa Yogananda's teachings about habits, I slowly tried to replace the habit of going to bed late with a habit of going to bed at a more sensible, stipulated time. At first it was very difficult, since the habit was so deeply engrained. I gradually developed a nighttime routine of drinking a relaxing herbal tea, surrounding myself with positive images and thoughts, and going to bed with a spiritual book.

Consistently repeating these healthier behaviors, combined with daily prayer and meditation, made it possible to stop burning the midnight oil and start having a restful sleep. **–Loredana**, *Rome*

Another approach is to find a new habit that actually delivers the satisfaction you're seeking, without the negative side effects. If the bad habit you've chosen to eliminate is coffee-drinking, for example, and the main reward is that it gives you energy, the new habit could be a combination of natural energy-boosting vitamins and minerals, and practicing the Life Force Full Body Recharge* exercise, which gives the desired energy boost without side-effects and can be done virtually anywhere in the same time it would take to make or buy and drink a cup of coffee.

If overeating or food cravings are habits you want to eliminate, and the reward you're seeking is a feeling of being full and complete, a possible new habit might be a fitness regime, or doing pranayama breathing exercises when the craving strikes, as well as regular meditation that creates feelings of completeness and inner peace.

---

* See pages 275-291 in Part IV, Volume One.

How long will it take to establish a new habit firmly?

Yogananda points out the many variables involved in establishing a new habit pattern.

> Slow or rapid habit formation depends on the general state of health; on the condition of the nervous system, including that of the brain cells; on habit-forming methods, mental imagery, will.... Any habit can be installed in the brain, almost instantaneously at will, by creating brain-grooves through the power of deep trained attention....
>
> It does not take long to develop good mental habits. In fact, by exercising strong will, mental habits of health or success or wisdom may be formed at once. By concentrating with perseverance, courage, and faith in God and oneself on legitimate necessities, one can materialize them at will.... An intelligent, purposeful individual can easily form or substitute a good mental habit for a bad one, in a trice.[6]

The requirements needed for establishing a new habit quickly

- A strong nervous system and brain
- The ability to concentrate deeply – to focus the mind powerfully
- Strong will power and iron determination
- Courage and perseverance
- Faith in God and in oneself

HOW TO CREATE A NEW HABIT

We are often unable to bring all of the above-mentioned faculties to bear with full force. Therefore, let's consider a step-by-step process that, with enough commitment and perseverance, can bring us real inner freedom from habits. *You'll find a copy of the exercise in the Appendices for Part VII, to complete digitally or print.*

- **I choose and commit to create the following positive habit.** Describe the new habit you wish to put in place. You're affirming your commitment to achieve your goal, and giving it a concrete reality in writing. It isn't necessary to set a fixed timeframe for creating the new habit, unless you feel it will help motivate you.

- **The benefits I hope to experience.** What are the ways you expect that you and your life will improve?

- **This is what I will look like and how I will feel when I've succeeded in developing this new habit.** Try to visualize yourself and describe in words how you'll look and feel once you've succeeded in this worthwhile endeavor.

- **This is the affirmation that I will repeat every day very consciously in order to engrave the new habit-grooves on all levels of my awareness.** Create a short phrase that encompasses your goal, and the inner feeling the goal holds for you.

Some years ago, I created an affirmation for myself to develop a habit of being more supportive of others: "I am sweet, I am kind. I am the friend of all. I see the good in all." An affirmation for creating a habit of regular morning meditation might be: "My soul loves to meditate, and so do I. I am calm and creative throughout the day."

If the new habit you want to develop is having a more positive attitude to replace a mental habit of skepticism and negativity, consider these words of Swami Kriyananda.

> Develop a habit, in response to every challenge, of saying, "I can!" "I can!" is the yes-saying principle in action. Unwillingness must be nipped in the bud. Let your first instinct be, rather, to affirm your openness to new possibilities. Habitual skepticism kills opportunity. The time exists, indeed, for reasoned consideration, but this time comes after one has affirmed his willingness to approach a new idea constructively.[7]

- **Other thoughts I will use to trigger** the new habit pattern. Let's say your goal is to replace coffee with the Life Force Full Body Recharge. Some motivating thoughts might be: "Time for a natural energy boost!" "I will take a drink from the fountain of pure prana." "Energy and joy flood my body cells." What thoughts will help you stay motivated in establishing your chosen new habit?

- **Demotivating thoughts that might arise.** We should expect that the ego will try to counter our good intentions with negative thoughts: "You've tried this before and you've failed. You'll never succeed." When you're getting ready to exercise, you may find the ego protesting: "You're too tired! It's too cold!"

  Jot down some of the demotivating thoughts you expect the ego will offer to dissuade you from your new habit. When the ego assails you with these thoughts, how will you respond? It's a good idea to be prepared with a number of strong responses.

- **Plan ahead.** Success in any endeavor requires careful preparation. Before cooking a meal, a good chef prepares the pots, the ingredients, and the cooking area. Before a concert, a musician prepares the instrument, practices the required skills, and makes sure that all the necessary equipment will be on the stage.

  When we're establishing a habit of morning meditation, there's a great deal we can do to prepare.

  ~ Dinner the evening before needs to be light, and not too late.

  ~ Adequate sleep is required.

- You'll need an alarm that will actually get you out of bed. You can set your smartphone to ring with a loud sound, music, or voice that will motivate you to get up.
- It's good to get up at a time when you can meditate without feeling rushed to start your daily activities.
- It's good to have a comfortable seating arrangement – chair, meditation bench, cushions, etc. – that meets your needs.
- It's very helpful to dedicate a small area of your home to be used only for meditation, where you won't be disturbed, and a meditative vibration will develop over time.
- You may need to arrange for someone to care for your children and pets during your meditation time.

Write down all of the preparations you'll need to make to ensure the success of your new habit.

- **My action plan.** A new habit becomes engraved in the subconscious mind by our oft-repeated thoughts and actions, accompanied by a feeling of satisfaction.

> **DETERMINATION + AFFIRMATION + VISUALIZATION + ACTIONS + REPETITION = NEW HABIT**

We need to perform every action with our full awareness and deep concentration, to imprint it in the memory banks of the subconscious.

> Attention is the needle that forms the grooves of mental good or bad habits. It is by deep attention to an evil experience or good experience that a bad or good habit is formed in the brain. These good or bad habits remain in the brain like good and bad records of human experience. As ordinary phonographic records can be played by a needle, so the good and bad records in the brain grooves can be played and brought forth by the needles of attention.[8]

The helpful actions need to be repeated frequently. The key to rapid habit formation is conscious repetition with deep concentration. Over time, through trial and error, you'll establish a routine that you'll be able to rely on, much like the morning hygiene routine that turns you out clean, fully awake, fresh and ready for the day. Write out a step-by-step plan to develop your new habit.

- **Stepping stones along the way.** New habits are generally formed one step at a time, incrementally, possibly by setting small goals and enjoying small victories along the way. If your goal is to develop a habit of "Doing It Now!" to replace an old, unwanted habit of putting things off, you could start by doing a single specific thing that you formerly resisted doing. Having formed a habit of doing that one small thing right away, you can proceed to the next thing you habitually resist doing. At some point, you can expect that the energy you're investing will reach a critical mass and overwhelm the old procrastination habit, and from then on you'll naturally and happily do all tasks promptly.

- **Supportive environments.** If your desired new habit is regular meditation, you'll be greatly helped by creating lots of positive energy around the new habit – for example, by choosing a meditation nook that is thoroughly to your liking, with proper temperature, fresh air, a favorite incense if it helps, and so on. No matter how chaotic the rest of your house might be, this will be your private oasis of peace where you can meditate, do yoga, read, and listen to spiritual inspiration. A friend of mine transformed her children's outgrown tree house into a delightful meditation space – little chance of being disturbed up there!

In fact, nature can offer us many wonderful environments for meditation. You may find it helpful to meditate in a secluded peaceful place outdoors where you won't be disturbed. The Himalayan yogis traditionally seek rivers, forests, mountains, lakes, and the ocean for meditation.

Places where people have often meditated and prayed, where holy persons have lived, and where healings have occurred can carry powerfully uplifting vibrations that will enhance your meditations and help you stay motivated.

Write down some favorable environments nearby that will help reinforce your new habit.

- **A network of supportive friends.** Write down a list of people who are strong in the habit you want to develop, and try to spend more time in their company. They will inspire you, and introduce you to a whole new world of ideas, people and places.

- **Other resources that can inspire and motivate me in my new endeavor.** Which writings, workshops, conferences, and other motivational resources might help you keep your enthusiasm alive?

- **Expect setbacks, and plan ahead.** It's unrealistic to imagine that our old habits will simply wither away. They are bound to bob up, time after time, especially when we are threatening to replace them.

> It is only when [we] mean business and make repeated struggles to establish the generals of good habits in the Kingdom of Consciousness, that the bad habits become afraid and make furious attempts to oust the good intruders.[9]

- *You might consider keeping a journal* of your progress in developing the new habit. Record the benefits you are reaping from your new habit – this will motivate you to keep going. A journal will help you stay on alert for the attacks of old bad habits. The ego will often want to ignore, hide from, or lightly dismiss these attacks, but this isn't a helpful response. By noting them down in your journal as they occur, with the attitude of a good journalist – just reporting the facts without emotion or guilt – you will expose them to the clear light of day, where it will be much easier to deal with them than if they remained as no more than hazy subconscious influences.

Make a plan for how you will respond when the old habit re-emerges. How will you respond mentally? It can be a simple, lighthearted: "Aha! – I caught you!"

The moment you unmask the intruder, strongly repeat your new-habit-affirmation, over and over.

Now, describe the first steps you will take to counter the old habit with a new one.

CHAPTER 5: *Points to Remember*

- You can re-direct the energy and willpower trapped in bad habits into healthy good habits.

- Establishing a new habit requires a firm resolve, a plan, and repeated thoughts and actions.

- When choosing a new habit to cultivate, consult your higher, intuitive Self that always has your best interests at heart.

- **Determination + Affirmation + Visualization + Actions + Repetition = New habit**

- Expect setbacks, and be ready for them.

PART VII   CHAPTER SIX

Superconscious Solutions

> All effects or seeds of our past actions (karma) can be destroyed by roasting them in the fire of meditation, concentration, the light of superconsciousness, and right actions, free from the selfish desire for the fruit of action.[1] –YOGANANDA
>
> An important factor in overcoming karma is meditation. Every time you meditate, your karma decreases, for at that time your energy is focused in the brain and burns up the old brain cells. After every deep meditation, you will find yourself becoming freer inside.[2] –YOGANANDA
>
> A person suffering from evil habits and evil-saturated brain cells can free himself by learning methods of meditation from spiritual teachers and practicing them regularly until his evil habit is transformed by good habits of calmness and peace, and his evil-saturated brain cells are cauterized by divine energy and charged into good-saturated brain cells.[3] –YOGANANDA

Eliminating a bad habit – especially a deeply-rooted bad habit carried over from past lives, and reinforced in this life – is a challenging task that will require steady determination, wise methods, and the help of divine intervention. To rely solely on our own power would be like riding a single-geared bicycle up a steep mountain. Calling on the divine help radically changes the dynamic – it's like climbing the mountain on a forty-gear bike with a silent partner Who does three-fourths of the work.

> **The superconscious is that level of awareness which is often described as the higher Self. It is from this level, for example, that great inspirations come. It is through the superconscious that divine guidance descends and true healing takes place.[4]**

In recent chapters we talked about using the superpowers of the conscious mind – concentration, willpower, and visualization – to reprogram the subconscious, where most of our habit grooves are stored. Now, we want to enlist the support of the *superconscious* mind to help us eliminate the seeds of negative habit-karma, with the aid of time-tested spiritual practices.

Most of the habits we manifest in this lifetime were developed over many lives. We have seen how the karmic seeds (*samskars*) of our habits survive physical death. At our next birth, those seeds will

pass from our causal realm of ideas – the thought of the habit – to be stored in the astral energy centers of the spine, where some of them will awaken in this life, while others will remain dormant, their influence invisible yet subtly present, perhaps as subtle tendencies of which we aren't consciously aware.

Yogananda taught that these seeds of habits are lodged in various places:

> *Pre-natal actions (are) entrenched in the superconscious and subconscious territory in the cranial region of man. Post-natal actions are entrenched in the tract of the conscious body of man.*[5]

Life Force / **174**

The conscious mind uses reason and logic, which can be labored and time-consuming. The superconsciousness, on the other hand, with its intuitive powers, can directly, and even instantaneously, eradicate harmful habits, awaken seeds of good habits, and create entirely new habits.

In this chapter, we will consider several ways to activate the power of superconsciousness, meditation being the most effective for this worthwhile endeavor.

How superconsciousness deals with habit grooves

Our habit patterns lodge in the brain, where Yogananda likens them to **"groove-like shelves in the convolutions of the grey matter."**[6]

The frequency of the repetition of a habit pattern over time and incarnations determines the depth of its groove and how firmly the seeds are buried there. But the soil in which those furrows and seeds exist can be tilled by the practices in this book, and the habit weeds removed by their very roots.

> As acids can dissolve a record, so the mental and physiological grooves in the brain cells of an error-stricken individual can be obliterated by the transmission of Life Force. Erroneous habits can be changed to good habits in individuals.[7]

In a state of superconscious awareness, we can bring life force to bear on the task of removing the habit grooves in the brain:

> In deep meditation the energy accumulates in the brain .... withdraws the life force from the muscles and nerves, and concentrates [it] in the brain cells where the evil mental habits are grooved .... seeking out the evil habits and cauterizing them.[8]

Although the seeds of our karma may be seemingly endless, Yogananda promises we can eliminate them all – even in one lifetime.

> If a soul is determined enough and meditates a great deal, he can destroy all the bad karma of his past lives in this one life. People suffer the lengthy effects of their actions because they don't use the antidotes by which they can destroy the hidden tendencies accruing from their past bad actions...The fire of deep and constant meditation cauterizes the brain grooves which contain the records of bad karmic tendencies of past lives, and thus overcomes their hidden evil.[9]

PRACTICES TO DISLODGE HABITS

The following meditation exercises will help you direct your attention to the brain and mentally release the seeds of long-standing habits.

~ Release habit seeds ~

- As you meditate, let the breath flow of its own accord, in its own rhythm. The cycles of breath will not follow an established pattern or rhythm; they will vary from one cycle of inhalation/exhalation to the next.
- Focus your attention and your gaze calmly, with relaxation, at the spiritual eye.
- Observe the flow of the breath at the spiritual eye.
- Imagine that each cycle of breath is causing the point between the eyebrows to be filled with light. This light will, with further practice, eventually permeate the brain.
- As the breath continues to flow and the light intensifies, the seeds of karma and bad habits will become dislodged from the grooves in the brain.
- With each inhalation, bring them to a focus at the spiritual eye, and with each exhalation disperse them. Try to visualize this process: the gathering of habit seeds in a ball

of energy at the spiritual eye during inhalation, and their complete dispersal during exhalation.

- You can accompany the process by mentally repeating an affirmation – for example, saying "I am" during inhalation, and "free" during exhalation – or "Habits" with inhalation, and "be gone!" with exhalation as they disperse. (You can create your own affirmations.)

~ Toss the seeds in a bonfire ~

Relax, and sit comfortably in any meditation pose.

- Center your attention at the spiritual eye. Visualize there a bonfire where you will toss the *samskars* that are located in the *sushumna* and *chakras*.
- Imagine a current coming up the center of the spine very slowly from the base to the medulla oblongata, and then through the brain to the point between the eyebrows. (The duration of this ascent should be not less than one minute.)
- Feel each chakra as you draw the current through it; chant AUM there, if you like, and visualize the rays from that chakra turning upward toward the brain.[10]
- Imagine the seeds of karma in each chakra being released into the upward-flowing current.
- When they arrive at the spiritual eye, cast them into the bonfire with the affirmation, "I am free!"

~ Shine a laser beam of light ~

The following technique was fashioned from numerous instructions by Yogananda and can be practiced at the conclusion of each meditation:

- In deep meditation, focus your attention and life force calmly at the spiritual eye.

- Transform the energy into a sphere of blazing light, and with willpower and imagination, shine the light throughout the brain, burning the habit seeds lodged in the grooves there.
- Pass the cauterizing light through the brain many times.
- If you wish, you can link the process to the breath, inhaling as you focus on the power of the sphere of light, and exhaling as you pass its rays through the brain.
- You can accompany the exhalation with a mental affirmation: "I am free, ever free!"

You can then use the ray of light to heal any body part, by passing it from the brain, down the spine, and outward through the nerves to the weak or diseased part, infusing the affected cells with the light of perfect health. This practice is in accordance with Yogananda's technique of Life Therapy: **"To effect direct healing by the rays of inner Life Force."**

> During meditation the Yogi feels the power of concentration in the will centre, i.e., at the point between the eyebrows, and also experiences a feeling of complete peace throughout his body. Whenever he wants to scour from the brain cells the seeds of past failure or sickness, he must turn that peace-and-concentration power on the whole brain. The entire peace feeling of the body as well as the power of concentration felt between the eyebrows must be transferred and felt in the entire brain. In this way the brain cells become impregnated with peace and power, and their chemical and psychological hereditary composition is modified.[11]

You can use this same technique to awaken past good habits that are stored in the superconscious. The intention with which we practice the technique will determine its results – whether our intention is to eliminate harmful habits or awaken good ones.

❄ On laser beams of healing light ❄

Having been in delicate health for years, particularly with back and intestinal pain, I decided to attend a course at Ananda Assisi on changing thought patterns in the brain.

Following a suggestion by Yogananda, we meditated and affirmed: "I and my Father are One." When the instructor asked us to find an unhealthy thought form, I discovered one that surprised me: *"I don't want to be well."* Using a technique in which I visualized healing light focused like a laser beam, I removed the negative thought, and then used the laser beam to create a new thought pattern. I chose: "I love life."

I immediately felt a powerful sense of well-being pervading my body. It felt like a miracle. For nearly a year, I felt well, without physical discomfort. Whenever some aches and pains would return, for example back pain, I would look for the thought that was blocking the flow of energy. I would ask myself, "Are you working too much? Is there something you don't want to do?" I would then ask God to take away the thought pattern and fill my mind with His unconditional love. With the laser beam of healing light, I directed the healing thoughts: "I am well. Everything is possible for me. I am worthy." And again, the discomfort disappeared.

Now, whenever I feel pain, I look for the energy-blocking thought and bring it into the light, and then I create a healing thought pattern in its place. Most of the time, it works quickly, though at other times it may take a while.

Whenever my body isn't feeling well, instead of rushing to take an external remedy, I use this practice. I work with the grooves nearly every day. I have learned that we are children of God and that we are therefore co-creators of our reality. –**Monica**, *Torino*

❄   ❄   ❄

Kriya Yoga

Possibly the most ancient of all scientific meditation techniques is Kriya Yoga. It was reintroduced to the modern world in the late nineteenth century by Mahavatar Babaji. Paramhansa Yogananda brought Kriya to the West in 1920. He wrote about it extensively in *Autobiography of a Yogi* and taught it personally to hundreds of thousands of aspirants.

Kriya meditation is remarkably effective in its ability to eliminate the seeds of our past karma, by targeting them in the astral spine – the *sushumna* and *chakras* – and in the grooves of the brain.

> The practice of Kriya Yoga.... helps to free one of the samskars (subtle tendencies) that block the upward flow of Kundalini. These samkars – the "seeds" of karma, as they are called – are the result of repeated actions (karmas) of the past – not only of this life, but of many past incarnations. Each samskar constitutes a subtle vortex of energy. There are countless such vortices in the spine. Until the energy in them has been released to flow upward, Kundalini's upward movement will be slow, her progress impeded. In fact, Kundalini in her upward surge gradually "roasts" these karmic seeds of samskars. Once "roasted" they can never again sprout into outward actions.[12]

Kriya practice can erase even deeply rooted habits, as told here.

❋ La dolce vita ❋

Were it not for Kriya, I would be lost in this world of illusions. I was always attracted to the pleasures of this world: dancing, drinking, eating well, traveling, dining in expensive restaurants, and staying at luxury hotels. I often travel to South America where the people revel in the good life. Along the way, I picked up some not-so-favorable habits: smoking, drinking, and to some extent using drugs.

One morning after partying and drinking late into the night, I woke up with a fever, feeling sick and broken inside. Until that point my spiritual practices had been irregular and superficial, but on that day I decided that I would practice Kriya every day, morning and evening, putting it at the center of my life.

I have since lost my taste for those old worldly pleasures. When someone invites me to go out drinking and dancing, I politely decline. There is a joy inside me that is so much more fulfilling than the best party or the most exclusive club could give. The best thing is the exhilaration I feel in freeing myself from those old bad habits. –*Ivanha*, *Verbania*

Old mental habits of thought that block the flow of the life force can be "roasted" and removed by Kriya.

✻ SELF-OFFERING ✻

No one knows how habitually plagued I am by thoughts of low self-esteem. Even my husband thinks I have great self-confidence. Through meditation, I have become aware of the downward-pulling tendency of these unwelcome thought patterns, and I have been using Kriya to help me break free of them. When I see them creeping into my mind, I stop whatever I'm doing and find a quiet place. I'll take a moment to invoke the presence of God and my Master, and then I practice Kriya. With each inward breath, I consciously offer the negative thoughts up to be transmuted at the spiritual eye, and with every outward breath I feel God's unconditional love descending upon me. Breath by breath, I feel that Kriya is pulling out the roots of this mental habit, and day by day I realize that my self-confidence is being born of my growing consciousness of the higher Self. –*Anonymous*

Although Kriya can be received only through an initiation ceremony conducted by an authorized *Kriayacharya*, the steps on the path to qualify for Kriya initiation are open to all sincere seekers. You can find more information about Kriya in the Endnotes to this chapter.[13]

CHAPTER 6: *Points to Remember*

- Our good and bad habits survive the death of our physical body and return in each life as *samskars* stored in our astral body and in the grooves of our brain.

- By deep meditation, we can eliminate or overwrite the grooves of bad habits with good habits.

- Kriya Yoga is an ancient science of meditation that can give us the power to eliminate the seeds of past bad karma.

- Seeds of good habits can be awakened through meditation and visualization practices.

NOTES | PART SEVEN

Title Page
1 Yogananda, "The Power of Habit," *East-West*, August 1933.
2 Yogananda, "How Yoga Frees from All Obstacles," *Spiritual Interpretation of the Bhagavad Gita, Inner Culture,* October 1938; and "Wisdom Guided by God," *Inner Culture,* July 1939.

Chapter One
1 Yogananda, "The Power of Habit," *East-West*, August 1933.
2 Kriyananda, *Awaken to Superconsciousness,* 67.
3 Yogananda, "Control Your Habits," *The Attributes of Success.*
4 Yogananda, *Super Advanced Course No. 1*, Lesson 6.
5 Yogananda, "The Law of Attracting Abundance," "Second Coming of Christ," *Inner Culture*, May 1938.
6 Yogananda, "Law of Karma," *Inner Culture*, November 1938.
7 Kriyananda, *The Hindu Way of Awakening,* 266.
8 Yogananda, "Mental Responsibility for Chronic Diseases," *Scientific Healing Affirmations.*
9 Kriyananda, *Art and Science of Raja Yoga,* 400.
10 Kriyananda, 220-221.
11 Kriyananda, *The Light of Superconsciousness,* 179.
12 Yogananda, "Did Jesus Believe in Rebirth?", "Second Coming of Christ," *Inner Culture*, January 1940.
13 Kriyananda, *Rays of the Same Light,* Vol. 3, 140.
14 Yogananda, "Ladder of Self-Realization," *Inner Culture*, March 1937.
15 Yogananda, "Curing Bad Habits," *Scientific Healing Affirmations,* 103.
16 Yogananda, "What Is Freedom?" *Inner Culture*, April 1941.
17 Yogananda, *Super Advanced Course No. 1*, Lesson 8.

Chapter Two
1 "Optimism and your Health," Harvard Health Publishing, May 1, 2008, https://www.health.harvard.edu/heart-health/optimism-and-your-health.

Defining the optimist: The optimist...does not assume blame for negative events. Instead, he tends to give himself credit for good news, assume good things will last, and be confident that positive developments will spill over into many areas of his life.

Coronary surgery: Optimists were only half as likely as pessimists to require re-hospitalization. In a similar study of angioplasty patients, optimism was also protective; over a six-month period, pessimists were three times more likely than optimists to have heart attacks or require repeat angioplasties or bypass operations.

Blood pressure: An American study of 2,564 men and women who were 65 and older also found that optimism is good for blood pressure.... People with positive emotions had lower blood pressures than those with a negative outlook. On average, the people with the most positive emotions had the lowest blood pressures.

Heart disease: Scientists from Harvard and Boston University evaluated 1,306 men with an average age of 61. Each volunteer was evaluated for an optimistic or pessimistic explanatory style as well as for blood pressure, cholesterol, obesity, smoking, alcohol use, and family history of heart disease. None of the men had been diagnosed with coronary artery disease when the study began. Over the next 10 years, the most pessimistic men were more than twice as likely to develop heart disease than the most optimistic men, even after taking other risk factors into account.

General health: A large, short-term study evaluated the link between optimism and overall health in 2,300 older adults. Over two years, people who had a positive outlook were much more likely to stay healthy and enjoy independent living than their less cheerful peers… Over a 30-year period, optimism was linked to a better outcome on eight measures of physical and mental function and health, including better cardiac health, a stronger immune system, better lung function, and lower mortality risk, among others.

Biological benefits: A 2008 study of 2,873 healthy men and women found that a positive outlook on life was linked to lower levels of the stress hormone cortisol, even after taking age, employment, income, ethnicity, obesity, smoking, and depression into account …. Other possible benefits include reduced levels of adrenaline, improved immune function, and less active clotting systems.

Longevity: A study from Holland evaluated 941 men and women between the ages of 65 and 85. People who demonstrated dispositional optimism at the start of the study enjoyed a 45% lower risk of death during a nine-year follow-up period. A 2019 study found both men and women with the highest levels of optimism had an average 11% to 15% longer life span than people who practiced little positive thinking. In fact, the highest-scoring optimists were most likely to live to age 85 or beyond.

2 Yogananda, "Second Coming of Christ," *Inner Culture,* February 1938.

Chapter Three

1 Yogananda, "Intuitional Whispers," Interpretation of the Bhagavad Gita, *East-West,* October 1932.
2 Yogananda, "Curing Bad Habits," *Scientific Healing Affirmations,* 103.
3 Yogananda, *Praecepta Lessons,* Vol. 2, 43/2.

Chapter Four

1 Yogananda, "Curing Bad Habits," *Scientific Healing Affirmations,* 103.
2 Yogananda, "Fixing Habits in the Brain at Will," *East-West,* January 1926.
3 Yogananda, *Super-Advanced Course No. 1,* Lesson 6.
4 "Benefits of quitting tobacco," MedlinePlus, https://medlineplus.gov/ency/article/007532.htm.
5 "Benefits of quitting," Centers for Disease Control and Prevention, https://www.cdc.gov/tobacco/quit_smoking/how_to_quit/benefits/index.htm.
6 Yogananda, "Foreword," *Psychological Chart.*
7 Yogananda, "For Curing Bad Habits," *Scientific Healing Affirmations.*
8 Yogananda, *Inner Culture,* October 1938.
9 Yogananda, "Conquering Temptation," Interpretation of the Bhagavad Gita, *East-West,* May 1933
10 Yogananda, "The X-Ray of Soul Wisdom," Interpretation of the Bhagavad Gita, *East-West,* February 1933.
11 Yogananda, *Whispers from Eternity,* No. 80.

Chapter Five

1 Yogananda, "Forward," *Psychological Chart.*
2 Kriyananda, *Material Success Through Yoga Principles,* Vol. 1:191.
3 Yogananda, "Steps Toward the Attaining of Consciousness," "Second Coming of Christ," *Inner Culture,* August 1934.
4 Yogananda, "Is It Possible to Forgive Sins?", "Second Coming of Christ," *Inner Culture,* February 1938.
5 Yogananda, "Curing Bad Habits," *Scientific Healing Affirmations,* 104.
6 Yogananda, "Installing Habits of Success, Health, and Wisdom in the Mind at Will," *Super-Advanced Course No. 1,* Lesson 6; and "Fixing Habits in the Brain at Will," *East-West,* January 1926. These articles are in the Appendices.
7 Kriyananda, *26 Keys to Greater Awareness.*
8 Yogananda, "How Jesus Healed," and "Second Coming of Christ," *Inner Culture,* September 1938.
9 Yogananda, "Victory Through Meditation," Interpretation of the Bhagavad Gita, *East-West,* March 1934.

Chapter Six

1 Yogananda, "Law of Karma," *Inner Culture,* November 1938.
2 Yogananda, *The Essence of Self-Realization* 10:17.
3 Yogananda, "Is It Possible to Forgive Sins?", "Second Coming of Christ," *Inner Culture,* February 1938.
4 Kriyananda, "Introduction," *Affirmations for Self-Healing,* 11.
5 Yogananda, "Intuitional Whispers," Interpretation of the Bhagavad Gita, *East-West,* October 1932.
6 Yogananda, *New Super Cosmic Science Course,* Lesson 3.
7 Yogananda, "Steps Toward the Attaining of Consciousness," "Second Coming of Christ," *Inner Culture,* February 1937.
8 Yogananda, "Uprooting Subconscious Habits," "Second Coming of Christ," *Inner Culture,* June 1938; and "How Jesus Healed," September 1938.
9 Yogananda, "Overcoming Bad Karma," *Inner Culture,* August 1939.
10 Kriyananda, *The Art and Science of Raja Yoga,* 409.
11 Yogananda, *Super Advanced Course No. 1,* Lesson 8.
12 Kriyananda, *The Art and Science of Raja Yoga,* 400.
13 Information about Kriya Yoga can be found at https://anandaindia.org/meditation/.

PART VIII

SCIENTIFIC HEALING AFFIRMATIONS

❈ Taming the Lion ❈

I overheard the other patients – radiation therapy could burn out cancer cells, but the x-rays burned all over the body, and it was very painful.

I had survived the surgery – but could I survive the thirty sessions of radiation? I turned to Yogananda's healing techniques. Before each session, I prepared myself by visualizing rays of light emanating from Yogananda's hands and entering my body, transforming the aberrant cells into pure light.

I also repeated an affirmation throughout each session:

"I open myself to your Light, to your Love, to your Strength, Give me the necessary energy to heal my body, my mind, my soul."

In none of the sessions did I experience burning or pain – the oncologist couldn't believe it!

Five years later, the cancer reappeared – another lump in the breast. My first reaction was self-pity, mixed with anxiety that clearly wasn't making the situation any better. This time I found an affirmation that resonated with me in Yogananda's book *Metaphysical Meditations*.

"God is within me, around me, protecting me, so I shall banish the gloom of fear that shuts out His guiding light."

Not long after I began this practice, my anxiety vanished, replaced by a calmness, detachment, and deep peace.

At that time, I had a dream – I was in the house where I'd grown up. I was with my mother – we were walking from room to room, and we realized that a lion was following us. Anxiously, I closed the doors behind us to keep the lion at bay as we continued our walk.

Then a man appeared. He easily put a leash around the lion's neck. Then he said to me: "Even lions can be tamed."

I woke up immediately, wide awake and alert. It was the middle of the night. I said aloud, "I get it – the lion is the cancer that is attacking me, but even cancer can be tamed!"

And so it was. The lion has been tamed for the past twenty-five years. –**Gabriella**, *Pisa*

PART VIII CHAPTER ONE

The Truth Shall Make You Free

> And ye shall know the truth, and the truth shall make you free. [JOHN 8:32]
>
> The truth simply exists. It cannot be created; it cannot be distorted; it cannot be denied. One may play with it as shrewdly as one likes; one may put on a superb show and convince many people: Truth always wins in the end.[1] —KRIYANANDA

The audience is quiet, the musicians are waiting on the stage. But where is the conductor? A lone figure enters and a few neophyte concert-goers begin to clap, then stop. To the veteran concert goers the concert master is familiar. He is respected by the musicians, and now he mounts the podium and commands their attention. They take up their instruments, and he nods to the oboist, who plays a single note. The musicians tune their instruments to the note, and cacophony reigns, then harmony, then a suspended, unified silence. Only then does the conductor arrive, and the performance begins.

Each of our body's cells and organs has a role to play in the symphony of our life. How well they will perform depends on who is setting the tone – is the Soul or the Ego playing the role of concert master of our thoughts?

We have met these characters earlier in Volume One.* When our orchestra is being conducted by the Ego, our thoughts are tainted by the Big Lie: the misery-making suggestion that we are this perishable body, separate from and essentially different from Spirit. The result is disharmony and disease in the body, as the cells and organs struggle in chaos and confusion.

---
* See Part I, Volume One, for a discussion of the soul and the ego.

The single note that the Soul intones is Truth: the Truth that we are one with the Infinite Spirit and all Creation. We find this central Truth expressed by Jesus Christ, when he said, "I and my Father are One" – as well as by a mantra from the ancient Vedas: *"Aham Brahmasmi"* – "I am Brahman, the absolute, universal consciousness."

In his song "Brothers," Swami Kriyananda refers to the underlying note that unifies us all.

> *Though words and customs vary*
> *Like waves upon the sea,*
> *One life beneath the surface*
> *Binds everyone to me.*
> *Who knows the truth knows all men as brothers.*
> *Who knows the truth knows all men as –*
> *Brothers!*

As the single note of the oboe helped the musicians tune their instruments, only the ultimate divine Truth can align and create harmony among the seemingly disparate instruments of our body, mind, and soul.

The power of Truth

Healing affirmations are those which are infused with vibrations of Truth. When intoned with deep concentration and conviction, they can penetrate all the levels of our consciousness – persuading the conscious mind, etching grooves in the subconscious, drawing the all-healing power of the superconscious, and awakening us to our true, highest Self.

Truth has power – it vibrates in harmony with the structure of the universe, and it can set all the structures of our lives in alignment with its celestial harmonies. Just as the musicians in an orchestra can play as one only after tuning their instruments to a single pure note, when our minds are tuned to Truth, the healing power of the universe can flow freely through us.

Affirmations are most effective when they are spoken by people who are honest, and who always strive to speak truth. Lying to ourselves and perpetuating falsehood to others weakens our inner power. It leads, in time, to illness, and contributes to the degradation of society.

In his *Yoga Sutras*, Patanjali includes "non-lying" as one of the ten primary virtues (the *yamas* and *niyamas*).* Patanjali tells us that the perfection of each virtue gives us a specific power. Thus, he promises that those who are unfailingly truthful will receive the power to **"attain the fruits of action without even acting. His mere thought, his mere word will be binding on the universe."** [2]

In his autobiography, Yogananda recalls an early experiment with the power of thought. He was sitting with his sister, when...

> Uma complained of a boil on her leg, and fetched a jar of ointment. I smeared a bit of the salve on my forearm.
> "Why do you use medicine on a healthy arm?"
> "Well, Sis, I feel I am going to have a boil tomorrow. I am testing your ointment on the spot where the boil will appear."
> "You little liar!"
> "Sis, don't call me a liar until you see what happens in the morning." Indignation filled me.
> An adamant resolution sounded in my voice as I made slow reply. "By the power of will in me, I say that tomorrow I shall have a fairly large boil in this exact place on my arm; and *your* boil shall swell to twice its present size!"
> Morning found me with a stalwart boil on the indicated spot; the dimensions of Uma's boil had doubled...Mother instructed me never to use the power of words for doing harm. I have always remembered her counsel, and followed it.[3]

The power of words

A single word, uttered with the power of Truth, can change the entire course of our life. Hearing the simple words "I love you" can impel us to change our work, move to another city, even profess a different religion. The words have no intrinsic value – it is the speaker who imbues them with meaning.†

A lecturer can say all the right words, but fail to convince or motivate us. Another speaker can say essentially the same words with a very different result. One who lives the Truth can change hearts and minds.

---

* The *yamas* and *niyamas* are mentioned in Chapter Four of Part II, Volume One.
† An exception is the power of mantras, which will be discussed in Part XII.

> Thoughts are things. Words, which are crystallized thoughts, have immeasurable power, especially when we speak them with concentration.[4]

> Words that are saturated with sincerity, conviction, faith and intuition are just like highly explosive vibration bombs, which when let out, are sure to explode the rocks of difficulties and create the change desired.[5]

Jesus resurrected a friend with words that were infused with the divine power of his oneness with God: "Lazarus, come forth!" Bernardo de Quintavalle, a rich merchant of Assisi, became St. Francis' first follower after he heard the saint uttering a simple prayer through the night: "My God, my all!"

Hearing Francis preach in the courtyard of the church outside her home, Claire Offreduccio left her wealthy family to become the first woman follower of Francis, and the founder of the Order of Poor Claires. Her words, saturated with faith and conviction, later attracted her mother and sisters to the Order.

Words can also be infused with a power of evil, as witnessed by the words and actions of dictators and tyrants throughout history.

The power of healing affirmations to change our lives depends not only on the power of Truth which they express, but the depth of sincerity with which we repeat them.

> Man's word is Spirit in man. Words are sounds occasioned by the vibrations of thoughts. Thoughts are vibrations sent forth by the Ego or Soul. Every word that leaves your mouth ought to be potent with your genuine soul vibration...Every word you utter you must mean it: every word you put forth must represent not only Truth, but some of your realized soul force. Words without soul force are husks without the corn.[6]

Truth versus fact

An affirmation is simply a statement. It can be positive or negative, true or false. When used to heal ourselves, affirmations draw upon the power of Truth and Light to dispel untruth and darkness.

How can we sincerely affirm "I am strong, I am well!" if we are too sick to get out of bed? The body may, in fact, be so ill as to require bed rest, but that condition will pass. Meanwhile, health is an expression of a deeper truth that is unchanging.

> Fact and truth are not always synonymous. A statement may be factual without bearing any relationship to higher truths.[7] Truth, after all, is both universal and eternal. It never changes.[8]

Facts are subject to interpretation. Our interpretation of the facts may be clouded by ignorance, fear, negativity, wickedness, or unawareness of the actual facts. But the divine Truth is beyond doubting. In *Rays of the One Light,* Swami Kriyananda begins each chapter: **"Truth is one and eternal. Realize oneness with it in your deathless Self, within."**

One of the greatest powers of cosmic delusion (Maya) is that it tries to convince us that the present "facts" of our life define who we are. When we are ill, especially if we are suffering from a serious chronic disease or a deeply entrenched mental bad habit, the mind may be hypnotized by the insistent, habitual thought that our present condition is what we are and what we will always be. Negative affirmations such as "I am sick," "I am weak," "I have an incurable disease" are both false and paralyzing.

> Most people cannot heal themselves because their own thoughts are poisoned by the habit of thinking of chronic sickness. It is strange that the people who are always well never seem to believe that they can become sick; but if they happen to become sick after having enjoyed fifty

years of good health, and are then unable to keep well for three months, they believe that they can never get well again....No one can heal us except through the hidden power of our own thoughts.[9]

Are the following statements facts or truths?

"I have a bad flu."
"I am addicted to coffee."
"I don't have enough money to make ends meet."
"My boss doesn't like me and my co-workers are ganging up on me."
"I am impatient and judgmental."
"The sun isn't shining today." (*Your thought on a rainy day.*)

We may indeed have a terrible flu, but it will pass with proper care. Yes, our colleagues may be treating us unkindly, but by modifying our attitude and behavior, they may change their behavior toward us. A coffee habit, once we've decided that it's harming our health, will, in time, be only a distant memory. Even though it's raining, the sun is shining somewhere, if you were to rise above the clouds.

What are the eternal truths that will free us from delusion?

- Our inherent nature is perfection, not sinfulness.
- Love conquers all.
- God and the forces of spiritual evolution are on our side.
- Energy is infinite, and it is instantly accessible.

Yogananda urged us to affirm these eternal truths of our being.

I am strong, I am strength.
I am healthy, I am health.
I am successful, I am success.
I am blessed, I am bliss.
I am peaceful, I am peace.
I am Immortal, I am Immortality.[10]

In the following story, Rosa's daughter tells how her mother was able to distinguish the difference between the facts and the Truth.

I Told You So

The oncologist said that the tumor was inoperable – perhaps chemotherapy might slow its progress. That was exactly ten years ago, and I want to tell you the story of my mother, Rosa, and her journey of self-healing.

Mother was seventy-eight when a routine checkup revealed that she had stage-four uterine cancer with metastases in various parts of the abdominal area. Always the realist, Rosa wanted to know the complete truth, and she was committed to receiving whatever therapy was recommended. If she were to die, she said, "It means my time has come." At the same time, she suspected that the doctors were wrong, because she felt fine.

When she began the first cycle of chemotherapy, surprisingly, she experienced none of the anticipated side-effects. Each session found her ever more positive, serene, and absolutely convinced that she was perfectly fine. Her joy for life was increasing – it was obvious in her demeanor – and she wouldn't let us speak of her as a sick person or even mention the tumor. Her recurring firm statement was: "I feel great. I think the doctors are wrong."

Since Rosa had tolerated the first round of chemo so well, the doctors decided to accompany the second round with radiation therapy. Rosa continued to arrive serenely for the treatments, joking with the doctors and nurses, and continuing to tell them that there was nothing wrong with her.

The doctors were indeed surprised when exams showed that the malignant masses were decreasing in volume, and that an operation might be possible. Yet, unsure of their diagnosis, they referred Rosa for further consultation to a hospital with a more advanced oncology department.

Once Rosa was admitted and given a series of tests, the doctors and nurses began to whisper about her case. All they would tell her was that more tests were needed.

My sister accompanied Rosa to the final consultation, where the oncology department head launched into an explanation filled with incomprehensible medical jargon.

"Excuse me, Doctor," my sister interrupted. "Would you kindly tell us if my mother's cancer is operable or not?"

"Madam, your mother is not operable for a simple reason – there is nothing left to operate on! The tumor is gone. Your mother is completely and miraculously cured." From "no operation is possible" to "no operation is needed" was a journey that utterly confounded the doctors.

That was eleven months after the original diagnosis of inoperable cancer, and only my mother wasn't surprised. She had been certain all along that the doctors were wrong. Holding strongly to this conviction and to her increasing joy in living, my mother had cured herself.

I wanted to be sure that the original diagnosis hadn't simply been switched with someone else's, so I checked the original records – Rosa had definitely had a malignant tumor with metastases.

Rosa is ninety now. She fell recently, breaking a femur, and had surgery to insert a prosthesis. For some months she was confined to a wheelchair, but thanks to her remarkable mental vitality and willpower she is now walking without a cane. How grateful I am to be the daughter of such a remarkable woman! –**Candida**, *Pescara, Italy*

❊ ❊ ❊

Truth and Life Force

Scientific healing affirmations activate and empower all of the other self-healing techniques, the master key that opens us to receive the full flow of the divine healing life force. This is because every cell in the body obeys the powerful commands of the mind.

> **Life-affirming attitudes of joy, willingness, or love actually *generate* energy in the body. And life-negating attitudes of sadness, unwillingness, or animosity actually sap the body's energy.**[11]

When the mind is consumed by the thought that we are tired and cannot go a step further, the muscles shut down. Marathon runners talk about the experience of "hitting the wall." I had this experience while running a marathon. From one step to the next, I felt utterly exhausted, as if my body's fuel had been instantly and thoroughly depleted. Warding off the thought "I can't go on," I said aloud forcefully: "Prana sustains me!" In that instant, I felt a rush of energy and finished the course without slowing.

> Mental cure is superior to all methods of physical cure because...[it] directly acts from within and [is] the motive power that stimulates and directs the Life Energy to accomplish any definite task.[12]

There's a charming children's story, "The Little Engine That Could," that has been a favorite of children and their parents and teachers for more than a century. (It was made into a Disney animated film.) It tells the story of a train laden with children's toys that breaks down while climbing a steep mountain. Big engines try to pull the train over the pass, but fail. Then the exuberantly willing and energetic Little Engine decides to try. As it pulls its heavy load over the mountain pass it affirms again and again: "I think I can! I think I can! I know I can! I know I can!" And, of course, it succeeds.

Truth and Honesty

Despite these stories that affirm the power of willingness and enthusiasm, the road to self-transformation must always begin with an honest assessment and an understanding of the facts of our current situation.

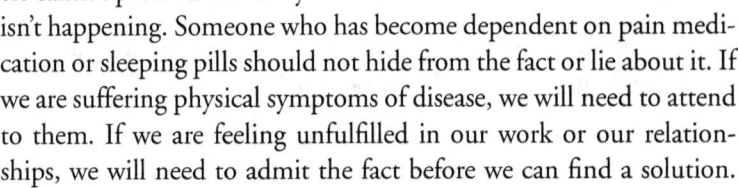

A person suffering from abuse by others cannot pretend or merely affirm that it isn't happening. Someone who has become dependent on pain medication or sleeping pills should not hide from the fact or lie about it. If we are suffering physical symptoms of disease, we will need to attend to them. If we are feeling unfulfilled in our work or our relationships, we will need to admit the fact before we can find a solution.

We must acknowledge the facts of our lives, without believing that they represent our true nature and our permanent destiny. Being honest is an important first step toward self-healing.

However, we should be careful about sharing our insights and opinions about other people's lives. Yogananda teaches that Truth is always beneficial and helpful.

> To be truthful, then, does not necessarily mean to be literally factual...Truth is always beneficial.[13]
>
> [...]a statement of fact may be either beneficial or harmful. If there is a chance that a statement will do harm, it must not be considered a truth in the highest sense. If you cannot speak sincerely without the risk of inflicting harm, the best alternative is to remain silent.[14]

CHAPTER 1: *Points to Remember*

- Every thought we think and every word we utter influences our health.

- The practice of scientific healing affirmations accesses the power of Truth to align the structure of our bodies and minds with the universal divine harmony.

- Affirmations of Truth are like a tap that opens us to a flow of life force.

- The facts about our present circumstances never represent our true identity and destiny.

- The words of a person who speaks and lives by the highest Truth carry a power to inspire and motivate others.

PART VIII   CHAPTER TWO

Choose Your Affirmation

> Will, or imagination, or reason, or feeling, cannot of themselves effect a physical cure. They only act as different agents which, according to the different temperaments of different individuals, can stimulate the life energy to awaken and cure a certain ailment... internally electrify[ing] the diseased body cells and restore them to their original healthy condition.[1] –YOGANANDA

A unique feature of Yogananda's science of healing is the adaptation of affirmations to the particular temperament of the person using them. As with any categorization of personality qualities, an individual will exhibit some or all of them at different times, depending on the circumstances. That being said, each person will express one of these qualities more than the others.

Yogananda described four basic human temperaments: **Reason, Will, Feeling, Imagination**. Which best describes you?

> Imagination; convincing reason; faith, emotion or feeling; or will or conation can be employed according to the different specific imaginative or intellectual or emotional or conative nature of the individual... During the different affirmations, the attitude of the mind should be different, e.g., will affirmations should be accompanied by strong will; feeling affirmations by devotion; reason affirmations by intelligence and devotion; imagination affirmations by firm fancy and faith.[2]

Yogananda suggests that while practicing an affirmation, we focus our attention at specific centers in the body.

> During the different affirmations, notice should be taken of the physiological centers where the attention should be directed – i.e., the heart is the center where feeling is concerned, the medulla is the source of energy, and will proceeds from the spot in the center of the forehead. Attention is unconsciously directed to those centers, e.g., when we feel, the attention is centered in the heart and we feel it to the exclusion of all other parts of our bodies. We want to cultivate a conscious power over the direction of attention to the centers of thought, will and feeling.[3]

Reason

Reason is the conscious mind's capacity to analyze a situation and understand its logical implications. Many people have a well-developed intellect, from birth or by their training, that they can call upon as a powerful aid to help heal themselves.

If reason is your dominant inclination, you will want to choose or create an affirmation that appeals to the rational mind. Here are suggestions from Yogananda.

> I demand my Divine birthright
> because I intuitively realize
> that all wisdom and power already exist in my soul.
> I am constantly surrounded
> by the immortal currents of His Omnipresence,
> and no disease germs can harm me.
> If they attack me,
> they will be electrocuted by His overcoming power.[4]

> In wisdom's chambers
> Thou dost roam
> Thou art the reason in me
> O Thou dost roam and wake
> Each lazy little cell of brain
> To receive, to receive
> The good that mind and senses give
> The knowledge that Thou dost give.
> Myself will think, myself will reason
> I won't trouble Thee for thought
> But lead Thou when reason errs
> To its goal lead it right.[5]

> My body cells are made of light
> My fleshly cells are made of Thee
> They are perfect, for Thou art perfect
> They are healthy, for Thou art health
> They are spirit, for Thou art so
> They are immortal, for Thou art living.[6]

You can create your own reason-based affirmations to deal with specific situations. For example, if you've decided to start an exercise program, your core affirmation could be: "My metabolism improves (or "my immunity grows stronger") every time I exercise." Or "Fresh oxygen and fresh blood are purifying my body cells."

If your goal is to be more compassionate and kinder in your interactions with others, and your temperament is more rational than feeling, you might choose an affirmation such as: "When I am kind to others, they are kind to me."

Will

Another strong weapon of the conscious mind is willpower. A strong will can bring a powerful flood of cosmic energy to bear on any situation. If you are an energetic, enthusiastic, willpower type who loves to get things done, you may want to choose or create affirmations that appeal to your self-reliant, independent, "do-it-now," can-do nature.

> A strong affirmation of will can change old habits in a day...Indeed, strong affirmation can change those patterns with a single breath! [7]

It would be wise for people of strong willpower to invite the power of the universe to guide them before they act – as Yogananda recommends in *Whispers from Eternity*:

> I will reason, I will will, and I will act, but guide my reason, will, and activity to the right thing that I should do.... Teach us to use independently the human will (since Thou gavest that to us to use freely), in tune with Thy wisdom-guided will. [8]

In his *Yogoda Course* Yogananda gives these instructions:

> *Concentrate your vision and feeling in between the eyebrows, close your eyes and repeat the following thrice:*

"I will, with my own will, which flows from the Divine Will, to be healthy, to be well, to be prosperous and spiritual, to be well, to be well. [9]

In *Scientific Healing Affirmations* he recommends:

> *Concentrate will on the Medulla and on the spot between the eyebrows, simultaneously, and repeat the following, first loudly and then gradually in whispers.*

"I will my life to charge
With Godly will I will it charge
Through my nerves and muscles all
My tissues, limbs and all,
With vibrant tingling fire
With burning joyous power
In blood and glands
By sovran command
I bid you flow
By my command
I bid you glow
By my command
I bid you glow." [10]

Life Force / **202**

Even if you are not predominantly a willpower type, you are bound to find yourself occasionally in situations that call for an affirmation of the will. Returning to the example of starting an exercise program, you may need a forceful affirmation to help keep you going. For example: "I will put on my workout gear today, and every day at 5 p.m."

Will-based affirmations can help us overcome habits and addictions – a good example is this one, from *Scientific Healing Affirmations:*

Oh ye brave good soldier habits
Drive away the dark, dark habits
Drive away the dark, dark habits.
I am free, I am free.
I have no habits, I have no habits
I will do what is right, I'll do what's right
Uncommanded by habits' might
I am free, I am free. [11]

Swami Kriyananda suggests the following affirmation for overcoming desires and attachments – notice how it combines willpower and devotional feeling:

"With the sword of devotion I sever the heart-strings that tie me to delusion." [12]

Feeling/Devotion

While some people implicitly trust their feelings, others need concrete verification. Jesus lovingly rebuked a disciple: "Thomas, because thou hast seen me, thou hast believed: blessed are they that have not seen, and yet have believed." (JOHN 20:29)

The devotional temperament inclines toward belief in a Higher Power. People of strong devotion find it easier to accept that everything that happens to them is coming from the hands of that benevolent Power. If this is how you customarily see yourself, or if you find yourself in situations where you feel a need to talk with God in a personal way, you may find the following affirmations of Yogananda appealing.

> Close your eyes, *concentrate on the heart throb* and repeat with devotion and feeling:

Thou art love, Thou art love,
I am Thine, Thou art mine,
I am Thine, Thou art mine,
I am love, I am love,
Love is healthy, Love is perfect,
I am healthy, I am love,
I am whole, I am perfect. [13]

O Heavenly Father,
Thou art in my affected bodily part.
It is well — for Thou art there.
O Heavenly Father, Thou art perfect.
I am made in Thine image. I am perfect. [14]

Imagination

Artists are not the only ones endowed with imagination. You might consider yourself bereft of artistic talent, yet be able to see things in your imagination, in your 'mind's eye.'

We have discussed in Part VI the third superpower of the conscious mind: visualization. Imagination is similar, but different in that it employs creativity in the inner seeing of something which has not necessarily been experienced. It is the ability to simulate things as you fancy they might be. Visualization is more the mental reconstruction of something already experienced or to be experienced. It does not necessarily involve fancy. French author Jules Verne used his imagination to conceive his science fiction novels. Athletes visualize their next performances to help them perfect their skills.

For those whose temperament is imaginative, Yogananda offers the following affirmations.

> *Concentrate on the navel* and imagine a luminous light there. Close your eyes. Feel the navel and repeat with imagination and devotion:

'Thou art Life, Thou art strength,
    Thou art mind, and imagination,
Thou art thought, Thou art fancy, I am thought, I am fancy.
In every way, in every way, I am like Thee, I am like Thee,
I am whole, I am like Thee.' [15]

> *Concentrate ...on the forehead*, and repeat the following:

I think my life to flow
I know my life to flow
From brain to all my body to flow.
Streaks of light do shoot
Through my tissue-root.
The flood of Life through vertebrae
Doth rush through spine in froth and spray
The little cells all are drinking
Their tiny mouths all are shining
The little cells all are drinking
Their tiny mouths all are shining. [16]

Kriyananda suggests an affirmation for Self-expansion:

I feel myself in the flowing brooks,
in the flight of birds,
in the raging wind upon the mountains,
in the gentle dance of flowers in a breeze.
Renouncing my little, egoic self,
  I expand with my great, soul-Self everywhere! [17]

And to remind ourselves of our immortality, he suggests this one:

> I am a child of eternity!
> I am ageless.
> I am deathless.
> I am the changeless Spirit at the heart of all mutation! [18]

Create your own affirmations

Thoughts are reverberating in our minds during every waking moment of the day. Thoughts permeate our actions, and they can either motivate and inspire, or demotivate and discourage us. Instead of being passive victims of our energy-draining thoughts, we can write positive thought-scripts that will change our lives. We can fashion our own "storylines" throughout the day, keeping our mind flowing with positive, harmonious thoughts. We can, in fact, improve the quality of our lives by assigning a positive affirmation to various moments in daily life.

It is useful to have one core habit affirmation that you use upon awaking and going to sleep, and at the conclusion of meditation periods. You might experiment with different affirmations until you find one that truly motivates you. Throughout the day, you can add other encouraging affirmations.

New habit affirmation

In the previous section on Will, we saw the importance of using an affirmation to trigger new attitudes and actions. Returning to the example of starting an exercise program (so important for our health), you might affirm at appropriate times: "I can't wait to get out and exercise!" Or, "My muscles and cells are longing to get out and start moving!"

We can apply the same principle to start a habit of regular meditation: "My soul longs to meditate this evening!"; or "Meditation brings me clarity and joy!"; or "Before all else, I will meditate!"

A wake-up affirmation

Are you a "potato person" or a "toast person"? If you're "toast," you pop up bright and early, ready to face the day. If you're a "potato" you roll over and keep baking.

The way we wake up has a tremendous influence on the quality of our day. Train yourself to say, aloud (when it's appropriate): ***"I am awake and ready!"*** If you do this immediately upon waking, it will help you ward off tempting thoughts to sleep just a little longer: "I've got way too much to do today." "I don't want to do all the things on my to-do list." Perhaps you're able to overcome your reluctance gradually as the day progresses. But your days will be brighter and merrier if you can start them with a life-affirming burst of positive energy.

We will consider some other wake-up hints in Chapter Five, on affirmation with movement.

※ HEALTHY HAIR ※

Can our hair follicles respond to our affirmations?

With the hormonal changes of menopause, my hair started to thin. I was accustomed to a thick, full-bodied head of hair, and it was disconcerting when I showered to find my hands full of loose strands.

After searching online for remedies, I decided to reach into my bag of affirmations. Whenever I washed my hair, I affirmed: "My hair is healthy, vital and strong!" I followed Yogananda's directions to say the affirmation first in a loud voice, then softer and softer, and finally in a whisper, then mentally, allowing the words to imprint themselves on the subconscious, conscious, and super-conscious levels of my mind.

My hair today is a perfect reflection of the affirmation. But, equally important, practicing the affirmation helped me keep my mind in a positive state regardless of the changes my body was undergoing. –***Jenny***, *Switzerland*

Work affirmation

Another crucially important moment for setting a positive direction is when we begin our daily work. The conscious mind has two basic settings: "Wander" and "Focus." If we push the Wander button, we may squander hours or entire days of productivity. To avoid wanderlust, you might compose an affirmation to repeat when you start your work. Or you might consider this one, from Kriyananda's book of healing affirmations.

> Whatever I do in life, I give it my full attention. Like a laser beam, I burn from before me all problems, all obstructions! [19]

Relationship affirmation

When we're feeling swamped by the daily flood of verbal exchanges and emails, we can easily forget that each one represents a human relationship. To help us stay aware of the human factor and make each encounter meaningful and personal, consider creating an affirmation to think of before you pick up the phone or read an email.

For example: "I will take the time and make the effort to listen and understand." As an experiment, you might choose a particularly awkward relationship and create an affirmation to help you set a harmonious note at the start of each interaction, then repeat it mentally during the encounter.

Diet affirmation

One of the primary causes of disease is overeating and wrong eating. If mealtimes have become a temptation, establish a different tone by offering a prayer of gratitude before starting the meal. Pausing a moment to pray will help us make our meals a more conscious, nourishing activity for the body and soul.

> **TRY THIS**
>
> **YOGANANDA'S PRAYER BEFORE MEALS**
>
> Heavenly Father, receive this food.
> Make it holy.
> Let no impurity of greed ever defile it.
> The food comes from Thee.
> It is to build Thy temple. Spiritualize it.
> Spirit to Spirit goes.
> We are the petals of Thy manifestation,
> but Thou art the Flower,
> its life, beauty and loveliness.
> Permeate our souls with
> the fragrance of Thy presence.[20]

You might follow the prayer with the simple affirmation: "I eat less, I eat slowly, and I chew well." You could even abbreviate it: "Less. Slowly. Chew."

Unexpected events affirmation

Life happens – not always in the way we expect or might prefer. Events are constantly challenging our poise and threatening our sense of security. When faced with life's difficult situations, it's good to have a response ready, as the following story illustrates.

✻ EVERYTHING HAPPENS FOR THE BEST ✻

The prime minister was unlike the other ministers – he was more philosopher than politician, more interested in truth than self-advancement – and it was these rare qualities that had earned him the king's trust.

No matter the difficulty, disaster, or disappointment, the minister's counsel was the same. He would tell the king: "Everything happens for the best." Thus reassured, the king and his minister would calmly find a solution.

One day the king invited his court on a hunt. As a skilled archer, the king rarely missed his target. But this day disaster struck. The king's attention was distracted and he let go of the bowstring at the wrong moment, slicing off a portion of his thumb. As the courtiers huddled around giving their aid, the prime minister offered his usual counsel: "Be not concerned, my lord, everything happens for the best."

Writhing in pain, the king was infuriated – this was no time for philosophy! Angrily, he commanded his guards to take the minister to the dungeon.

As the weeks passed, the king's thumb healed and he returned to the pleasures of the hunt. While hunting with several of his closest courtiers one day, he spotted a deer and galloped after it, lance in hand. Deep into the thick forest he sped, leaving the courtiers far behind.

Further and further into the thickets he chased the deer, which eventually escaped along byways impenetrable to horse and rider. Disappointed, the king turned back – but where was the trail? The forest was a labyrinth, and as night descended, the king found no escape. Finally, he dismounted, resigned to wait until morning.

Shivering against the cold, he managed to build a small fire to warm himself and ward off any wild animals. But a tribe of primitive forest dwellers were attracted by the firelight, and delighted to find the object they had been seeking: a human sacrifice to offer to their god. The king was summarily bound and taken to the tribe's encampment, where a bonfire was prepared. As they divested the king of his clothing, necklaces, and rings, they came upon his half-severed thumb. Uncertain, they called to the headman, who sauntered over to inspect the king.

"Impure! Imperfect!" he roared – "Unworthy to be offered to our God! Cast him out!"

So it was that the king set out on the long walk to his palace. As he trudged, he suddenly remembered the prime minister's words when he had injured his thumb: "Everything happens for the best!" And now, filled with remorse, he realized that that the seeming misfortune had saved his life.

As soon as he arrived at the palace, he hastened to the prison and released the minister from his cell. As he recounted the harrowing story, the minister nodded serenely. "Yes, my lord, everything does happen for the best."

The king was moved by the firmness of the minister's faith, yet a question arose in his mind. "My good fortune is clear, but how have these events benefitted you, who've spent months in the company of rats and vermin?"

The prime minister smiled. "My lord, if I had not been here, I would have accompanied you on the hunt, and as you can see, my thumbs are whole. So these months of discomfort have saved my life. Everything indeed happens for the best."

When unexpected events happen in your life, remember the minister's wise affirmation: **"Everything happens for the best!"**

CHAPTER 2: *Points to Remember*

- The mind is speaking to us constantly with positive or negative affirmations.
- By practicing positive affirmations throughout the day, we can keep negativity at bay.
- When using an affirmation, adapt it to your unique temperament – reasoning, willful, feeling, or imaginative – and to the situation at hand.
- Create your own affirmations to help you in the unique situations you must face in your life.
- Our first waking thoughts set the tone for the day. On waking, affirm: "I am awake and ready!"
- The affirmations you choose need to be crafted and repeated giving emphasis, meaning, conviction and energy to each word. They will then have the power to penetrate the conscious, subconscious and superconscious dimensions of your mind.
- You will find many powerful affirmations in Yogananda's book, *Scientific Healing Affirmations*, and in Kriyananda's book, *Affirmations for Self-Healing*.

PART VIII CHAPTER THREE

Affirmation Recipe

> Impregnate your affirmations with your devotion, will and faith, intensely and repeatedly, unmindful of the results. Results *will* come naturally as the fruits of your labors.[1] —YOGANANDA

Before we can prepare a meal worthy to delight the most discriminating gourmet, we will need top-quality ingredients and a time-tested recipe. In the next chapter we will consider the scientific healing affirmation technique. In this chapter, we will assemble the ingredients.

Understanding

The first ingredient we need to make our affirmation practice as effective as possible is that we clearly understand that the affirmation represents our own truest, higher Self. Before beginning our practice, it will help to explore the various subtle meanings hiding in the affirmation, and how they are relevant to our own situation.

> In an affirmation, one should both say and feel deeply the meaning of the thought behind the words; then the thought will go deeply into the conscious mind, then into the subconscious, and then into the superconscious... Always affirm with intelligence and devotion until your thought goes consciously through the subconscious mind into the superconscious mind.[2]

Conviction

The more deeply we are able to understand the high truths expressed by an affirmation, the more profoundly we will be persuaded of its power to effect the desired change. Rest assured, the ego will try to dissuade us from our practice by presenting doubts about its effectiveness. Thus we will need to be vigilant against the cross-currents of uncertainty and doubt that can derail our efforts.

> In affirming "I am healthy," or "I am wise," the positive affirmation must be so strong that it crowds out completely any subconscious, discouraging, negative enemy thoughts which may be whispering to you, 'you fool, you will never succeed. You are a failure; wisdom is impossible for you.' You must know that whatever you wish strongly, you can materialize in short order.[3]

Yogananda told his audiences that they should not blindly believe what he was telling them, but that they should try the techniques for themselves and see if they were effective. The value of affirming high truths, even if we are unable to believe in them wholeheartedly in the beginning, is that it opens us to receive a living experience of the Truth. We need not be thoroughly convinced that true love is knocking before we open the door.

Attention

By bringing one hundred percent of our attention to bear on the affirmation, repeating it with understanding, conviction, and power, we can imprint it on all levels of our consciousness.

> Affirmations should be practiced...with ever-increasing intensity of attention and continuity. The attention from the very beginning of affirmation must steadily increase and should never be allowed to flag.

> Flagging attention should be again and again brought back like a truant child and repeatedly and patiently trained to perform its given task.[4]

Yogananda said that success in every undertaking depends on the intensity and continuity of our efforts.

> Intensity of mental effort while practicing, and duration of practice—both are needed.[5]

Faith and devotion

Once we have overcome our doubts, and we've begun to see results from our practice, we will want to add the element of faith.

> Faith is another vitally important principle. To do a thing really well, one must believe in it wholeheartedly. Faith is intuitive recognition of the truth of a thing. It is not passive acceptance, but committed belief, belief put into practice. Faith transcends petty victories and defeats. It is not commitment to things, merely, but to truth... Rejoice in the power within you, a power shared by all mankind, to achieve your own highest potential.[6]

Power

An affirmation is not an incantation; the words in themselves are not magically endowed. Even using the affirmations created by a realized master will have little effect unless we infuse them with the power of our own conviction and faith.

> Always during affirmations or prayer vibrations feel that you are using your own but God-given power

> to heal yourself or others. Always believe that it is not God only but yourself also who, as His beloved child, tries to employ His-given will, reason, etc., to react on the difficult problems of life. A balance must be struck between the old idea of wholly depending on God, and the modern way of sole dependence on the ego.[7]

Yogananda scolded a young disciple, who protested, "I know my fault, but how can I change without your blessings?" "Well," the Guru replied, "my blessings are there already. God's blessings are there. It is *your* blessings that are needed!"[8]

Repetition

A single, constant drip of water falling on a rock will over time carve a channel. Even so, when we practice an affirmation patiently and continuously, it will alter the neural pathways in our brain and change our behavior and our life.

> In all affirmations the intensity of attention comes first, but continuity and repetition count a great deal, too...Attentive, intelligent repetition and patience are the creators of habits, and as such, these ought to be employed during all affirmations...
>
> Always avoid mechanical repetition... Repeat affirmations firmly and with intensity and sincerity, until such power is gained that one command, one strong urge from yourself would be sufficient to change your body cells or move your Soul to the performance of miracles.[9]

Visualization

We can amplify the power of an affirmation by visualizing the truth behind the words. The mind is impressed more deeply by combining images, feelings, and words than by words and thoughts alone. An unknown word will evoke no understanding or feelings. The Italian word *arcobaleno* may elicit our curiosity, but seeing a photo of a rainbow will evoke a sense of awe, a happy memory, a feeling of hope.

When we can link the words of an affirmation to a visual image, it will be more deeply etched into our consciousness. Yogananda's affirmations are rich with visual imagery. The little body cells are said to be "drinking." Streaks of light are "shooting." He speaks of the myriad-hued atoms, the doors of space, and the Fountain of Light. Strong visual images bring his affirmations, chants, poems, and prayers very vividly to life.

Even if an affirmation is intended to stimulate our willpower or our reason, it will help to link it to mental pictures. Affirming that we are healthy, well, and prosperous, becomes even more effective when we can see ourselves in each of those states, and more so if we can conjure up the feeling of *being* healthy, well and prosperous.

Notable are Yogananda's instructions for using visualizing together with this reason-based affirmation.

> Close your eyes, and *feeling or visualizing the light there*, repeat:

> "Thy cosmic current flows in me, flows in me,
> through my medulla flows in me, flows in me.
> I think and will the current to flow, in all my body
> the current to flow, in all my body the current to flow.
> I am charged, I am cured, I am charged, I am cured.
> Lightning flash goes through me.
> I am cured, I am cured." [10]

Whether the images that come to you are photographic or abstract, whether your mental artist tends more to Caravaggio, Monet or Dali, it is worthwhile to make the effort to use at least one strong visual image with each affirmation.

"Visualization" usually refers to visual images, but it can involve the other senses as well. The memory of the fragrance of incense may strengthen an affirmation about meditation. The memory of soft wind in the trees, or an ocean breeze, might enhance an affirmation about inner peace. Associating sensory experiences with affirmations helps them become more deeply etched in our consciousness.

With these ingredients in hand, we can proceed to the technique of scientific healing affirmations.

PART VIII CHAPTER FOUR

Scientific Affirmation Technique*

> First, affirm for wisdom and Bliss, then for harmony, then for health, then for true happiness for all mankind. Affirmations remind the Soul of what it already has, and what it does not have, because of forgetfulness.[1] –YOGANANDA

To make our affirmations effective, we need to proceed in three stages. First, we need to understand the affirmation clearly with the conscious mind. Then, by continuous repetition with deep attention and focused energy, it needs to penetrate the subconscious mind, where it will begin to create a new pattern of thought and behavior. Finally, it needs to attract the supreme power of superconsciousness that will guarantee its effectiveness.

We need to engage all three dimensions of our consciousness.

> Chronic mental or physical diseases have always a deep root in the sub-conscious mind...That is why all affirmations practiced by the conscious mind ought to be impressive enough to stay as mental habits in the sub-conscious mind, which would in turn again automatically influence the conscious mind. Strong conscious affirmation thus being reinforced reacts on the mind and body through the medium of the sub-conscious. Still stronger conscious will or devotion affirmations not only reach the sub-conscious but the Super-conscious, the magic storehouse or factory of all miraculous mental powers. [2]

---

* The primary resources for these practices are Yogananda's *Scientific Healing Affirmations* and his *Advanced Super Cosmic Science Course, Lesson 1* (which you'll find in the Appendices); Kriyananda's *Affirmations for Self-Healing*; and his *Art and Science of Raja Yoga*.

Nor is it enough, even, to affirm change on conscious and subconscious levels. For we are part of a much greater reality, with which we must live in harmony also. Behind our human minds is the divine consciousness....Affirmation should be lifted from the self-enclosure of the mind into the greater reality of superconsciousness.[3]

How to begin [4]

- First, sit calmly. Quiet the fanciful, subconscious mind. Stop the conscious mind from being restless. Induce the all-powerful superconsciousness by meditating deeply.

- Sit facing north or east.

- Close your eyes (concentrating your attention on the medulla, unless otherwise directed). Keep the spine erect, chest high, abdomen in. Relax completely. Take deep breaths and exhale thrice.

- Relax the body and keep it motionless. Empty the mind of all restless thoughts, and withdraw it from all sensations of bodily weight, temperature and sounds, etc.

- Fill your mind with devotion and with will, feeling the former in the heart and the latter in its physiological center of generation in between the eyebrows. Cast away anxiety, distrust, worry. Realize calmly that the Divine Law works and is All-Powerful only when you do not shut it out by doubt or disbelief. Faith and concentration allow it to operate unhampered. Hold the thought that all bodily states are changeable and curable and that the consciousness of anything being chronic is a delusion.

- Forget what it is that you want to be healed.

- Before beginning your affirmation practice, broadcast your message, "My Father and I are One" until you feel this over-powering, all-solacing Bliss of God. When this happens, you have made contact.[5]

THE TECHNIQUE [6]

Choose your affirmation, and with deep concentration:

- Repeat it first **loudly**,
- Then **softer** and more **slowly**,
- Until your voice becomes a **whisper**.
- Then gradually affirm it **mentally** only, without moving even the tongue or the lips.
- Affirm mentally until you feel that you have merged into deep, unbroken concentration, with a conscious continuity of uninterrupted thought.
- If you continue your mental affirmation and go deeper, you will feel an increasing joy and peace coming over you.
- In deep concentration the affirmation will merge with the subconscious stream, to return later, reinforced by the power to influence the conscious mind through the law of habit.
- During the stage when you are experiencing increasing peace, the affirmation will penetrate into the superconscious reservoir, to return later laden with unlimited power not only to influence your conscious mind but to fulfill your desires in very real, material ways.
- The affirmations must be practiced with the proper loud intonation, fading into a whisper, and above all with attention and devotion, taking the thought from the auditory sense to the understanding or conscious mind, thence to the subconscious or automatic mind, and then to the Superconscious, with conviction about their efficacy and truth.

The voice

In recordings of Yogananda speaking in public,* we experience the power of his voice to transform our consciousness. He is demonstrating also the quality and degree of power we want to bring to our own voice while repeating affirmations to heal ourselves and change our lives. During the phases of the practice when we speak softly, the voice should still be saturated with vitality.

At the beginning of our practice, we are urged to repeat the affirmation loudly, to capture the attention of the conscious mind. The voice should be strong, and infused with conviction and faith.

> Your conscious mind must be made awake and ready before it can go deep into the spirit of the affirmation...
> Either at bedtime, or sitting upright in meditation, repeat your affirmation out loud to begin with to generate energy and command the attention of all your conscious thought.... Remember, then, put your whole self joyously into your affirmation. Then gradually let the words resound from deeper and deeper levels of feeling and awareness. As you do so, you will notice that the outward sound of the words automatically decreases, until it becomes only a whisper. Sink the words down deeper still, until you feel no desire to speak or to chant them outwardly at all, and the affirmation becomes purely mental. Go deeper still, carrying the thought into the subconscious, zealously changing the mental patterns there.[7]

After repeating the affirmation loudly a number of times, our intonation becomes softer. The rhythm slows as, with deepening concentration, the affirmation begins to penetrate the subconscious mind. The intonation then becomes a whisper, as our concentration deepens and the affirmation influences the subconscious ever more deeply.

In the last stage we repeat the affirmation only mentally, offering it into the superconscious, from where it will return to influence our conscious awareness and our daily life. We should continue to repeat

* https://yogananda.org/paramahansa-yogananda-engage-listen.

the affirmation mentally for a long time, so that we can experience joy and peace as a sure confirmation that the affirmation has reached the superconscious level.

The position of the eyes

Swami Kriyananda said that our habitual gaze reflects the level of our consciousness. In normal waking consciousness the eyes are fully open and tend to look straight ahead. Kriyananda recommended that we begin repeating the affirmation consciously – thus, in a loud voice and with *open eyes*.

The eyes tend to lower as we drift into subconsciousness. As we repeat the affirmation more softly, we can enhance its effectiveness at the subconscious level by closing our eyelids and *lowering our gaze*.

The gaze of the eyes spontaneously turns upward in superconscious states. We see this in paintings of saints portrayed with uplifted gaze, and more recently, in photographs of people in ecstatic states, such as the visionaries of Fatima, Garabandal, and Medjugorje. While repeating the affirmation mentally, we can more effectively direct it upward to the superconscious by keeping our *eyes relaxed and uplifted*, with closed or half-open eyelids.

> You will find, when you look down, that the mind tends more easily to drift into subconsciousness. When you look straight ahead, it is easier to shake off sleep's lethargy. And when you look up, it is easier to soar up into higher consciousness and to feel inspiration.
>
> *Practice this exercise:*
>
> 1) Look down, closing your eyes. Feel yourself drifting downward as if sinking through water—through forests of waving seaweed—ever deeper into a green, misty world of fantasy. Enjoy this pleasant sense of freedom from earthly responsibility, from demanding projects, from fears, from worldly ambitions. Affirm mentally, **"Through slowly drifting waters, I sink into subconsciousness."**

2) Now, with a quick burst of will power, open your eyes and gaze straight ahead. Shake off the last clinging tendrils of passivity. Affirm, **"With a burst of energy I rise to greet the world!"**

3) Remain in that state a few moments. Then look upward and affirm, **"I awake in Thy light! I am joyful! I am free! I awake in Thy light!"**

Practice alternating between these three states of consciousness, accompanying them with a corresponding shift in the position of your eyes. Gradually, you will gain the ability to control your states of consciousness at will.[8]

When to practice

The most effective time for repeating affirmations is when the mind is transitioning from wakefulness to sleep.

> When you want to affirm something, make a special point of doing so as you go to sleep. Carry that thought into the subconscious. The next morning as you wake up, while the subconscious is still open, make that affirmation again. You can change your life for the better, thereby, very quickly.[9]

Another favorable time to repeat your affirmation is at the end of your meditations, when the mind is more attuned to superconsciousness.

Group practice [10]

Meditating and practicing affirmations in the company of those who share our aspirations will enhance their effectiveness. When practicing alone or in groups, we should sit perfectly still. Yogananda offers these guidelines for group practice.

Life Force / **224**

In group affirmations the leader should read the affirmations rhythmically while standing. The audience should repeat after him with his same rhythm and intonation.[10]

All loud affirmations by a group may be started loudly or softly, but must end in chanting them mentally for some time in silence, until the words change into vibratory messengers of thought let loose in the ether to execute their desired errands.[11]

During group affirmations for curing physical or mental disease in self or others, care should be taken to affirm with an even tone, even mental force, even concentration and even sense of faith and peace. Weaker minds lessen the united force born of such affirmations and can even side-track this flood of force from its super-conscious destination. By all means do not make any bodily movements or become mentally restless or disturb your neighbor. Merely keeping still is not enough, you must remember your concentration or restlessness will materially affect the desired result favorably or unfavorably.[12]

In the next chapter, we will discover how we can use affirmations to help us at other times.

PART VIII   CHAPTER FIVE

Affirmation in Motion and Music

> Affirmations become potent to the extent that they can be made to resound in inner depths.[1] –KRIYANANDA
>
> Put your whole self joyously into your affirmation.[2] –KRIYANANDA

Research has shown that we learn more quickly and permanently when we engage the body and senses in the process – the neural pathways are more powerfully stimulated, and the new mental patterns are more quickly and lastingly engraved.

Mentally repeating an affirmation, as described in the last chapter, can transform our lives, and adding movement to our affirmations can magnify their effects and accelerate the results. Often, a simple bodily gesture will be enough to direct our energy and attention with greater focus. For example, when mental fatigue sets in, we can rescue ourselves from the spiral of unwillingness and mental dullness by raising both arms overhead while looking upward and mentally or loudly shouting the simple affirmation: "YES!"

Awake and ready

When you wake up, try to capture your first thought. Is it life-affirming, or life-negating? Does it express enthusiasm and willingness or reluctance and resignation? Training the mind to affirm "I am awake and ready!" with a positive burst of energy can set the tone for the day.

My experience is that while the mind adjusts quickly to this practice, its effects will be negated if I follow my "Yes!" affirmation by turning off the alarm, rolling over, and pulling the blankets over my head. But if I combine the affirmation with positive movements, the odds are better that I'll get out of bed.

While repeating the affirmation, I engage in a series of physical actions to reinforce its effects. For starters, I open my eyes and smile.

Yogananda recommends doing the Life Force Full Body Recharge* in bed on waking. Several cycles of full-body tension and relaxation, followed by tensing and relaxing each body part in turn, generally do the trick for me. The next step is sitting up in bed and continuing the affirmation while rapping my skull vigorously with both knuckles, then strongly massaging the scalp. Finally, I stand and repeat the process.

The days when I succeed in completing the sequence are golden.

The importance of rhythm

The rhythm and cadence of an affirmation are important – they are an essential element of the technique.

Kriyananda recommends: **"Make your affirmations rhythmic, in a rhythm commensurate with the nature of your resolution."** [3] At a time when he was experiencing serious heart problems, he created this rhythmic affirmation:

> *Thy light pervades my body cells:*
> *Thy light pervades my heart.*
> *Thy light perfects my body cells:*
> *Thy light perfects my heart.* [4]

Aside from practicing affirmation in a meditative state, as previously discussed, we can use them whenever we're engaged in rhythmic activities such as walking, running, bicycling, dancing, or an individual sport requiring an even pace.

---

* See pages 275-291 in Volume One.

❋ A Flowing River ❋

A prime ingredient of my walks is affirmations. I use them to boost my vitality and improve my outlook for the day. Especially when I'm feeling tired, I'll go for a walk and repeat: "I am a bursting river of unlimited power and infinite energy!" As I repeat it in synchrony with the rhythm of my steps, its power seems to become deeply fixed in my mind. When I finish, I feel truly recharged and enthusiastic. Wow! –**Monica**, *Turin, Italy*

❋ Winter Dreariness ❋

The Russian winters are cold and depressingly long. A variety of physical and psychological ailments would routinely visit me in this dreary season. I especially remember a year when I was suffering from a painful disappointment. To lift myself out of the doldrums, I started going for short runs, and synchronizing my steps and breath in rhythm with a mental affirmation: "I am healthy! I am well!" If there were no people around, I would repeat it aloud.

The runs got longer, the affirmation got stronger, and my willpower reawakened. It took about six months to pull myself up completely. My affirmation reached its zenith when I took it along on a three-week hike in the beautiful mountains of the Altai region in southern Siberia, which is a very special place of power, beauty, and healing.

Nowadays there is always an affirmation in my mind that keeps me positive, healthy, and doing my best in the face of the ever-new challenges on the path to my goal. – **Sunita**, *Russia*

❋ ❋ ❋

Ananda Yoga for Higher Awareness

The health benefits of the Hatha Yoga postures have been thoroughly documented. By releasing tension, the *asanas* permit life force to flow more strongly and harmoniously, repairing and nourishing the body cells and organs.

The *asanas* originated from the bodily positions assumed spontaneously by spiritually advanced souls while in states of higher awareness. While attuning himself to those states of consciousness, Swami Kriyananda perceived an affirmation for each of the basic postures that vibrationally reflects and stimulates those superconscious experiences. This practice is now known throughout the world as Ananda Yoga. The affirmations are given in his books *Ananda Yoga for Higher Awareness* and *The Art and Science of Raja Yoga*.

❀ STRENGTH AND COURAGE ❀ FILL MY BODY CELLS

When I began sharing Swami Kriyananda's affirmations for higher awareness with my yoga students, they initially received them as a rather unusual, then a welcome experience.

One of the students, the chief physician of the neurology department at a large hospital in Rome, suggested that we collaborate and use the postures and affirmations for patients with Parkinson's disease. Thus began one of the most rewarding experiences of my life.

Parkinson's is considered incurable, though there are drugs that attempt to improve the quality of life.

We began to use yoga as an adjunct to the drug therapies. Working with the patients individually and in groups, we introduced them to some of Yogananda's Energization Exercises, to help them feel their bodies come alive. We then moved on to the traditional yoga asanas, adapting them so that they could be done sitting in a chair, combined with the affirmations, which we repeat aloud.

The affirmations have had a twofold effect. Repeating them helps the patients enter and remain in the posture, and it encourages them to express their feelings, including the hopes in their hearts.

With *garudasana*, we affirm: "In the center of the storms of life, I am serene." With *gomukhasana*: "Free in my heart I live without fear." With *ardhachandrasana*: "Strength and courage fill my body cells." And with the balance pose, *vrikasana*: "I am calm, I am poised."

This practice has improved their balance – almost all of the patients are able to stand as we affirm: "I am Positive! Energetic! Enthusiastic!" In fact, this affirmation has become our motto, the culmination of every session, and it is inscribed on the Certificate of Participation.

The results have been so remarkable that I was encouraged to adapt these practices for people who suffer from anxiety, phobias, panic attacks, and eating disorders. Working with a psychiatrist and a psychotherapist, we are now collaborating with the neuroscience department of the American National Institutes of Health (NIH).

My experience with hundreds of patients offers convincing proof that our quality of life depends to a great extent on our mental attitudes, which are entirely within our power to control through the practice of affirmation.
–**Sonia**, *Rome*

Superconscious Living affirmations

Swami Kriyananda contributed another significant expression of the practice of affirmation by introducing a series of Superconscious Living Exercises.

> Superconscious living means to trust
> one's life to the flow of a higher wisdom.
> Superconsciousness arranges things
> in ways that we might never imagine...
> seeing life as a flow, and the universe
> as living and conscious.[5]

Each exercise combines an affirmation with a brisk physical movement that strengthens the impact of the words on the mind. The set can be done in a few minutes, assuming each exercise is repeated six times. You can use them in the morning to generate a positive outlook for the day, then repeat them as often as needed to keep yourself centered, positive, and creative. You can also use them as a mental and physical warmup before meditating.

SUPERCONSCIOUS LIVING EXERCISES*

Repeat each exercise several times, or as much as you like.

① Walk vigorously in place before meditating. Affirm: *"I am awake and ready! I am awake and ready!"*

②

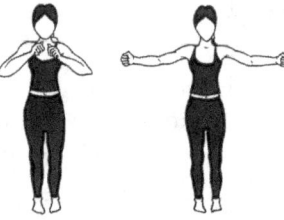

(a) Begin at the starting position

(b) From there, fling the arms out to the side. Affirm: *"I am positive!"*

(c) Bring the arms back briefly to the starting position, then thrust them out in front of you. Affirm: *"Energetic!"*

(d) Bring the arms back briefly again to the starting position, then fling them high above your head, coming up onto the toes. Affirm: *"Enthusiastic!"*

 **③** Rap your knuckles lightly on the forearms and upper arms, first with the right fist, then with the left. Affirm: *"I am master of my body, I am master of myself!"* Repeat this exercise several times.

④ Rub your arms, legs, hips, chest, and other parts of the body. Affirm: *"Awake! Rejoice, my body cells!"*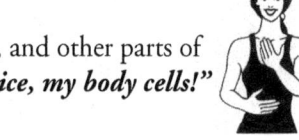

 **⑤** Rap your scalp lightly with your knuckles. Affirm: *"Be glad, my brain! Be wise and strong!"*

⑥ Massage scalp lightly all over with your fingertips. Affirm: *"Awake, my sleeping children! Wake!"*

---

* You will find an instruction video in the Appendices.

Affirmation in music

Just as movement can help to imprint an affirmation more rapidly and deeply in the subconscious mind, music can amplify the affirmations in much the same way.

Research has shown that students learn better in the presence of appropriate music. Certain music activates the left and right brain hemispheres at the same time, maximizing learning and improving memory. It has been found that listening to favorite music greatly enhances the emotional, behavioral, and communication skills of Alzheimer's patients.

Music penetrates our consciousness more effectively than the spoken word. Music can create a mood and an environment of peace and harmony, disharmony and disease, or violence and destruction. We can use music to very good effect together with the practice of affirmations. Kriyananda suggests: **"It is helpful to combine prayers, and even affirmations, with the uplifting influence of music."** [6]

If you are musically inclined, you can create, or adapt, a melody to your chosen affirmation. Yogananda's chant *Door of My Heart* includes an affirmation in the refrain: "Night and day, night and day, I look for Thee night and day."

Another chant of Yogananda's affirms: "I am the bubble, make me the sea. Wave of the sea, dissolve in the sea." And another of his *Cosmic Chants* affirms: "I am Aum. I am Aum. Omnipresence, I am Aum, All-pervading, I am Aum."

Kriyananda's song lyrics often contain affirmations.

> Nothing on earth can hold me!
> Rise, oh my soul, in freedom!
> Rise, oh my soul, in freedom,
> Nothing to fear anymore.

Another chant declares:

> I awake in Thy Light!
> I am joyful, I am free,
> I awake in Thy Light!

The following short affirmation, from Yogananda's mystical poem, "Samadhi," was set to music by a disciple.

From joy I came,
For joy I live,
In sacred joy I melt.

You can sing affirmations in the shower, while walking, together with friends, and at the start and end of your meditations – even during the meditation, to bring the wandering mind back to what you're trying to accomplish.

We will further explore the healing effects of music and singing in Part XII of Volume Three, "Vibratory Healing."

PART VIII   CHAPTER SIX

Healed by Affirmations

> **WHEN I ASKED FRIENDS TO SHARE**
> their experiences on this topic, I received
> countless incredible stories. These accounts are
> so inspiring that they deserve their own chapter.
> May they inspire you to experiment with
> affirmations for your own healing.

※ THE EARTHQUAKE STOPPED ※

I only really began to discover Yogananda's affirmations on the day my histology test results came back. It was the news I most feared: I had breast cancer. An earthquake erupted in me, and I couldn't think straight.

I was still trembling when I received a message from a spiritual sister. She sent me one of Yogananda's affirmations and encouraged me to repeat it continuously:

> *My body cells are made of Light,*
> *They are perfect because You are perfect,*
> *They are healthy because You are health,*
> *They are spirit because You are spirit,*
> *They are immortal because You are living.*

I perfectly remember the moment I began to repeat the affirmation. I felt the words resonating in every part of my body – I could feel that every cell was being affected. "Something" had been set in motion that I could not explain, even though I experienced it. The earthquake stopped – I was no longer afraid. Strangely, I felt joy.

No longer debilitated by fear, and with this powerful tool in hand, I met the test with courage and assurance. The cancerous cells were removed, and no chemotherapy was needed, only radiation. Now, more than three years later, I continue to use the affirmation, together with another that helps me ward off anxiety before my quarterly checkups:

> *I am immersed in the Eternal Light,*
> *It pervades every particle of my body,*
> *I live in that Light,*
> *The Divine Spirit envelops me entirely inside and out.*
> *God is in me, He surrounds me and protects me!*
> *I will eliminate every fear that precludes me*
> *from His Light.*
>
> —**Stefania**, *Milan, Italy*

✵ COVID THERAPY ✵

The first three nights, I could only succumb to the symptoms: fever, sore throat, stuffy nose, weakness, sleeplessness. Anxiously I thought, "It has me in its grip – I am powerless against this Covid."

And then, suddenly, I remembered a healing affirmation by Paramhansa Yogananda that a friend had sent me:

> *"I am immersed in the Eternal Light!*
> *It pervades every part of my being.*
> *I live in this Light!!!*
> *Divine Spirit fills me*
> *Inside and outside!"*

Mentally I immersed my body in the light. I imagined that every cell of my body was filled with this healing light!

Did my fever fall immediately? Did my sore throat go away?

No – but my mood began to improve. I no longer gave my attention to the disease that was trying to *force* me into the blues.

In that moment I realized that my condition was strongly linked to my thoughts, and that I could give in to the disease and admit that I was sick. But instead, I imagined myself

Life Force / **236**

completely healthy and filled with joyful energy. I could feel that the disease was retreating. It was a turning point.

I continued to repeat the affirmation continuously, visualizing the divine Light inside and around me. There was a sense of joy, of lightness and strength, and I felt a flow of bliss inside me. Though my body was still weak, I felt a blossoming joy along with the affirmation.

I made a conscious choice to hold on to the stream of positive thoughts, regardless of my external circumstances. From that moment the disease retreated quickly, and I recovered completely, with no lingering effects. I had taken an antiviral medication and Vitamin D, but my main medicines were my positive thoughts and affirmations of light and healing.

I've shared my experience with friends who were infected with Covid, and the affirmation is working for them.

–**Snezhana**, *Russia*

A PRINCESS ON THE THRONE OF PEACE

My husband was scheduled to undergo a simple gallstone operation. I had full confidence in the surgeon, but when my husband unexpectedly had a stroke during the surgery, my whole world changed overnight.

My husband had been my point of reference for all that we had shared, and now I had to take on countless responsibilities on my own. While affirming a positive attitude and a constant smile as I cared for him, I was managing the family business, my husband's affairs, and the many medical matters.

My reference points now were God and Guru. In the midst of my despair, Yogananda whispered to me: *"God gives you the trials you can bear!"* This inner response gave me the strength to go on.

To calm myself while I devised a new plan to organize my life, several of Yogananda's affirmations came to me spontaneously from my heart, including this one:

"I am the princess of peace and I rule my kingdom of activity, sitting on the throne of calm."

I repeated the affirmation when I was about to confront my husband's business associates, whose only concerns were financial. The circumstances were beyond me, but with this calming affirmation I could see things more clearly.

As I walked and talked with my Guru, He sent me this affirmation: "The shining light of divine truth dissolves the darkness of ignorance. I am protected by that light; in dharma there is victory!"

Slowly I began to live my new life, spending all day at the hospital, teaching classes in the evenings, and giving evening classes in yoga and meditation for my clients and students. Meanwhile, I was busy finding new cures for my husband.

This routine continued for more than four years, until the financial problems with his partners were finally resolved.

My husband and I understood that the time for a separation had come. At that point, I felt that I had to let him go.

I knew that our Guru was with us and would guide me in my new life alone. –**Lucilla**, *Monte Visconti, Italy*

❋ LIVER TRANSPLANT ❋

"Why me, God? What have I done?" I'd been living a clean life, with no smoking or drinking and a good diet. How was it possible that I was suddenly *dying*?

When the stomach problems began, I went to the doctor. My condition didn't seem serious, but it rapidly got much worse. The doctors ran several tests and told me that my liver was completely destroyed by cirrhosis, whereupon they began to look for an organ donor, which was my only hope to survive.

I was hospitalized immediately, and for some time I was in a semi-coma state. When I was finally able to grasp the situation, my life came crashing down. I lost all hope, and even after a donor was found I was so depressed that I said I wouldn't go through with the process, and that I would rather die. The operation was delayed by the onset of the Covid pandemic, and after a month or so I was discharged in a wheelchair to go home and take complete rest while following a strict diet and taking liver-support medication.

During this time, I saw the image of my cousin's wife while I was in a half-waking state. Thinking it might be a sign, I asked my mother to call her – I didn't know it, but she was experienced in spiritual healing practices, and we began healing sessions through the internet, as she was in Delhi and I lived in Mumbai.

We had several sessions each week. She taught me the Superconscious Living exercises, and at first I had to do them while sitting in bed. Each session included gentle diaphragmatic pranayama breathing exercises, and most important, affirmations with visualization.

From feeling helpless and hopeless, I began to feel better with each session. As we practiced the healing affirmations, I felt that they were beginning to change my mental outlook. Following her guided visualizations, I began to see my body as pure light, and as I practiced, my body began to heal. Each day she sent me encouraging quotes from the teachings of Paramhansa Yogananda, and my mood began to change as well.

As hope returned, I was more open to having the liver transplant, but because my condition was steadily improving the doctors had taken my name off the list. After two years of regular sessions with my healing angel, my liver is now completely free of cirrhosis and I am back at work, trading stocks and leading a normal life. The only medication I take is vitamins, together with daily affirmations and our regular healing sessions online.

I don't think I will ever know what karma brought about the degeneration of my liver, but I can say with confidence that the love and support of my family and friends, and the affirmation and visualization sessions with my healing angel brought hope back into my life and wrought a medical miracle. –**Nishit**, *Mumbai, India*

ALPINE TRAINING

My friends were in admirably good shape. I met up with the group in Mendoza, Argentina, and while we shared the goal of climbing to the top of Mt. Aconcagua, the highest peak in the Americas at 6960 meters (22,841 feet), we were from vastly different backgrounds. Most of them had been training for years, and many went to the gym for rigorous daily workouts. One had cycled across Canada from Montreal to Vancouver.

I was one of two women in the group, the second-oldest climber at age fifty-four, and the only one who had done no training to speak of. I had never been to a gym, and the longest hike I had done was six hours in the Surrey Hills of my native England. How could I hope to climb the highest mountain in the Americas and in the Southern Hemisphere?

I was here to be healed: to leave technology behind, immerse myself in nature, gladden my heart, refresh my spirit, and lift my consciousness – and, as it turned out, to test my willpower and my faith in the power of the affirmations and prayer-poems of Paramhansa Yogananda that I loved.

I recited them to myself continuously, finding in them the strength to keep climbing every day of the two-week expedition. The following are some of the words that saw me through to the end:

"Bless me, Father, that I may fly with Thee from peak to peak..."

To prevent any negative thoughts, fears, or doubts from taking over, I also drew upon these words and images:

"I now know that I am a lion of cosmic power. Bleating no more, I shake the error forest with reverberations of Thine almighty voice. In divine freedom I bound through the jungle of earthly delusions, devouring the little creatures of vexing worries and timidities, and the wild hyenas of disbelief. O Lion of Liberation, ever send through me Thy roar of all-conquering courage."

I was one of just five climbers to reach the top. As I stood on the summit, in awe of the magnificence and majesty of the surrounding mountains, I thanked Yogananda for the power in his words, mentally saying:

> "The scenery of mountains painted on the
> ever-changing azure canvas of the sky,
> the mysterious mechanism of the human body,
> the rose, the green grass carpet,
> the magnanimity of souls, the loftiness of minds,
> the depth of love – all these things
> remind us of a God who is beautiful and noble."
>
> —**Fiona**, *England*

NOTES PART EIGHT

Chapter One
1 Kriyananda, *Education for Life*, 163.
2 Kriyananda, *Art and Science of Raja Yoga*, 103.
3 Yogananda, *Autobiography of a Yogi*, 12-13.
4 Kriyananda, "Introduction," *Affirmations for Self-Healing*.
5 Yogananda, "Spiritual Power of Man's Word," *Scientific Healing Affirmations*, 15.
6 Yogananda, 15.
7 Kriyananda, *Awaken to Superconsciousness*, 72.
8 Kriyananda, *God Is for Everyone*, 36.
9 Yogananda, "Steps Toward the Attaining of Consciousness," "Second Coming of Christ," *Inner Culture*, July 1934.
10 Yogananda, *Yogoda Course*, Lesson 1.
11 Kriyananda, *Self-Expansion through Marriage*, 103-104.
12 Yogananda, "Evaluation of the Science of Curative Methods," *Scientific Healing Affirmations*, 28-29.
13 Kriyananda, *The Art and Science of Raja Yoga*, 103.
14 Kriyananda, *Awaken to Superconsciousness*, 73.

Chapter Two
1 Yogananda, "Cure According to Temperament," *Scientific Healing Affirmations*, 21.
2 Yogananda, 20.
3 Yogananda, "Psychological Centers," *Scientific Healing Affirmations*, 50.
4 Yogananda, Meditations & Affirmations," *Inner Culture*, April-June 1941.
5 Yogananda, *Scientific Healing Affirmations*, 73.
6 Yogananda, "Wisdom Affirmation," *Scientific Healing Affirmations*, 78.
7 Kriyananda, "How Old Are You?" unpublished article.
8 Yogananda, *Whispers from Eternity*, No. 2.
9 Yogananda, *Yogoda Course*, Lesson 8.
10 Yogananda, "Will Affirmation," *Scientific Healing Affirmations*, 70.
11 Yogananda, "Curing Bad Habits," 105.
12 Kriyananda, "Devotion," *Affirmations for Self-Healing*, 36.
13 Yogananda, "Art of Spiritual Healing," *Yogoda Course*, Lesson 8.
14 Yogananda, *Whispers from Eternity*, No. 92.
15 Yogananda, "Art of Spiritual Healing," *Yogoda Course*, Lesson 8.
16 Yogananda, "Thought Affirmation," *Scientific Healing Affirmations*, 69.
17 Kriyananda, "Self-Expansion," *Affirmations for Self-Healing*, 82.
18 Kriyananda, "Immortality," 116.
19 Kriyananda, "Concentration," 80.
20 Yogananda, *Whispers from Eternity*, No. 15.

Chapter Three
1 Yogananda, "God Given Power of Man," *Scientific Healing Affirmations*, 6.
2 Yogananda, "How to Find God," *Inner Culture*, October 1941.
3 Yogananda, *Super-Advanced Course No. 1*, Lesson 6.
4 Yogananda, "Mental Responsibility for Chronic Diseases," *Scientific Healing Affirmations*, 9.
5 Yogananda, *Yogoda Course*, Lesson 5.
6 Kriyananda, *26 Keys to Greater Awareness*.
7 Yogananda, "God-given Power of Man," *Scientific Healing Affirmations*, 5-6.

8 Kriyananda, "Grace vs. Self-Effort," Written for *The Hindustan Times*, January 29, 2004.
9 Yogananda, "God-given Power of Man," and "Individual and Group Directions," *Scientific Healing Affirmations*, 56-57.
10 Yogananda, *Yogoda Course*, Lesson 8.

Chapter Four
1 Yogananda, *Advanced Super Cosmic Science Course*, Lesson 1.
2 Yogananda, "Mental Responsibility for Chronic Diseases," *Scientific Healing Affirmations*, 8-9.
3 Kriyananda, "Introduction," *Affirmations for Self-Healing*, 11.
4 Yogananda, "Healing by Spiritual Affirmation and by Astral Food," *Advanced Super Cosmic Science Course*, Lesson 1. You will find the complete article in the Appendices.
5 Yogananda, "The Surest Way to Prosperity," *East-West*, October 1932.
6 Yogananda, "Individual and Group Directions," *Scientific Healing Affirmations*, 54, 55, 47.
7 Kriyananda, *Art and Science of Raja Yoga*, 223, 224.
8 Kriyananda, *Awaken to Superconsciousness*, 111-112.
9 Kriyananda, *Money Magnetism*, 115.
10 Yogananda, "Individual and Group Directions," *Scientific Healing Affirmations*, 59, 55-56.
11 Yogananda, *Scientific Healing Affirmations*, 59
12 Yogananda, "Healing by spiritual affirmation," *Advanced Super Cosmic Science Course*, Lesson 1.
13 Yogananda, *Scientific Healing Affirmations*, 55-56.

Chapter Five
1 Kriyananda, *Art and Science of Raja Yoga*, 193.
2 Kriyananda, 224.
3 Kriyananda, *Money Magnetism*, 117-118.
4 Kriyananda, *Awaken to Superconsciousness*, 187.
5 Kriyananda, 244, 245.
6 Kriyananda, *Art and Science of Raja Yoga*, 245.

PART IX
DIVINE GRACE

IF YOU WANT HIS ANSWER [1]
by Paramhansa Yogananda

Whether He replies or not
Keep calling Him.
Ever calling in the chamber
Of continuous prayer.
Whether He comes or not
You must believe He is ever
Approaching nearer to you.
With every command of your
    heart's love,
Whether He answers or not
You must keep entreating Him
Even if He makes no reply
In the way you expect,
Ever know He will respond
In some subtle way.
In the darkness of your deepest
    prayers,
Know He is playing hide-and-seek
With you.
And in the midst of the dance of
    life,
disease, and death,
If you keep calling Him,
Undepressed by His seeming
    silence,
You will receive His answer.

PART IX CHAPTER ONE

Who Is Listening?

> Feel that just behind the screen of your devotional demands, God is listening to the silent words of your soul. Feel this! Be one with your heart's demand—and be thoroughly convinced that He has listened to you. Then go about your duties, seeking not to know whether God will grant your demand. Believe absolutely that your demand has been heard, and you will know that what is God's is yours also.[1] –YOGANANDA
>
> You must not be discouraged because of ill health, poverty, or moral weakness. Remember, sin is only a temporary graft; in reality you are eternally a Child of God. Even if the world condemns you and casts you away, God will ever seek to find you and bring you back home.[2] –YOGANANDA
>
> My religion consists of a humble admiration of the illimitable superior spirit who reveals himself in the slight details we are able to perceive with our frail and feeble mind." – ALBERT EINSTEIN

※ **ALBERT AND THE ABYSS** ※

Eager to escape from the drudgery of his engineering job, Albert signed up for a safari in Africa. The safari guide harshly insisted that the members of the group stick together – and he was graphic in his descriptions of what could happen if they didn't. Albert was sure he could keep up, so he wasn't worried.

An avid photographer, Albert was eager to capture the rare flowers that bloomed briefly in the desert. Thrilled to take pictures of flowers he had never seen, Albert failed to notice that he had fallen behind the group. Albert didn't know where they had gone, and their footprints had been swept away by the wind.

Wandering aimlessly, Albert came to the attention of a lion in search of its dinner. As he ran, he didn't see the precipice until too late, and over he went. Only a slim branch growing on the cliff side saved him from certain death.

Albert wasn't a religious man. He believed in a strict scientific model of the universe. But now he felt he should examine his options.

"Hello! Hello! Is anyone up there?" he called. "God, if you exist, please help me!"

A soothing voice replied: "My son, I've been hoping you'd call."

"Is that you, God? Do You really exist?"

"Yes, my child, I am here. I see you're in trouble."

"I'll do anything for You – I'll promise You anything, build anything in Your name, if you'll just get me out of here!"

"You'll do anything I ask?"

"Yes, yes, anything – but please hurry!"

"All right. Let go of the branch."

"What?! It's the only thing saving me."

"Yes, I know. Let go."

Glancing upward, Albert observed the tiger licking his chops. Then, turning his gaze to the abyss below, he said: "Is there anyone else I can talk to up there?"

Whether we think of ourselves as open-minded agnostics, "scientific" atheists, or dyed-in-the-wool believers, there appear to be powers in the universe that operate outside of known physical laws*. Some call these powers miraculous. Others dismiss them as merely phenomena waiting to be explained. For those who maintain that science and spirituality are incompatible, respected scientists offer their perspectives:

> Everyone who is seriously involved in the pursuit of science becomes convinced that a spirit is manifest in the laws of the Universe – a spirit vastly superior to that of man, and one in the face of which we with our modest powers must feel humble.
> —ALBERT EINSTEIN

> Gravity explains the motions of the planets, but it cannot explain who sets the planets in motion.
> —SIR ISAAC NEWTON

In Part I of Volume One we discussed the vibratory origins of the universe. In Part XII of Volume Three, we will discover that the material creation consists of varying vibratory frequencies.

Pythagoras, the Greek philosopher and mathematician, proposed that vibration creates sound, which in turn creates precise mathematical, archetypical shapes which are the building blocks of creation, from the most massive galaxies to the smallest subatomic particles. There is order in the universe, and physical scientists continue to discover its orderly laws.

Yogananda observed that the scientist seeks to understand the nature of the Infinite from outside, while the spiritual scientist approaches the Infinite from inside. There are universal, cosmic, metaphysical laws that manifest on the material plane as the laws of physics.

* See, for example, the story "Antigravity" on p. 210 in Volume One.

> Divine truths are applicable on all levels of reality, from the sublime to the most mundane. In physics, the Law of Karma manifests as the law of action and reaction. The Law of Love manifests as the law of gravity. Cosmic energy manifests in living creatures as the life-force; in matter, as electricity. Spiritual magnetism is echoed in the laws of electro-magnetism. In human affairs, the longing for divine immortality manifests in the ego's struggle for survival.[4]

Underlying these laws are the twin forces of duality: on one hand, the power that is actively drawing every creature back to its source in Spirit, and the equally magnetic power that is forever trying to pull us outward away from that source.

In his autobiography, *The New Path,* Swami Kriyananda recalls a puzzling conversation with his guru.

> Master posed me an unexpected question. 'What keeps the earth from shooting out into space, away from the sun?'
> Surprised, and not as yet familiar with the cryptic way he often taught us, I assumed he simply wanted information. 'It's the sun's gravitational pull, Sir,' I explained.
> 'Then what keeps the earth from being drawn back into the sun?'
> 'That's the earth's centrifugal force, pulling it constantly outward. If the sun's gravity weren't as strong as it is, we'd shoot off into space, out of the solar system altogether.'
> Master smiled significantly. Had he intended more than I realized? Some months later I recalled this conversation, and understood that he had been speaking metaphorically of God as the sun, drawing all things back to Himself, and of man as the earth, resisting with desires and petty self-interest the pull of divine love.[4]

These two equally powerful and perfectly balanced forces are at play: God's Love—the power that draws us toward infinite inner expansion and freedom; and Maya—the Cosmic Deluder, the hypnotic power that is always busily trying to keep us distracted from our true goal, and entrenched in material identifications and pursuits. This is the battle that is the backdrop for the Bhagavad Gita, in which the armies of the Soul, the instruments of God's love, are arrayed against the soldiers under the command of the Ego, the instrument of Maya.

How is it possible to win against the formidable forces of Maya? By doing as Arjuna does in the Bhagavad Gita: calling into play the power that supersedes all others—the Grace of God. In the battle of daily life, our efforts to overcome our tests, temptations, and trials are enormously enhanced when we call upon God's power of love to help and guide us. **"Without grace from above,"** Swami Kriyananda writes, **"no way exists for man to escape from delusion."** [5]

Cooperating with Grace

Yet, if God's love for each of us is boundless, total, and unconditional, is His grace automatically present when we are in need? Does it come to us by God's will, or ours? Does it come on its own, perhaps dispensed only to certain worthy people in certain circumstances, or must we call on it?

> God's grace flows into us, the more we open ourselves to Him. It doesn't come to us from outside. It is the operation, from within, of our own higher reality. Grace comes, the more we live in soul-consciousness, and the less we live centered in the ego.[6]

> Ultimately... what liberates the soul is divine grace.
> It is unrealistic, however, to claim that man
> plays no part in the process. Nectar cannot
> fill a chalice that is turned upside-down.
> One must cooperate consciously with grace.
> To wait passively for grace to descend
> may mean waiting a long, long time! [7]

To be helped or healed in any situation is not exclusively the result of a spontaneous gift of God's grace. Nor is it due to our own, personal efforts alone. It almost always requires an elegant blending of both.

> The spiritual path is twenty-five percent the disciple's
> effort, twenty-five percent the guru's effort on his
> behalf, and fifty percent the grace of God.
> Don't forget, however... that the twenty-five percent
> that is your part represents one hundred percent
> of your own effort and sincerity! [8]

While seventy-five percent of the effort is, in a sense, a free ride, the remaining twenty-five percent is up to us, and will require the full force of our energy and will. Our own effort is essential to activate the Law of Grace.

> Many people ask what the relation is between grace and self-effort...How often people ask God for His blessings – but what a rare few stop to consider the part they themselves play in attracting those blessings! Grace is like the sunlight shining impersonally on the side of a building. God has no favorites: He loves all equally. Paramhansa Yogananda once told his first disciple in America, "God loves you just as much as he does me. He is our common Father."

> If those who live in a building want to receive the sunlight, they must keep the curtains of their windows open. It is we ourselves who keep out the sun of divine grace, by closing our mental curtains.... Prayer and meditation are the best ways to part the curtains of the mind, making it receptive.
>
> God's grace flows constantly in our lives. He is always with us. If we would receive that grace, however, we must open ourselves to it. It is our hearts, especially, that must be held open by love, and calmness, and a willing spirit.[9]

The techniques that we will now consider can help us focus our efforts to achieve the highest results as quickly and effectively as possible. Activating the Law of Grace requires that we apply tested, scientific methods, using our own, focused effort.

Activating the seventy-five percent

> It is certainly true that we cannot be redeemed by self-effort alone. It is equally true, however, that we can and must cooperate, by an act of conscious will, with the flow of grace. It is also true that, with such cooperation, there are no spiritual heights that cannot be achieved.[10]

While the Law of Inertia tells us that an object tends to remain in motion until it is acted upon, the metaphysical Law of Grace says that if we can enter the stream of Grace, it will keep us moving toward the ultimate divine happiness and freedom. In other words, our own efforts will be blessed and amplified by God's Grace.

Before we can experience the fullness of Grace, we must discover the rewards of *humility*: the willingness to invite the divine help, and the humility to admit that the journey is longer and more difficult than we imagined, and that it will require greater strength than we alone possess.

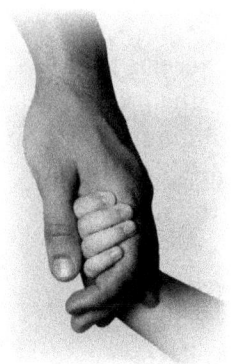

Whenever we find ourselves in difficult circumstances, the ego – ever Maya's willing helper – tries to persuade us that we can overcome the trial by ourselves. But it takes only a little honest introspection to realize that whenever we've taken the reins of our lives entirely in our own hands, we have rarely succeeded.

In the experience of people who have overcome serious addictions, humbly seeking divine aid has been the turning point that miraculously changed their lives. The Twelve Step program of Alcoholics Anonymous includes as Step Three the "decision to turn our will and our lives over to the care of God as we understand Him."

When we reach out to God for His help, we inevitably find the ego mightily opposing our efforts. Yet we can take comfort from Christ's promise: *"Ask, and it shall be given you; seek, and ye shall find; knock, and it shall be opened unto you."* (LUKE 11:9)

God's grace comes through channels, in cosmically creative ways. Many have testified how they have experienced it in unexpected, seemingly serendipitous circumstances, or through individuals who were mysteriously sent to help them, or to whom they were guided by the divine Hand.

Among the individuals God sends to help us, the most important is the spiritual guide whom God Himself has chosen as the principal channel for His grace to us, individually. Every soul will, in time, discover the helpmate who has been divinely appointed to guide him or her. It usually takes many lifetimes to discover our divine guide, and even longer to enter fully into the relationship of disciple and guru. Our God-appointed guru will not only assume spiritual responsibility for our lives; he or she will also serve as a channel for God's divine power to guide, teach, discipline, and increasingly, liberate us.

A friend told me about a dream in which he saw himself standing before a pile of garbage so high that he could barely see the top. He had a little pail, the kind children play with at the beach, and a little shovel with which he would repeatedly fill the tiny pail and carry it off and dump it, then come back for more. After working for a long time, he realized that he had scarcely made a dent in the big pile. And then he heard a loud motor on the other side of the garbage heap. Curious, he strolled around the pile and saw his guru waving at him from a huge tractor with a front-end loader with which he was effortlessly removing large portions of garbage.

There will be many helpers whom the Divine sends to help us. Whether they are friends living now on earth, or angels, they are waiting for God to call them to His service. Evolved souls who have served others in their earthly lives can continue to serve from the astral world.

> Inhabitants of the astral world have no difficulty observing our activities on earth. Relatives may come to us in dreams to express their love to us—or, perhaps, to warn us, in the event of an impending calamity in our lives...Angels roam the streets of man. They inspire with uplifting thoughts and beautiful ideas those whose minds and hearts are open to them. They inspire scientists in their search for new discoveries for the benefit of mankind. They suggest inspiration to artists who long to express truth and beauty through painting, or music, or literature, in order that others, through their works, might achieve more understanding and joy in their lives.
>
> Angels visit hospitals to give strength and comfort to those who suffer physically. Sometimes, they heal those for whom the doctors have abandoned all hope. Often, they help to ease the dying in their struggles to win release from their physical bodies.[11]

❖ Protected by St. Francis ❖
and Archangel Michael

The diagnosis was terrifying, and the prognosis was dire – it was an inoperable, fast-growing bronchial cancer with metastasis in the brain. With intensive chemotherapy and radiation treatments, I might live for six months. That was forty-eight months ago, in 2019.

Years ago, while visiting friends at Ananda Assisi, I learned of St. Francis, and in my meditations I developed a deep inner relationship with him.

When I told an Ananda Assisi friend about my situation, she suggested that I might visualize something that would bring me comfort during the treatments on my head.

During the first session, I mentally began to create the following story.

I am living in the year 1200. St. Francis is staying with his brothers at the Porziuncola, and I'm walking through the forest toward that tiny church, where I find a golden cloak hanging on the door. I undress completely and put the golden cloak around me, then I enter and go to Francis, and as I kneel before him, he puts his hands on my head and keeps them there for the duration of the treatment. I feel his blessing and protection, and when the treatment ends, I hang the golden cloak on the door and walk out of the forest.

I repeat the story for eight days. On the ninth day, I lose my hair. When I tell Francis about this, he says, "It doesn't matter – as long as you don't lose your faith, everything is fine." When the treatments are done, the metastases have disappeared.

I ask the Archangel Michael to help me with the radiation treatments on the bronchials. When I visited St. Michael's church in Perugia, I was deeply affected by the peace I felt there. During the thirty treatments, I visualize myself in the church, and I see the Archangel Michael carrying a golden flaming sword. He is standing on a dragon, but he doesn't kill it. Rather, he keeps it in check and draws power from it.

I ask Michael if he can help me with that power. He is standing before me with his left hand raised. I walk toward him with my hand raised, and our palms touch. We stand like this for the duration of the treatments. At the end of the cycle, the tumor has shrunk significantly.

Recently, the radiologist was able to remove two metastases that had returned in the brain. The most important result, however, is that these years have been the happiest and most rewarding of my life. Whatever the future may bring, I am happy, and I have no fears about tomorrow.

I wake up at four in the morning and I again experience this space between the spiritual and earthly worlds. I see Francis, and I ask him if he can tell me how it is with death.

He says, "Someday I will come to you, take you in my arms, and say that we must go now."

I turn to him and say, "Then I will gladly go with you."
–*Joachim*, *Germany*

God is actively on our side

> Remember that no matter what you do, God's on your side. He's not going to judge you— he's going to help you in every way He can, but you have to let Him help you.[12]

When something in our lives goes wrong, we may be tempted to feel guilty, and may try to hide it from ourselves, from others, and from God. While we are all too ready to judge ourselves and fear others' judgment, God is never judgmental, and He is certainly not vengeful. Elsewhere in this book, we have pondered the utter uselessness of guilt, and how it merely paralyzes our will to improve.

Why are parents patiently tolerant and supportive when their children make mistakes? Because they know that learning from our mistakes is an invaluable part of our growing up – as the following story shows.

☀ GOD'S MEMORY LAPSE ☀

The abbot of the monastery was close friends with a rabbi who lived nearby. It was widely whispered that the rabbi talked with God often, and that he received the Lord's answers. One day the abbot asked the rabbi for a favor – when he next spoke with God, would he ask Him if He had forgiven his sins? The rabbi agreed, and when the abbot returned the next day, he said that he had a message for him: "God said that He has forgotten your sins."

It requires courage, willpower, and humility to talk openly about our mistakes with God and ask Him to help us not err again. In In an unblished letter to a sincere disciple, Yogananda offered his support.

> Your troubles I do not mind. I will never give up my job about you. It is better to conquer one evil and not live with it forever. Never for a moment identify yourself with momentary flashes of error.... Have no fear even though I am gone from your visible eyes. You will never be alone.... Keep unceasingly trying to conquer.... A smooth life is not a victorious life—and I will give you lots of my good karma, so you will get through.

CHAPTER 1: *Points to Remember*

- There is a conscious force that is drawing the universe and everything in it toward ever-greater expansion, the ultimate goal of which is complete oneness with the unbounded joy of God's consciousness.

- There is an opposite, conscious force of inertia that is always trying to block the universal urge to expansion by keeping everything fixed and static.

- Our journey to Self-realization is a collaboration between our own efforts, which amount to twenty-five percent of the total effort required; the efforts of a spiritual master on our behalf, which count for another twenty-five percent; and God's grace, which accomplishes fifty percent of our salvation.

What are the most effective ways to attract the help of a higher power? These will be revealed in the following chapters.

PART IX CHAPTER TWO

Who Is Asking?

> Every begging prayer, no matter how sincere, limits the soul...Most of us beg and pray without first establishing, in our own minds, our divine birthright; that is why we are limited by the law of beggary....
>
> We do not have to beg, but to reclaim and demand from our Father that which we, through our human imagination, thought to be lost....
>
> We must think, meditate, affirm, believe and realize daily that we are sons of God. This realization may take time, but we must begin with the right method, rather than gamble with the unscientific beggary of prayers and consequently be subject to disbelief, doubts or the jugglery of superstition. It is only when the slumbering ego perceives itself not as a body, but as a free soul or son of God, residing in and working through the body, that it can rightfully and lawfully demand its divine rights. [1] —YOGANANDA

The Bible urges us to make full use of the metaphysical law of prayer.

> Ask, and it shall be given you; seek, and ye shall find; knock, and it shall be opened unto you: For every one that asketh receiveth; and he that seeketh findeth; and to him that knocketh it shall be opened. (LUKE 11:7-11)

"Ask, and it shall be given you." The metaphysical law of prayer mirrors the physical laws of cause and effect. Thus, in the scientific laboratory of prayer, the act of asking with the required sincerity and pure intent should bring us the scientific result of receiving.

Can it be that simple? That easy? When it comes to something as personal and sensitive as prayer, there will be subtleties that we will need to sort out. A good one to begin with might be the simple question: "Who is asking?"

A loving parent will eagerly make every effort to fulfill a child's valid requests. Parents will attempt the impossible to meet their children's needs and support their talents. The child knows this and will therefore approach the parents with love, confidence, and trust.

Yogananda said that this should be the attitude with which we approach our divine Parent in our prayers: not as beggars or sinners, but with the simple trust and confidence of a child.

> The word prayer smacks of beggary. We are the children of God. He are made us in His image. Why should we beg? The word prayer is antiquated and carries with it the consciousness of supplication. The psychology of supplication consists of doubt as to whether the Father will grant what we ask. We, being children of the Almighty Father, can claim everything which He possesses, namely, wisdom, immortality, happiness, and abundance.[2]

A beggar's pittance, or a prince's inheritance?

A warm-hearted king will lovingly press a coin in a beggar's hand, but if the king's own son and heir asks his father to increase his monthly allowance, the king will gladly grant the request. Yogananda urges us always to affirm and know this truth: ***"I am His Child, the Prince of the Cosmos, Born of the Omnipotent."***[3]

> A beggar has no choice; he receives whatever is given to him out of kindness. But a son has a perfect right of possession over his father's treasures... When we beg, we are limited. We receive then only according to the measure of our merits and the limitations of our environment. But when we demand as heirs of our Universal Father, we have access to perfect health, balanced prosperity, and deep wisdom.[4]

In countless lives we have fallen prey to the delusive thought that our fulfillments lie outside ourselves, and that we must control our circumstances in order to be truly happy. But this world has a way of eluding our control, and so our experiences have engrained in our minds a terrible sense of lack: that we do not have enough of what we need; that others have more of the earth's riches than we do; and that we must beg, steal, or manipulate the world to even the score.

This desperate need for control distorts our relationship with the infinite Source of all plenty. In our ego-self, we are convinced that we know what we need, and that we could get it if only God would help us take control. But prayers that are born of the ego's desperate longings close the doors to the Infinite Abundance.

> A beggar's plea is of a fawning, groveling, cringing nature; a child's demand is straightforward, sincere, and lovingly unafraid. Most people beg from God; hence they receive a beggar's pittance instead of a son's share. Those who demand as children receive everything the Father has.
>
> A beggar doubts that his plea will be granted; a true son knows that his demand will be fulfilled. You were a son, but your own weakness has made you a beggar; you must become a son again before you can claim your birthright. Therefore,

demand to be a son again before you demand anything else. First establish your identity with God, as Jesus did, by realizing, in the joy of meditation, "I and my Father are one." Do not beseech Him beggarwise, but unite your ignorance-separated soul with God by constantly remaining identified with the ever-new Bliss within you.[5]

A loving relationship

Yogananda's relationship to God was that of a trusting child. As a young boy, he sought places of worship that were dedicated to the Divine Mother, where, with childlike devotion, he would share his thoughts and hopes with Her. His childlike, trusting relationship with the Mother continued throughout his life.

In his autobiography, *The New Path,* Swami Kriyananda tells a charming story about his guru.

❋ SCOTTISH SHORTBREAD [6] ❋

Master, in his travels between Los Angeles and Encinitas, sometimes stopped in the town of Laguna Beach, in a little Scottish tea shop where shortbread was a specialty. On one occasion, all of the shortbread had been sold.

Surprised, Yogananda prayed, "Divine Mother, how come?" It wasn't that he was disappointed. Accustomed, rather, to receiving divine guidance in even the minor details of his life, he wondered whether some lesson might be intended in this unexpected denial. Suddenly he saw a shaft of light shine down onto the little shop. Moments later the door opened; the owner came out.

"Wait! Wait!" she called. Hastening over to the car with a little package, she said, "I was saving this order for a local customer. But I want you to have it. I can make more for him."

Master had had no real desire for the shortbread. What touched him deeply about this episode was the divine love it exemplified. For the more inconsequential the need to which God responds, the greater, in a sense, the proof of His love. Divine intervention in time of serious need might be attributed to other motives—perhaps the wish to see some important work finished. But what motive could there possibly be for such intervention in trivial matters, save love alone?

If we speak with a friend only when we want something from him, the relationship will not be fruitful for either of us. A child who is estranged from his parents will find it difficult to ask for their help. But in a closely knit family or among close friends there will be an easy exchange of giving and receiving.

It's natural that we will want to stay in touch with the people we care about and who care about us. So it is with our divine Parent, who is pleased to be included in all our thoughts and activities. No telephone is needed, only a silent, ongoing conversation in which we include God in our daily undertakings. By sharing our joys and sorrows and our struggles and achievements with Him, we develop a relationship of intimacy and immediacy.

Like a doting parent, God is never far from us. I remember Swami Kriyananda saying: "He is as close to you now as He ever will be."

To establish a loving relationship with God, Yogananda suggests this prayer.

> My Infinite Beloved, I know that Thou art nearer than these words with which I pray; nearer even than my nearest thoughts. Behind my every restless feeling, may I feel Thy concern for me, and Thy love. Behind my awareness, may I feel sustained and guided by Thy consciousness. Behind my love for Thee, may I become ever more deeply conscious of Thy love. *If you continuously pray to Him in this way, and if you pray with all sincerity, you will feel His presence suddenly as a great joy in your heart. In that bursting joy you will know that He is with you, and that He is your very own.*[7]

Are we truly worthy?

Our relationship with God has nothing to do with our merits and accomplishments, or our worthiness. Remember these words from the last chapter: *"Paramhansa Yogananda once told his first disciple in America, 'God loves you just as much as he does me. He is our common Father.'"*

It is difficult to imagine, and even harder to accept, that God loves each of us every bit as much as He loves Jesus, Buddha, and any other fully Self-realized master. Yet His love is unwavering, *especially when His children go astray,* as demonstrated by the parable of the prodigal son. [LUKE 15]

As we progress in our practice of prayer and meditation, we slowly but surely begin to experience our true identity as children of the Infinite. Yogananda's teachings are noteworthy for their emphasis on our relationship with God not as sinners, but as eternally beloved children who are inseparably part of His blissful consciousness. The ancient *Vedas* of India declare, *"Aham Brahmasmi"*–"I and the infinite cosmic consciousness are one."

> Broadcast your message,
> "My Father and I are One" until you feel
> this over-powering, all-solacing Bliss of God.
> When this happens, you have made contact.
> Then demand your celestial right.[8]

CHAPTER 2: *Points to Remember*

- Silently affirm throughout the day and at the beginning of each meditation and prayer: "I and my Father are One."

- Be in touch with God not only when you need something from Him, but include Him lovingly in all of your thoughts and activities.

- "And all things, whatsoever ye shall ask in prayer, believing, ye shall receive." (MATTHEW 21:22)

PART IX   CHAPTER THREE

Scientific Healing Prayer Demand

All my discoveries have been made in answer to prayer. —Sir Isaac Newton

If any of you lack wisdom,
let him ask of God, that giveth
to all men liberally, and upbraideth not;
and it shall be given him.
[James 1:5]

Half-hearted prayer brings at best a
half-hearted response. Effective prayer demands
that we offer it up with strong will power,
with complete confidence in the rightness
of the outcome, and with an awareness
of the energy required for results. [1]
—Kriyananda

The prayer that I have in mind is no matter
of routine, it is deliberate and earnest. It is not
tied down to a fixed timetable, rather it is
a state which endures by night and day.
—Saint John Chrysostom

• • •

※ **A candid conversation with God** ※

Where I come from, prayer means different things to different people. If you are a devout Buddhist, you will recite long, involved mantras in the Pali language before you go to bed. Because the emphasis is on phonetic expression rather than inner comprehension, reciting and praying are one and the same to the average Thai.

Another way to pray is to ask a favor from a mystical being. Shrines that house supernatural entities are found throughout Thailand, each specializing in a particular human desire. A student wanting to pass an exam might go to one shrine, while a sick person will seek a miracle at another. There is a common thread: payment. It is customary to promise something in return if your wish is granted. Perhaps you will commission a performance by the temple's dancers, or take a vow of renunciation for a time. Not to pay for what you have promised to the gods is considered the ultimate in bad luck.

Thus, praying felt, to me, like either an incomprehensible ritual, or a business deal. Neither deepened my faith.

When I was unexpectedly diagnosed with a brain tumor, it consumed all of my attention. I was continually getting tests done to determine its severity, or answering questions about it to my tearful mother, or reading about it long into the night.

It was during this time that I started speaking with God candidly. I had never done this before, and at first it felt strange. I spent days searching for the right words: a poem to touch God's heart, a spell to soothe my jittery mind.

Then the right prayer came: "Let everything that's keeping me away from You be concentrated in this tumor, and may all of it be removed successfully." I repeated this prayer demand every chance I got, and I continued to repeat it as I entered the operating room.

It has been three months since the successful operation, and I'm still speaking candidly to God. I have come to understand God not as an exalted Being, but a kind of confidant. With that realization, praying is no longer an exercise in dry formality – rather, it is a soothing, nurturing conversation with a best friend.

> I needed this perspective on prayer, which has made a huge difference in how I approach the spiritual path. In this world of increasing isolation, we all need someone to count on when things get tough. For me, a brain tumor is a small price to pay for the realization that God is right by my side always. —**Peeti**, *Thailand*

Once we know, or we're at least willing to hypothesize, that there is a loving, benevolent, listening Presence, and once we are convinced, or at least willing, to entertain the possibility that we have a hereditary claim on the infinite abundance, what remains is the request itself. Are there prayer requests that are more valid than others? Are there some requests that God rejects, and others that He might take under consideration, and some that He will immediately satisfy?

As we saw in the last chapter, when we approach God, the source of infinite abundance, health and happiness, as His children, He is ready and willing to fulfill our need. In this chapter, we will consider what Yogananda meant when he spoke of "prayer demands," and the practical aspects of when and how we can "demand" from His abundance.

What kind of prayer to offer

The conscious, intelligent force of evolution supports us in our endeavors to make spiritual progress. We can legitimately ask to be granted what we need in this regard, and like a human parent, God will provide. We need, however, as Yogananda councils, to discriminate between what we actually *need*, and what the ego wants.

> Why concentrate on unnecessary "necessities" or go on constantly multiplying self-created useless desires for more? To create such meaningless demands for luxuries is to be engaged night and day, giving one's life blood in the pursuit of getting things which one does not need.[2]

> Differentiate between your "needs" and your "wants." Your "needs" are few, while your "wants" can be limitless. In order to find freedom and Bliss, minister only unto your "needs"; stop creating limitless "wants" and pursuing the will-o'-the-wisp of false happiness. The more you depend on conditions outside yourself for happiness, the less happy you will be.[3]

> To live in luxury, riding in Rolls-Royces... among starving human brothers, is the sin of all sins. The Divine Spirit does not like the children who revel in luxury while some of His other children are suffering.[4]

While egoic desires are the bane of spiritual progress, the soul desires that which will serve its mission of ensuring a steady march towards higher consciousness.

> Reinforcing the soul with good desires which yield joy is extremely beneficial...Good desires lead the soul to perpetual happiness.[5]

Such desires might include a peaceful home environment; a supportive companion; a work that brings joy and is challenging; a work environment that is harmonious, creative, with supportive colleagues; the ability to participate in uplifting activities like seminars, retreats, pilgrimages; money for Self-improvement and for serving others.

> It is sufficient to overcome all your useless desires. The fulfillment of all worthwhile desires is the attainment of the Divine.[6]

❋ California Dreamin' ❋

When someone asked if I wanted to travel to California for the centennial celebration of Yogananda's birth, I was surprised to find myself responding with an enthusiastic "YES!"

Nevertheless, I wondered how it would be possible, and I asked Yogananda to help.

While waiting for his answer, I continued to meditate every day. After each meditation I placed a coin in a jar, symbolizing my willingness to help meet the expenses of the trip.

I would leave in July, which happened to be the most inconvenient time for my factory shifts. At times, I was tempted to give up the dream. Then my boss asked me to coordinate my vacation with the other person who worked in my sector, and to my amazement he begged me to take my holiday in July so he could take his in August. I immediately accepted and silently thanked Yogananda for arranging matters so precisely.

When my boss heard about my vacation destination, he spontaneously added an extra day to help me prepare for my departure, and a day to rest when I returned. The divine plan is precise – and generous, too! –**Roberto**, *Brescia, Italy*

Yogananda cautions us: "Every desire must be fulfilled, every action brought to completion." [7]

Jesus offered us the following advice to help us understand which desires we can safely pursue and which we should let go.

> **And seek not ye what ye shall eat, or what ye shall drink, neither be ye of doubtful mind. For all these things do the nations of the world seek after: and your Father knoweth that ye have need of these things. But rather seek ye the kingdom of God; and all these things shall be added unto you.** (LUKE 12: 29-31)

Mental whispers

We often think of prayer as a last resort, to be saved for times of desperate need. A more satisfying approach is to think of it as a constant inner dialogue with God.

A friend told me about a religious convention that her father attended, where Rev. Frank Laubach gave the opening prayer. Laubach wrote a wonderful book about his experiences with prayer, *Letters by a Modern Mystic*.* His prayer was not a flowery oration or impassioned exhortation; he merely raised the volume of his inner conversation with God, which had clearly been in progress for some time, and then lowered it again as he left the stage.

> You can ease your conscience by claiming that pressure of business prevents you from praying and meditating, but you can have no excuses for not offering Him deep mental whispers at any time, in the temple of activity or on the altar of silence. No matter what you may be doing, you are always free to whisper your love to God, until you consciously receive His response. This is the surest way to contact Him in the mad rush of present-day life.
> To rouse God, to receive His response, you must offer Him your mental-whisper songs unceasingly. No matter what you are doing, offer deep, inward mental-whisper prayer-demands.[8]

How to get your prayers answered

Every religion enjoins its followers to pray, yet too often what's meant is the rote recitation of standardized prayers. In stark contrast, Yogananda urges us to offer God the spontaneous, personal, heartfelt "prayer-demands" of our hearts, with an intensity and sincerity that would ensure that our prayers would reach their destination and elicit a loving response.

* Laubach, *Letters by a Modern Mystic*: https://www.amazon.com/Letters-Modern-Mystic-Frank-Laubach/dp/1583310916.

1. Approach God only with **legitimate desires.**
2. In your mind, **convince yourself** that you are a child of God. Yogananda recommends using this affirmation before praying: *"I am Thy child. Thou art my Father. I and my Father are One."*

> The most important prayer-demand you can utter is to re-establish your unity with the Divine Father-Mother as His/Her eternal son.

3. Hold no expectations about the response to your prayers; keep an attitude of complete **openness** and neutrality. While the request may be specific, the manner in which it is answered may be surprising and completely unexpected.
4. Offer your prayer-demands **lovingly,** not as presumptuous commands. A loving prayer will always receive a loving response from the God of love.

> Since God is also above law, devotion is necessary to call His attention. The devotional call, if sincere, deep, and continuous, and if it is supplemented by sincere efforts at deep meditation, will bring divine response. Devotional demand is greater than law, for it touches the heart of God and makes Him answer His naughty and good children alike. Law is based upon mathematical precision, but devotion is based upon claiming God as our own true love, for did He not make us in His own likeness? Law is exacting in its demand, while love causes God to surrender Himself to the devotee. God can never hide from the person who exercises devotion, love, the law of meditation, and the soul-call.[9]

5. **Believe** that your prayer will be answered. If half of your mind wants something and the other half is doubting that you'll receive it, your request will essentially be nullified.

> By demand I don't mean you should try to force your will on Him, as though anticipating His reluctance to accede to your wishes. I mean, pray with the firm conviction that He wants to give you everything you need, and that He will give it.[10]

Believing that our prayers will be answered doesn't mean that we should assume they will be answered in the way we expect. It may not be in our best interests to get a specific job, or to be accepted to the university of our choice, or to marry the Prince Charming of our dreams.

> God never fails to listen to all Soul-Calls, but He does not always respond in the way that we want Him to. He has His own mysterious ways.[11]

6. Make your prayer-demands **calmly**. Prayers are often needed in moments of desperation, anxiety, or fear. Yet our prayers will be more effective if we can prepare ourselves with the calming breathing exercises or meditation techniques mentioned in Volume One.

> [The] mind microphone must be repaired by deep silence, or by the practice of the technique of concentration and physical discipline, preceding your prayer of loving demand. When you feel calm, your mind microphone is repaired, and then it is time to broadcast your first and foremost loving demand: "Father, make me realize again that Thou and I are One."[12]

7. When you formulate your request, instead of limiting it to specifics – "I need $500 to pay the rent this month" – **give God lots of leeway to respond** in the manner that will be best for you, without setting limits or conditions on His generosity.

❊ THE HEAVENLY JUNKYARD ❊

When Henry arrived at the Pearly Gates, St. Peter greeted him and led him on a tour of heaven. Henry was delighted with all that he saw, but he was perplexed by a high-walled enclosure. When he asked what was behind the wall, St. Peter replied: "That is the heavenly junkyard that holds the things people threw away or rejected during their life on earth."

His curiosity aroused, Henry asked if they could go inside and look around. Peter agreed, and when Henry looked at the piles of worldly goods people had rejected, he was astonished. There were priceless jewels, luxurious vacation villas, gleaming yachts, designer clothes, and sportscars. When Henry wondered aloud who could have rejected that bright-red Ferrari, Peter said with a knowing smile, "Well, it's interesting that you should ask about that car, because it was you who refused it." "Impossible!" Henry exclaimed. "I would never turn down such a wonderful car!"

"You certainly did," St. Pete replied. "Whenever you prayed for a car, you asked for a Volkswagen."

The "winning" approach in prayer is to express your needs simply and directly, as if to a beloved parent or friend – "My financial situation is making it hard to pay the bills." Then ask God to inspire you with the right solution: "Guide Thou my reason, will, and activity to the right course in everything."[13]

❊ ❊ ❊

8. **Concentrate** wholeheartedly on your prayer request – give it your full, undivided attention.

> God answers all prayers, but restless prayers He answers only a little bit... Get control over your mind. When you can pray with concentration, the Lord will know that you mean what you are saying. He will answer you, then, in wonderful ways. [14]

9. Don't become discouraged if you don't immediately receive an answer. Use your **willpower**, and be persistent.

> Pray and use your dogged will steadily day after day, week after week, year after year until the cosmic silence of ages is broken and you find your answer. [15]

How to use prayer demands

Often referred to as a book of poetry, Yogananda's *Whispers from Eternity* contains specific guidelines for his "prayer-demands." [16]

- Select a demand from the contents according to your need.
- Take only one paragraph at a time from any demand, mentally picture the meaning, and visualize the imagery of the figure of speech.
- Then calm your mind by sitting motionless on a straight chair, with spine erect.
- With eyes closed, or lifted (if open), meditate on the meaning of the demand selected by you, until it becomes a part of you.
- Then saturate the demand with devotion and meditate upon it.
- As your meditation becomes deeper, increase your devotion, and mentally offer the demand as your own heart's outburst.
- Demand until you establish your divine rights.

- Demand unceasingly that which belongs to you, and you will receive it.
- Imbue yourself with the faith that your heart's craving, expressed through this specific demand, is being felt by God. Feel that just behind the screen of your devotional demands, God is listening to the silent words of your soul. Feel this! Be *one* with your heart's demand! Be thoroughly convinced that He has listened to you;
- Then go about your duties, seeking not to know whether God will grant your demand. Believe absolutely that your demand has been heard, and you will know that what is God's is yours also.

What weakens our prayers?

Doubt is the greatest enemy of prayer, and the biggest obstacle to success: doubting that there is a benevolent, conscious Power that wants to help us. Doubting that we are worthy to receive Gods' gifts. Doubting that we truly are God's children. Doubting that prayer actually works. The rational mind is the prime breeding ground for doubts – left to its own devices, it raises one doubt after another, each leading to the next.

Another nemesis of prayer is **restlessness**: not being able to focus wholeheartedly on the sacred act of prayer.

> The prayer-plant should be protected from the storms of doubt, distraction, mental idleness, leaving-meditation-until-tomorrow (the morrow that never comes), absent-mindedness, and thinking-of-something-else while imagining the mind is wholly on the soul of a prayer. Such parasites on the prayer-plants should be destroyed by the germicides of self-control, determination, and loyalty to a teaching. Thus, daily the glowing, immortal roses of inspiration may be gathered from the plants of these prayer-demands.[17]

Does God respond to our "trivial" prayer requests?

We tend to think that God only listens to impassioned prayers offered in moments of great need. Can we also confidently expect Him to answer our requests for help with mundane concerns? Should we ask Him to help us gather the money for a vacation trip? Should we pray for good weather for an outdoor event? What about praying to find a favorite pastry for a special dinner? Is it all right spiritually to pray for the fulfillment of our most trivial desires – when, after all, it is our desires that keep us bound in delusion?

When we offer our seemingly insignificant desires to God, we find that He delights in giving to those who seek the Giver over His gifts.

> To the sincere devotee... God's lesser gifts are meaningful in one sense only: as demonstrations of His love.[18]

❋ This car is yours ❋

I believe that when we put our lives in God's hands, He takes care of us better than we could imagine.

I had recently moved to Ananda with a sixteen-year-old daughter and little money. Every morning, I drove my daughter to school in Assisi, then I returned to the Ananda community center where I worked.

One day, I loaned my car to a friend who needed to drive to town to buy materials to finish some work he was doing on my house. He returned very late, on foot: "I'm so sorry!" he said ruefully. "Through no fault of mine, I had an accident, and although I survived without a scratch, your car was destroyed."

Well, I felt it wasn't only the car that was wrecked, but my life. What a disaster! How could I manage without a car?

For a moment, I felt lost, but then I thought, "Divine Mother, the car was Yours, and You had the right to do with it whatever You wanted."

When I entered the communal dining room to tell my friends what had happened, one of them said immediately,

"You can borrow my car. In fact, I can sell it to you for a very good price." And the person responsible for the accident paid for the new used car and transfer fees. In all, I had been without a car less than five minutes! –**Clarita**, *Ananda Assisi*

Yogananda reminds us to keep things in perspective.

> It is all right to pray to God for things. It is better still, however, to ask that His will be done in your life. He knows what you need, and will do much more for you than the best that you can imagine for yourself. Above all, seek Him for Himself, for His love. Pray to Him, 'Father, reveal Thyself!' If you call to Him in that way, sincerely, He will be with you always.[19]

Asking others to pray for us

How useful is it to ask others to pray for us? Yogananda often said, "God works through channels." Not only are the saints and realized masters capable of serving as His channels, but also anyone who sincerely wishes to serve in this way. In Chapter Five we will explore Yogananda's techniques for transmitting divine healing energy to others.

✷ THE SERENITY TO ACCEPT ✷

I asked the members of my prayer group to pray for me – and how glad I am that I did!

The operation was scheduled to be done laparoscopically – a relatively simple procedure where surgical instruments are inserted through a narrow opening without no need for a large incision.

Unfortunately, the operation went awry. An inexperienced surgeon tried for hours to complete the procedure without success, and then another surgeon had to be called in to open the abdomen and remove a long section of bowel.

When I woke up and learned about the harrowing procedure and the outcome, instead of feeling angry or despondent, I felt as if I was wrapped in an embrace of deep peace. An inner voice reassured me, and I accepted the situation without assigning blame. I am convinced that it was my friends' prayers that enabled me to remain calm and to accept this unpleasant situation with serenity. –**Wilma**, *Trento, Italy*

Prayer-demand for peace and harmony

When I was a child, my father told me that the Messiah would arrive when peace came on earth. Every night, I asked God to resolve the wars I heard about on the radio (television hadn't entered our home). I would name the conflicts I could remember, but soon there were too many to recite at bedtime. Even though my childish prayers were sincere, the conflicts continued unabated.

What use is it to pray for peace? The darkness that is engulfing the world seems to take little heed of our prayers.

Peace and conflict are states of consciousness – peace being the higher and more powerful of the two. Those who are themselves peaceful, and emanate love and compassion through their prayers, set into motion vibrations of higher consciousness that work on subtle levels.

When the forces of light or darkness predominate on earth, it is because people are serving more powerfully as channels for the expression of positive or negative forces. Our own choices and actions on behalf of the power of Light will subtly influence the overall balance of light and darkness in the world, even if the immediate effects aren't obvious.

When we pray for peace with an attitude of detachment and neutrality, knowing that God is acting through us and that He is responsible for the outcome, the power of light within us grows and inevitably influences our immediate environment.

Yogananda suggested a prayer demand for the healing of the world. It was particularly espoused and promoted by one of his direct disciples, Brother Bhaktananda, and it has become known as the "Peace and Harmony Prayer."*

---

* "The Peace and Harmony Prayer," *Triumph of the Spirit*, https://bolstablog.wordpress.com/2011/10/10/peace-and-harmony/. You will find a link to a short video that you can watch while practicing the prayer at home.

 *Lord, fill this world with peace and harmony; peace and harmony.*

This prayer is presently offered by individuals and groups all over the world to channel vibrations of higher consciousness to the planet. It is also effective for resolving interpersonal conflicts, as Bhaktananda suggests:

- Visualize the person or people who hurt you, and mentally surround them in divine light.
- Then deeply pray, "Lord, fill them with peace and harmony, peace and harmony, peace and harmony," over and over, for a minute.
- Afterward, visualize yourself in divine light and pray, "Lord, fill me with peace and harmony, peace and harmony," for fifteen seconds.
- Do this five times a day, and you will see a change come over those whom you're praying for.

After the terrorist attack on September 11, 2001, Swami Kriyananda sent a letter to the Ananda members worldwide:

> Each of us has the power to make an offering to God of this simple prayer: "Lord, use me! Let me channel your love impersonally to all." Divine Love is a force. It does not succumb weakly to evil, but opposes it with power to destroy it utterly—if possible, by transforming it into kindred love, but if necessary by cutting a swath through the forest in order that countless other trees be saved. If we understand that by loving rightly it is God's love we express, He will be able, through us, to uplift the world's consciousness. For that is how He works: through instruments; very seldom directly.

An ocean consists of countless drops. Although a raindrop adds but little moisture to the earth, Once it unites with many other drops a mighty current is created which flows down to the sea. We too, united with God's will, can help mightily in the struggle between the forces of light and of darkness. Thus, we may be instrumental in ushering in a period of peace and universal understanding.[20]

Yogananda's advice

- To receive God's response to your prayer-demands, ask only for that which you really need. The desire for superfluous material possessions ultimately brings misery and retards your spiritual progress.

- Before demanding anything of God, first establish your identity with Him through meditation. Then demand, as a child of the father, knowing that your request will be granted.

- Many prayers are said absent-mindedly, consisting of empty words forced from without. When you meet a friend after a long absence, you do not consult books on friendship in order to know how to express your love to him. God is your closest Friend; let your prayer-demands to Him be spontaneous outpourings, welling up from the depths of your heart.

- Whenever you have a real need, the thought of it is in your mind all the time, no matter where you are or what you are doing. Developing such deep, dynamic, inner whispers is sure to bring a response from Him. Constantly, unceasingly, whisper unto Him of your eternal love, of your burning desire to contact Him.

- Offer deep mental whispers in the temple of scientific meditation until you hear His answering whispers everywhere, audibly and distinctly.[21]

PART IX   CHAPTER FOUR

Inner Guidance

❉ REVELATIONS AT 4 A.M. ❉

On the day he received the Medal of Honor from President Theodore Roosevelt, as on every day of his adult life, he wore a flower in his jacket lapel.

He spoke with the flowers, the herbs and grasses, even the clay earth – and through them, God spoke to him.

George Washington Carver had taken the name of his slave owner, Moses Carver, who was a kind and gentle man. Because his health as a youth was delicate, George was given household tasks, and Susan Carver raised him as if he were one of her own children, teaching him to read and write, and to cook, work in the garden, and make simple herbal remedies.

George took a keen interest in plants. He experimented with natural pesticides, fungicides, and soil conditioners. Among the local farmers, he became known as "the plant doctor."

After just a year at the all-Black elementary school, George had already surpassed his teachers' learning, so he left Missouri to further his education in Kansas. In 1894 he became the first African-American to earn a Bachelor of Science degree. His professors, impressed by Carver's research on the fungal infections of soybean plants, asked him to stay on for graduate studies. After earning a Master of Agriculture degree, he accepted a professorship at Tuskegee University in Alabama, where he established a school of agriculture in 1896.

Every morning, George would rise before the dawn. By 4 a.m. he was seated under his favorite tree in the forest adjoining the university, keeping his appointment with God.

George asked God many questions: how to revive the agriculture-based economy of the South that had been destroyed in the Civil War. Which plants were best suited to the soil that had been impoverished by decades of cotton cultivation? How could the humble peanut and the sweet potato be used to improve health, and for other good purposes?

Every day God revealed a small portion of the plants' mysteries to George. Eventually, he discovered three hundred uses for the humble peanut, including for the manufacture of paper, shampoo, medicines, rubber, and glue, and for making peanut butter, pancake flour, and mayonnaise.

As for the sweet potato, God showed George how it could be used to feed both people and animals through the production of flour, starch, sugar, vinegar, candy, and chocolate, and to make dyes, paints, medicines, ink, and many other useful products.

A popular story about George's conversations with God is how, one day, he prayed: "Lord, can you reveal to me the purpose of life?" "I'm sorry, George," God replied. "That is much beyond your comprehension." "Then can you tell me the purpose of humanity?" "Neither that, George. It is quite a complicated matter. Ask me something of lesser magnitude." "All right, Lord, then please reveal to me the secrets of the peanut." "That is a good question, George, and something within your grasp. Let's get started."

Every day, we are compelled to make countless decisions. Most of them concern the routines of daily life – where to shop, what to have for lunch, how to arrange the day's activities. Other decisions may have more serious consequences – choosing a career path, deciding which job to apply for, arranging for medical care.

Every decision will have consequences. We make decisions influenced by our desires – we are guided either by our egoic desire for pleasure, power, and security, or we strive to align our decisions with the soul's impulse for expansion and inner joy. In time, with greater experience, we learn that the soul invariably knows the best way that will lead us most directly and effectively to greater happiness.

We met the superconscious dimension of the mind in Part VI. Perceptions that proceed from that state of awareness are known as intuitions. Yogananda describes intuition as **"tuition in"** or **knowledge from within, and does not depend upon any data whatsoever offered by the senses or the mind.** [1]

✺ My Inner Doctor ✺

I was at a colleague's funeral, when the cardiologist called. With urgency in his voice, he insisted that I rush to the hospital for a life-saving operation. I had lived a fulfilling life, despite a heart condition that I had managed to keep under control for about thirteen years, but recent symptoms had made it clear to my doctor that I would need surgery.

Yet a persistent voice inside was telling me that something else needed to be taken into account – I should have my thyroid checked. The doctor rejected the idea initially, certain that only the heart was involved. But the inner urging wouldn't abate, and I eventually convinced him to request the exam.

The doctor's urgent call that day was to report the alarming results of the thyroid test which showed a severe form of hyperthyroidism that was devastating me. It was an autoimmune disease that had caused nodules to grow in the thyroid, displacing the trachea. The thyroid had to be removed, but not before we could remedy the heart condition, which had deteriorated sharply because of fibrillations due to hyperthyroidism. The inner voice had known that more than heart surgery was needed.

In February, I had a seven-hour heart surgery. The recovery was very slow. I couldn't resume my normal activities, and there were setbacks that required me to return to the hospital for massive doses of intravenous antibiotics.

My eyesight was deteriorating due to the thyroid condition, to the point where I wasn't able to see anything clearly. A quick intervention with cortisone spared me from total blindness, as I awaited the operation to remove the thyroid. Post-operation, I had to continue with the cortisone and to undergo sixteen radiation treatments on my eyes.

Throughout this long healing journey, I have maintained an inner dialogue with my spiritual master, Yogananda, whose light has shone the way through every phase. My vision has returned, and I have never had side-effects from the medications. I am able to read, drive, play the piano, and teach music.

There are still ups and downs, but it seems the worst is over. The only big difference being that I am not what I used to be – my heart has been reborn, and I see with new eyes. A great calmness pervades me now – everything is filtered by peace, by a deep knowledge that comes from the inner voice that continues to guide me each day.
–**Paola**, *Verona*

The question

When confronted with difficult or puzzling situations, we tend to look outside ourselves for solutions. For instance, because I am a novice at cooking, I ask my smartphone, "Siri, potato and leek soup." And within a nanosecond she offers a dozen recipes. After looking at most of them, I feel more confident in what I had already surmised to be the proper ingredients and methods.

For queries that exceed Siri's purview, such as "Should I quit my job and start my own business?" – we can turn to family, friends, or consult a competent astrologer for advice. We might calculate the financial consequences of leaving the job, or look for financial backers for the new endeavor, and so on.

All of these avenues may be worthwhile, once we have become clear about what we are truly seeking. Perhaps the question isn't at all about whether I should quit my job, or if I should start my own business. It might be: "What is the next step to fulfill my life's goals?"

> A problem is half solved already once it is stated clearly. In seeking guidance, form a clear mental picture of what it is you need. Then hold that picture up to superconsciousness at the point between the eyebrows. People often struggle for a long time to find the inspiration they want. No time at all is needed: only sufficient mental clarity, and energy.[2]

Before proceeding to the actual techniques for receiving inner guidance, it's good to take a few moments to reflect on your own questions and write a few of them down. You might consider questions that deal with:

- ✔ **A current situation at home**
- ✔ **A health issue**
- ✔ **A long-term life direction**

Techniques

Yogananda suggests this technique for intuitively solving problems:

- Whenever you want to solve a problem intuitively, first **meditate deeply**, or use other practices for entering a state of inner silence and calm mental focus. Don't think of the problem while you are meditating or doing other practices.

- Meditate until you feel a sense of **calmness** filling the inner recesses of your body, and your breathing becoming calm and quiet.

- Finally, **concentrate simultaneously** at the point between the eyebrows (the Christ Center) and in the heart, while asking God to direct your intuition so that you will know which steps to take to resolve your problem.[3]

Swami Kriyananda offers suggestions for tuning in to higher guidance.

- **Ask for guidance** from the superconsciousness while keeping your eyes closed with gaze turned upward and gently focused at the Spiritual Eye.
- **Wait for a response** in the heart center.
- **Be completely impartial.** Don't intrude your personal desires into your prayers for divine assistance. Pray, "Thy will, not mine, be done."
- If you feel inner guidance, **never presume** on it. That guidance may tell you, metaphorically speaking, to go north, but if you cease listening you may not hear it when, at the next corner, it tells you to turn east.
- **Never use the claim** of inner guidance as an argument for convincing others to listen to you. The flow of superconsciousness is always humble, never boastful. It doesn't cooperate with attitudes that discourage others from seeking their own inner guidance. [4]

A word about *impartiality*: perhaps more than anything else, an attitude of impartiality is needed for receiving true superconscious guidance. To "be completely impartial" is seldom easy. Yet, being completely open to whatever guidance may come is a necessary prerequisite for receiving superconscious guidance.

If our prayer request is tinged with likes, dislikes, or other ego-preferences – "Should I accept this job which is closer to home and has good hours and good pay?" – we will likely find no answer forthcoming, or else the "answer" will come from own highly prejudiced subconscious mind. Or perhaps we won't be able to perceive the response clearly through the fog of our own biases.

If we have honest preferences, we will need to do some inward work to set them aside. We can, of course, share them frankly with the higher wisdom and ask it to help us step away from our desires. But getting into a calm, neutral state of mind is essential, whether through meditation, or new insights, or other means. It can take time – even days or weeks – to prepare ourselves to receive and accept and follow the guidance that comes.

The source of higher intuition doesn't usually respond instantaneously. **Here are some suggestions** for how we can proceed when no inner guidance seems to be forthcoming.

- Propose several alternative solutions at the Spiritual Eye. See if one of them receives special endorsement in the heart.[5]

- If you have no guidance at all, sometimes it is better just to start anyway, because often any action is better than none at all. But don't presume—take small steps. You'll find by doing a little, the energy starts to flow. As this happens, the guidance gradually comes into focus.[6]

- Guidance often comes only after an idea has been made concrete by setting it in motion. If, therefore, you receive no answer in meditation, act in whatever way seems reasonable to you, but continue to listen for guidance in the heart. To refuse to act until you receive inner guidance is good only if you can keep your level of energy and expectation high. For it is high energy and high expectation that attract guidance. If you must act because you have no other way of maintaining that level of energy, then go ahead and act. Often, it is better to act, even in error, than not to act at all.

    At a certain point, if your direction is right, you will feel the endorsement you've been seeking. But if your direction is wrong, suddenly you will *know* it is wrong. In that case, try something else, until the endorsement comes.[7]

Signs of true intuition

> You'll begin noticing that when a certain feeling comes, and you follow it, things work out well. Then there's a different feeling, less calm or clear. At first you may think it's got to be right, but over time you'll come to recognize this feeling as false guidance. Gradually you'll come to understand the difference from your own experience.[8]

Everyone will experience the feeling that accompanies a true intuition differently. It may come as an inner voice, or a visual image that appears in the still mind, or a simple inner knowing. But it will *always* include these three qualities: **calmness, clarity, and joy**.

> Intuition is always based in a deep sense of **calmness** and **detachment**. When you're trying to tune in to the superconscious mind, ask yourself if the guidance you've received makes you feel excited or restless. If so, then it's safe to assume that you're just going along with your own desires. Try to associate true guidance with a sense of calm acceptance...You'll experience a certain power with inner calmness, but it's also very steady.[9]

The second quality is a sense of **clarity** – a clear inner awareness of the right path. If the guidance comes as a mental impression, or in a dream, it will be important to distinguish whether it is a true superconscious message, or merely an impression from the realm of our own subconscious desires.

> Subconscious images tend to have a certain obscurity or cloudiness to them, and the colors appear dim or muddy. These signs indicate projections of the subconscious mind and shouldn't be trusted. In superconscious experiences, the colors will be bright, pure, and brilliant, and the images filled with clarity or radiance. The clarity of colors and images are strong signs that you've tuned in to true intuition.[10]

The third quality is a sense of **inner joy**.

> [If the guidance] makes you feel emotionally excited, then it probably only reflects the temporary happiness that comes when our desires are fulfilled.

> True guidance should have a joy that
> takes you inside rather than outside of yourself.
> Like a current of energy, this kind of joy should
> take your consciousness inward and upward—
> not inward in the sense of self-congratulation,
> but upward with a sense of soaring freedom.[11]

Negative signs

Sometimes, the higher guidance will come with a sense of nervousness instead of a calm inner clarity and certainty. This is an unmistakable warning sign that it would be best not to proceed in this direction, at least for the moment. Perhaps the direction or the project is right for you, but a refinement in your attitude or the components of the project is needed.

> Another sign to watch for is the effects of your
> guidance on other people. If it feels right to you,
> but it's creating disharmony all around, then the
> direction is probably wrong... If what you're doing is
> producing the disharmony, then you should question
> your intuition. When considering others' reactions,
> remember, too, that some people's opinions are worth
> more than others. Watch most closely the reactions
> of those with clear, impartial minds.[12]

How to test and follow your inner guidance

As suggested above, it takes time and experience to begin to feel comfortable with practicing these methods for developing our intuition and following the guidance that comes. When you feel inwardly guided, you may question whether the guidance is truly coming from the wisdom of the soul, or if it's simply expressing your own ego-born preferences and desires. Yogananda suggests ways to test your intuitions to know if they are true.

> A real intuition can never be wrong. It does not consist in believing a thing firmly or doggedly, but in knowing it directly and unmistakenly. An intuition does not contradict, but is always supported by right sense perception, reason and inference. All things known by intuition are invariably true both materially and intellectually, but the opposite is not always true.[13]

With every decision you make while following intuitive guidance, take special note of the results, inwardly and outwardly: the results in the real world, and the feeling during and after you act. In this way, you will learn to distinguish whether you are following your subconscious desires or true, superconscious guidance.

> In developing your ability to recognize intuition, it's important to test your guidance over a period of time. Unless you have no choice, don't make big decisions on the strength of intuition. It's better to begin with small decisions, and continually test your ability. You'll begin noticing that when a certain feeling comes, and you follow it, things work out well. Then there's a different feeling, less calm or clear... Gradually you'll come to understand the difference from your own experience.
>
> Another way to recognize intuition is to act it out and watch your reactions as you go. If you're doing the right thing, your inner feeling will gradually come stronger and clearer as you act. If you have no guidance at all, sometimes it is better just to start anyway... You'll find by doing a little, the energy starts to flow (and) the guidance gradually comes into focus.
>
> There's another method that has also worked for me over the years. If you're unsure of your guidance, try inwardly saying no to it and pushing it away. If the intuition continues to come back to you with strong energy, then it's probably more than just your own thoughts at work.[14]

Once we have received true inner guidance from the superconscious, we should not be tentative or equivocal. From the outset, we need to be determined to follow the guidance we've received. To hesitate, or to doubt the higher guidance, will block the flow of the supportive energy and grace that accompany it.

> We need to have courage to act on the guidance we receive. As you do this, you'll create a flow of energy that increasingly opens up the doorway to superconsciousness. And if you continue to act on your guidance, you'll reach a point where you're using your intuition all the time though you may not be aware of it." [15]

✹ WHEN A DOOR CLOSES, ANOTHER OPENS ✹

During the Covid lockdown I was no longer able to give yoga classes and I had to close my studio. How could I move forward?

I took advantage of the extra time to meditate and practice the Energization Exercises more often, and more intensely. I discovered that when my energy was high after Energization, my meditations were better. I began to receive inspirations about my career path. One would prove life-changing.

I had always had a passion for trekking, but I was not qualified as a professional guide. Now, an inner guidance prompted me to find out if my degree in tourism economics and my license as a professional tour guide would help me qualify as a licensed environmental hiking guide. I soon discovered that I could take the exam without having to complete any prerequisites – I had to study for the exam, but thanks to some clear guidance received in meditation, I was able to pass it fairly easily.

I am so glad that I trusted that intuition. Now I have two complementary careers: teaching yoga and leading "Holistic Experiences in Nature," both of which are giving health and happiness to me and many others. –**Annaluisa**, *Forlì, Italy*

While we should not harbor doubts about the intuitions that come, we *should* check their validity against the common sense of the conscious mind. A sensible approach is to take small steps in the direction indicated by the intuition, while confirming at every step of the way that the direction is still valid, as judged by a calm feeling of rightness in the heart. Very often, guidance in a certain direction will take us up to a point from which we will have to invite fresh guidance before we can go forward confidently in a new direction.

> Never presume that you're absolutely correct for the entire course of your actions. If you begin to feel too sure about a thing, you may streak for the horizon, whereas your intuition was only telling you to go to the next corner and turn right. Continually hold your feelings of guidance up for further refinement, and you'll eventually reach the point where you know when to veer off from your initial course. It's easy to make mistakes, but if you remain humble and avoid being presumptuous about your guidance, you'll be able to tune in to the superconscious level.[16]

Treasure hunt

As we follow the directions indicated by our intuition, we should continually look for concrete signs that either confirm or raise questions about the guidance. There are fascinating and creative ways in which the universe responds to our wish for confirmation. Looking out for these signs will resemble a treasure hunt, where one clue leads to the next.

> Superconscious guidance may come in ways that won't always be under your control, but because you've asked for it, the guidance will begin to lead you. When you get in tune with an intuitive flow, events seem to happen almost automatically that move you in the right direction... Even if our actions are going in the wrong direction, if we've sincerely asked for inner guidance, we will be redirected in the right course to take.[17]

✦ THE TALKING ROOF TILE ✦

From the start it was clear that renovating the old ruin on our property and turning it into a meditation center would be a long and arduous process. We were counting on Dad and his construction company, but that hope vanished when the workers disappeared at the start of the Covid pandemic. Without stonemasons, how could we even get started? Perhaps it was a sign to give up on the project.

One day while I was working on the roof, more than half convinced of the futility of the project, I asked for a clear sign: some divine guidance about whether we should struggle on or give up. Not five minutes later, I picked up a discarded tile and noticed that something was written on it. It said: "The last thing to lose is hope." To me, it was the clear sign I was seeking that the project was divinely sanctioned – and my non-carpenter friends and I continued our efforts with renewed hope.

About fifteen days after I chanced upon the message, one of the workers from the building company returned and finished the masonry. I took this as another sign that the project had the divine approval, and when he presented a bill for 108* hours of labor, there was no longer any doubt in my mind that we would be ready to do the interior work by autumn, and that by Christmas our hope of holding group meditations and celebrations in the restored building would be realized. To this day, I haven't been able to understand how the tile got all the way up on the roof, but I am grateful to be the beneficiary of His mysterious ways and wonders.
—**Luca**, *Modena, Italy*

[*Author's note:* the building was finished and inaugurated in time for Christmas.]

---

* There are 108 beads on the japa mala used by Hindus for the repetition of God's name and also for the practice of Kriya. This number represents the major *naḍis* in the astral body. See pages 178-180 in Volume One for information about the *naḍis*.

Obstacles

As with all worthwhile endeavors, particularly those with challenges beyond our current present experience and abilities, we can expect that obstacles will be part of the process, not only because of the dual fabric of the universe (consisting of the forces that attract us toward the light and the forces that oppose our progress), but also because we need to develop great inner strength before we can attain the heights of Self-realization.

> If you're sincerely asking for guidance, and inwardly feeling what you're doing is right, then you should look at the obstacles as challenges to your will power. As Paramhansa Yogananda said, "There are no obstacles, only opportunities." Try to see the blocks in your path as opportunities for you to put out more energy toward the accomplishment of your goals. [18]

INNER GUIDANCE CHECKLIST

- ✓ Clarify your question.
- ✓ Set aside all preferences and expectations.
- ✓ Meditate to calm the mind and emotions.
- ✓ Broadcast your request from the spiritual eye.
- ✓ Hold the heart open to receive.
- ✓ Write down your perceptions in a journal.
- ✓ Look for concrete confirmation of the guidance.
- ✓ Act on the intuition, but take one small step at a time.
- ✓ If no guidance comes, take the best course and evaluate the results.
- ✓ Keep asking for guidance before taking further steps.

CHAPTER 4: *Points to Remember*

- Asking for inner guidance before making important (and everyday) decisions helps develop our intuition.
- Be clear about the questions that are truly important at this time.
- When asking for inner guidance, first calm the mind in meditation, then focus at the spiritual eye while "broadcasting" your request and hold the heart in receptivity to receive any guidance that comes.
- Signs of true inner guidance are a feeling of calmness, clarity, and joy.
- Signs of false guidance are nervousness, a lack of clarity, and disharmony.
- If no guidance comes, consider the alternatives and immerse yourself in the feeling that accompanies each option to see if one of them resonates within you.
- If you are uncertain about the guidance, take a few small steps in the best direction you can, and listen in the heart for confirmation or an indication that you should try another way. Guidance will also come once you've begun moving forward, so long as you remain impartial and receptive.
- Inner guidance is directional – it says "Go in this direction, for now..." It is not absolute – it doesn't say "This is the direction you should follow forever." Thus, we need to keep checking our intuition at each step of the way.

PART IX CHAPTER FIVE

Channeling Healing Energy to Others

Learn to convert your hands into healing batteries, so that divine currents will flow through them at will. Through this means, when properly administered, diseases of body and mind, as well as the malady of soul ignorance, have vanished under this benign touch, whether administered at close quarters or from afar. Thus one becomes the fisherman of souls, that he may catch them in the net of his divine healing wisdom and present them unto God.[1] –YOGANANDA

Instantaneous mental healings are caused when the healer and the person to be healed are perfectly tuned to each other. If the healer has a strong will and imagination and the person to be healed has faith in the healer's ability to awaken his will or imagination, then the patient will be healed through his own awakened life-force.[2] –YOGANANDA

The more you act as a channel of blessing to others, the more you yourself will be blessed. Your magnetism will be enhanced, and your efforts to reach God greatly accelerated.[3] –YOGANANDA

❋ THE DUTIFUL DAUGHTER ❋

Thirteen years after her knee replacement operation, my mother is still in constant pain. When recently she fell and broke the same knee, she called me, feeling desperate, alone, and fearful of having to spend the rest of her life in a wheelchair.

I live far away and so am unable to assist her physically. But thanks to Yogananda's techniques for healing at a distance, I have been able to help her through video discussions with her.

I first pray to Divine Mother in the form of Mary, who I imagine transfigured in light. Then we start each session with a few breathing exercises and a short, calming guided meditation. Using my voice and the power of my faith, I guide her in a visualization. It begins by seeing a warm white light in her spiritual eye, and expanding that light into her brain, face, neck, shoulders, heart, and so forth down to her knees. I suggest that she see her cells being nourished by this restorative, healing light. We affirm: "Where there is light, there can be no darkness."

After this visualization, I ask her to lie down. Accompanied by the harmonium, I sing "Aum" for a long time, asking her to absorb the light through the sound. All the while, I am visualizing the Divine Mother transforming my mother completely into light.

After five of these healing sessions, her pains disappeared. The orthopedic doctor says that her knee is miraculously thirty percent more flexible. My mother has become more devout, and sometimes we pray together online, sharing with others the blessings we've received.

—*Gaia*, *Assisi, Italy*

In this chapter we will discover how we can serve as channels of healing energy for others. We will consider three primary concepts:

- **The existence of divine will and its power to heal**
- **Our own capacity to serve as channels for that power**
- **The openness of the people receiving the healing power**

In Chapters One and Two we considered that the immense **power that created the universe** is more than willing to respond to our personal needs, however seemingly important or insignificantly mundane.

For **our part in the process**, we need to understand that it is God's power that heals, and that it is His will that will decide whether, how, and when a person will be healed.

> When you try to heal people, you must understand that the real healing is of the soul. Sometimes, physical problems are a very important part of their growth... So yours is not the place to say that I will that this person be healed. It's ultimately God's will.[4]

Yogananda would often say: "God works through channels."

> Divine grace, again, like electricity, flows through channels. As electricity is passed on through transmitting stations, so also is grace: through the attunement of living persons.[5]

We need to learn to activate the divine healing power within ourselves, and then direct it toward the person in need, offering ourselves to serve as a bridge for God's healing light.

One of the best ways to channel the divine healing energy is with the aid of the Life Force Energization Exercises.* Yogananda introduced these exercises to help us develop the ability to use our willpower to open the doorway of the medulla oblongata,† where, Yogananda says, divine energy enters the body. While practicing the

---

* These exercises are discussed in Part IV, Volume One.
† See Volume One, page 198.

exercises, we use our willpower and concentration to first draw life force into the body, and then direct it where it is needed, for our own self-healing or to help others.

The third requisite for channeling healing energy is the **openness of the person who wishes to be healed.** As God never imposes His will on anyone, in respect for the free will with which He has endowed every human being, so we should be equally sensitive to their reality.

> Attune yourself... to that other person's center; try to feel where they are coming from and see whether it's what their deeper nature wants. Is it really the right thing for them? [6]

Who did Jesus heal?

Jesus was an *avatar*, a fully liberated world teacher; and as such, he was in full possession of divine healing powers. Although he could have healed anyone and everyone, he did not do so.

The story of how Jesus healed a woman who had suffered from constant hemorrhaging for many years is inspiring and instructive. She believed that Jesus was a true incarnation of the Divine on earth, and a transparent channel for God's power. And so her faith impelled her to make the effort to find him and get close enough to touch the hem of his robe. And it was in that moment that the hemorrhaging ceased.

Although Jesus was surrounded by hundreds of people milling around him and eager to touch him, Jesus responded only to the woman's delicate and fearful touch. He asked: "Who touched me?" And when his disciples protested that many people were pressing against him, Jesus repeated: "Somebody hath touched me: for I perceive that virtue is gone out of me." (LUKE 8:46) It was the woman's faith and sincerity that opened the channel for an instantaneous healing.

Another episode from the Bible highlights the need to play an active role in our healing.

On the Sabbath Jesus went to the temple, where he encountered a man with a withered hand. Jesus said to him: "Stretch forth thine hand."

The Bible tells us: "And he stretched it out: and his hand was restored whole as the other." (MARK 3:5) Yogananda commented on this episode.

> Jesus meant, "Make an effort of your will to stretch forth your hand and send the all-healing energy there. If you do so and are in tune with Me, My divine will, controlling the cosmic energy of the universe, also present in your will and your bodily energy, will heal your hand." The person healed had to do something to prepare his mental soil so that the seed of divine healing power coming from Jesus could sprout into the plant of healing.[7]

In these two episodes we witness important attitudes for those desiring to be healed: that they have complete faith in God's benevolence; that they draw the healing by their own efforts; and that they participate in the healing.

> Spiritual healing requires not only power on the part of the healer, but also dynamic, receptive faith on the part of the person to be healed.[8]

✵ HEALING CAN'T BE IMPOSED ✵

The baby was born prematurely at seven months and was struggling to breathe. The baby's aunt asked me to pray for him, and together with others in our prayer group, we began to send prayers for him.

But I had a strange feeling, as if the door wasn't open for a healing to happen, as if the baby's soul did not want to incarnate at this time, and that was why he decided to leave his mother's womb early.

I began to talk to his soul, telling him that I understood his fears of entering this world, but that he was not alone: that he had an aunt who was a disciple of a great guru, and that there were other people around him who would help him. That was when I felt that the door had slowly begun to open. The baby struggled for a time, but eventually stabilized sufficiently for the doctors to allow him to go home to his parents.

Later, when I talked with the others who'd sent healing prayers, they said that they'd had the same feeling at first – that there was a block, and that the boy's soul didn't want to accept a healing.

This experience made me more sensitive to the truth that we cannot impose a healing on anyone, no matter how fervent our prayers, because healing ultimately depends on the soul's willingness to accept it. *–***Hana**, *Belgrade*

What should we do when people either are not able to ask for prayers due to their condition, or when they don't believe in such "nonsense?"

If we are using the techniques with the right attitude and understanding – that it is God's energy and intelligence that are flowing through as His channels – then we will allow that higher Intelligence to provide what is necessary. I have the impression that even if a person rejects the divine healing energy, the energy is not offended, but that it remains nearby until there is an opening.

A primary purpose of these techniques is not so much that people find a healing, but that they learn to arouse the will to heal themselves. In serving as channels for divine healing energy, we are trying, as Kriyananda put it, to **"stimulate that person to be their own healer. That's the highest kind of healing of all."** [9]

What should be our attitude when we are trying to channel energy to those who may be dying?* Swami Kriyananda suggests:

> **Sometimes a person should die, and it's none of your business to try to prevent that process. It is your business to try helping in their transition, giving them the faith and encouragement of being in the Light of God.**[10]

* You will find more suggestions in the Epilogue, Volume Three.

How to be a channel

Offering ourself as a channel for divine healing energy is a sacred service. It means that we offer ourselves to serve as a bridge between the Divine and the person in need – similar to the role of Christian priests, Hindu pujaris, and native shamans. How can we become truly qualified to serve in this important way?

Of primary importance is to have a loving, constant, ongoing relationship with the divine consciousness. If we appeal to that power only in times of peril or great pain, the relationship will not be one of intimacy and trust. Daily contact through meditation, prayer, and other practices is needed.

We must also carefully consider our relationship with the person in need. Whether or not we know them intimately, we will need to be sincerely concerned for their wellbeing, but without being emotionally involved. If our minds and hearts are agitated with worries, those restless emotions will curtail or block our ability to serve as a channel.

Preparing yourself to serve as a channel

- **Align** yourself through meditation with the power of the universe.

> In healing others, one has to have control over his Life Energy and project a current into his patient's body which stimulates and harmonizes the disturbed Life Energy of the patient by the power of will or imagination.[11]

- **Massage** the area around the medulla oblongata to open the doorway through which the Life Force enters the body. Then, with concentration and willpower, draw that healing power into your own body: tense and relax the entire body many times, using the double-breathing with each cycle.

By consciously attuning yourself with the healing forces of the universe, you will feel the whole dynamo of power flowing through your body. That flow is everywhere. Realize that the power that you're drawing on is the same power that is all over the universe. To get in tune with healing, think of the generative power that produced the universe. [12]

- **Focus your attention at the spiritual eye**. Yogananda suggests that we massage and pinch that area in the forehead, using the sense of touch to draw our attention to the area. Kriyananda suggests that we mentally send a beam of light from that area to the spiritual eye of the other person, with the affirmation: "You are well, for God is in you." Repeat this numerous times until you are convinced of this truth and you feel that it has reached the other person, even though they may not be aware of it.

- **Contact the soul of the person in need**. Perceive them not as ill, but as healthy, whole, and as a manifestation of the Divine. If the person is present, gaze on them while trying to sense their essential nature as a child of God. If the person is not present, you can use a photograph to help you focus your attention on them. Or, with closed eyes, you can visualize them as a being of energy and light.

- **Dedicate time** for this practice when you are feeling calm, and if possible, in a place that is uplifting, where you can focus your attention without interruption. An ideal time is when you are feeling peaceful and calm after meditation. If you are called upon to send healing prayers at other times of the day – perhaps after receiving an emergency message from your prayer group – take a few moments to become centered, pray, and get in touch with the divine power you wish to channel, and with the soul of the individual in need.

You can now practice any of the following techniques.

YOGANANDA'S TECHNIQUE FOR CHANNELING DIVINE HEALING ENERGY

- Sit erect. Gently tense and relax the whole body. Calm yourself.
- Touch the medulla once, in order to make it easier for you to concentrate on it.
- Then visualize Cosmic Energy surrounding and entering the body through the medulla and at the point between the eyebrows, and pouring into the spine.
- Feel the energy flowing down the whole length of the two arms into the hands.
- Continue tensing and relaxing and feeling the life force flow from the medulla and the point between the eyebrows through the spine to the hands.
- Then stop tensing and relaxing, and firmly rub the entire bare left arm with the right palm (up and down, several times). Do the same to the right arm with the left palm.
- Relax, continuously visualizing and willing Cosmic energy to descend from the medulla through the arms into your hands.
- Now, with closed eyes, rapidly but gently rub your palms together about twenty times.
- Then separate the hands, and lift the arms upward. You will feel the life current flowing from the medulla into the spine, especially through both arms and hands, as a pricking, tingling sensation.
- Your energy-magnetized hands may be used either for curing any diseased part of your own body or for some other person, who need not be in your immediate vicinity, for it is not necessary to touch your patient. This life force passing through your hands has infinite power of projection. You must broadcast the healing force by moving your hands, electrified by the above method, up and down in space while willing the current to pass over your patient's diseased body part.
- Do this in a quiet room for fifteen minutes until you feel that you have accomplished your objective.[13]

AN ABBREVIATED PRACTICE
often used at the end of individual or group meditation

Prayer: "Divine Mother, Thou art omnipresent. Thou art in all Thy children. Thou art in [their name]. Manifest Thy healing presence in [his/her] body."

Practice: Rub the palms together briskly, then hold up your hands and chant Aum three times while sending energy to the person in need.

Pray again: "Divine Mother, Thou art omnipresent, Thou art in all Thy children. Thou art in [name]. Manifest Thy healing presence in [his/her] mind."

Practice: Rotate the hands around each other very quickly (right hand moving clockwise and the left hand moving counterclockwise), then hold up your hands and chant Aum three times while sending energy to the person.

Pray again: "Divine Mother, Thou art omnipresent. Thou art in all Thy children. Thou art in [name]. Manifest Thy healing presence in [his/her] soul."

Practice: Rub your palms together briskly, then hold up your hands and chant Aum three times while sending divine healing power to the person in need.

A SHORT FORM
for use in personal and group meditations

Visualize each person to whom you wish to channel healing energy, seeing them well and already healed. Send this affirmation from your spiritual eye to theirs: **"You are well, for God is in you."**

Pray: "Divine Mother, Thou art omnipresent, Thou art in these, Thy children. Manifest Thy healing presence in their bodies, in their minds, and in their souls."

Practice: Rub palms together briskly, then hold up your hands and chant Aum three times, sending energy to all those in need.

YOGANANDA'S TECHNIQUE
using only the mind and willpower

- Practice meditation until you are calm.
- Rub the middle of the forehead in between the eyebrows.
- Hold your skin at that place pinchingly.
- Concentrate all attention on the touch sensation caused by the pinch.
- Then strongly project will and try to see the Light.
- Concentrate with utmost faith and bridge your will with Divine will.
- Go on willing your patient to be cured, by thinking your will is running down through his forehead down his spine and body to the center of the affected area in his body.
- Doubt not, just refuse to investigate if your patient is cured. Just believe, cure and forget. Don't talk about your cure to skeptics. Never say, "I cured," Always think the Divine will, as your human will, cured the disease. Give the whole credit to the Divine Healing Power and Divine Energy." [14]

VI. A MINI TECHNIQUE

Another technique is to draw energy to your palms by rubbing them together briskly, thirty to sixty times. Then raise the hands high above the head, palms forward, and send the energy that you feel tingling in the hands to those for whom you are praying. Feeling the energy entering through the medulla and out through the palms, chant *AUM* three to twelve times, holding each tone as long as you can do so comfortably.[15]

Of note while practicing these techniques is the **use of the hands** as instruments for healing energy.

Convert yourself into a divine battery, sending out through your hands divine healing rays whenever and wherever they may be needed. Then your hands, charged with divine power, will throw healing rays into your patient's heart and brain. Thus his seeds of ignorance will be destroyed, and he will smile with the health of God-love.[16]

The laying of the hands on sick people is done to send the healing X-Rays of the hands into the body of the patient to electrocute the disease germs. There is no power greater than the Life Force flowing through the hands, provided it is made strong by an indomitable will. Man's strong will, which refuses to be discouraged by anything and which flows continually and energetically toward the accomplishment of an object, becomes divinely empowered. The strong will of man is Divine will.[17]

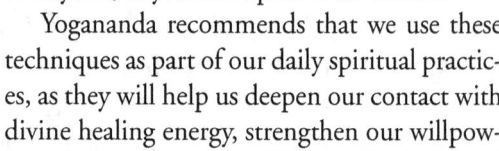

Magnetized additionally by moving them up and down, the hands can then be placed on our own body, or on the body of someone present, or used to project healing energy to anyone, anywhere. Space is no barrier.

Yogananda recommends that we use these techniques as part of our daily spiritual practices, as they will help us deepen our contact with divine healing energy, strengthen our willpower, serve as instruments to help relieve the suffering of others, and grant us the joy of experiencing the love of God flowing through us.

Are healing prayers effective?

Spiritual groups and movements the world over dedicate regular sessions to channel healing energy. Their websites and chat groups are replete with testimonials and expressions of gratitude for their service. The following testimonials were received from people who regularly send or have received channeled prayers.

✸ Praying for Strangers ✸

Belonging to a prayer group in Rome was a deeply felt need of mine: to know that in times of difficulty, I could ask my spiritual companions for prayer support. Even more so, I wanted to experience what it feels like to pray for someone I don't know.

I received a request to pray for someone's daughter who was in a coma following a car accident. She was the mother of a young child, and her family were in despair over the unbearable thought of possibly losing her. I submitted the request to our prayer group, and for months we prayed incessantly for her. The doctors said there was little hope, and the updates from my friend weren't encouraging.

We continued our prayers unabated, and there started to be small improvements: her vital signs began to stabilize and then slowly improve. Just a few weeks ago, she came out of the coma and regained consciousness, and now she has begun the first steps toward recovery.

This miracle strengthens me in the certainty of the power of prayer, the constant closeness of God, and His immense love, expressed through the channel of His sincere devotees. *–**Ramajyoti**, Rome, Italy*

✸ A Potentially Fatal Fall ✸

My granddaughter Alice loved horses, and had been an accomplished horsewoman since age thirteen. When she fell off her horse one day, we took her to the hospital, just to make sure everything was all right. The doctors found that she had severe internal injuries to her kidneys and spleen, and that immediate surgery was needed. For the next two weeks, she hovered between life and death.

I asked the many Ananda prayer groups in Europe, India, and the U.S. to pray for her. My daughter and I visited the hospital every day, and each time it felt, incredibly, as if we were walking on a carpet of light, and enveloped by many loving presences. The energy of all of these prayers helped us keep our spirits positive, and they had a remarkable effect on Alice's progress. The doctors wisely decided not to remove the kidney, which was very close to the aorta, and they were able to save her spleen.

Today, Alice is preparing to take her medical school entrance exams. Each year on April 13, the day of the accident, she celebrates by giving thanks for the prayers from around the world that made the miracle possible. –**Mira**, *Naples, Italy*

❋ PAINLESS POST-OP ❋

As I prepared for surgery, I was hoping that the number seven would bring good results. The seventh operation, they said, should definitively eliminate the endometriosis, but the surgery would be long, and the risk of complications would be high. The recovery, too, would be painful, and I was naturally anxious about those complications.

My good friend sent my name to the Ananda prayer group, and knowing that many people were praying for me, I entered the operating room with a great measure of calmness, surprising myself and the surgical team.

The surgery was a success, and the complications were minimal. The hospital had reserved a space for me for forty-eight hours in the post-operation ward. The prayer group was still actively praying for me, and it must have been due to their efforts that I never felt any pain. After only eighteen hours I was moved to the regular ward, where I resumed my meditation practice.

There seemed to be a bubble of grace around me, and those hospital meditations were filled with light and a strong feeling of lightness, as though I was floating on wings of joy. I offer my infinite gratitude to the prayer groups around the world and to Yogananda's technique for channeling God's healing power. –**Serena**, *Biella*

Prayers for those no longer on earth

Yogananda's guru, Swami Sri Yukteswar, reminds us that if we mistake the body for the soul, we perceive death as the final episode in life's drama: "Man *is* a soul, and *has* a body." [18]

> What is the use, anyway, of keeping
> the physical body indefinitely? Even were it
> to remain in perfect and glowing condition,
> the body — or, rather, the very ego that
> constructed it — is a prison!
> You aren't this body. You aren't this ego.
> You are the immortal soul. [19]

Prayers are a form of vibratory healing that can travel unimpeded through all dimensions of creation. Our prayers can also offer real and very valuable support to souls that have moved on from this physical world. We remain especially connected to those with whom we have enjoyed loving relationships. Our prayers can help them greatly as they continue on their soul's journey.

The channel is blessed

> Yogananda used to say, "The channel is
> blessed by that which flows through it."
> If you can give vibrations of peace,
> understanding and love, and above all
> joy to other people, so that they begin
> to get a little bit of hope and faith
> in their own destiny, your life will be worth
> a great deal to you. To whom else is it ever
> to be of worth, if not first to you? [20]

❋ Win-win ❋

I am part of a group of friends who meet every morning online to pray for a mutual friend who has suffered from severe anxiety over a variety of difficulties for which she hasn't been able to find solutions, despite a year of trying. From the time we began channeling light to her, her situation began to change. She became calmer, less worried, and practical solutions have started to appear.

As a fringe benefit, certain difficulties in our group living situation also began to improve from precisely the day when we started offering healing prayers for our friend. After six months of waiting, we now have electricity at our retreat center, and a number of challenges related to a program we are planning for this summer have been resolved in surprising ways.
—**Snezhana**, *Russia*

❋ At your service ❋

Every day after my morning meditation, I channel healing light to others. I do this practice also as a member of several prayer groups. We send prayers for a member of the group, and then for friends and relatives, and finally for the whole planet. When I invite the healing power to flow through me, it helps me connect with something big and deep that has no boundaries, and there is a sense of oneness with all Creation. I feel an immense joy and a deep gratitude to God for allowing me to serve others in this powerful way. —**Daniela**, *Cuneo, Italy*

CHAPTER 5: *Points to Remember*

- When we channel divine healing energy, we serve as a bridge between that healing Power and those in need.

- We must prepare ourselves for this sacred service by making a real inward contact with the divine healing power, and by raising our energy so that we can serve as a channel for its flow.

- The person receiving the healing also needs to be open and, if possible, should participate willingly and actively in the healing.

- While practicing the healing technique, we should visualize the person in their perfect, already healed form.

- We can help stimulate the recipient's will to heal him- or herself by repeating affirmations and transmitting the divine healing energy through our magnetically-charged hands.

- "The channel is blessed by that which flows through it." When we offer ourselves as channels for the divine healing Light, the Divine blesses us also.

NOTES | PART NINE

Title Page
1 Yogananda, *Inner Culture*, July-September 1941.

Chapter One
1 Yogananda, "Hints to the Reader," *Whispers from Eternity*, 9.
2 Yogananda, "The Law Behind Answered Prayers," *Inner Culture*, October 1941.
3 Yogananda, *The Rubaiyat of Omar Khayyam Explained*, quatrain 34.
4 Kriyananda, *The New Path*, 212.
5 Kriyananda, "A New Dispensation."
6 Yogananda, *The Essence of Self-Realization* 11:4.
7 Kriyananda, *God Is for Everyone*, 190.
8 Yogananda, *The Essence of Self-Realization* 10:19.
9 Kriyananda, "Grace vs. Effort."
10 Kriyananda, *Rays of the Same Light*, Week 27, 107-108.
11 Kriyananda, *How to be a True Channel*, 58-60.
12 Kriyananda, *The Light of Superconsciousness*, 106.

Chapter Two
1 Yogananda, "Hints to the Reader," *Whispers from Eternity*.
2 Yogananda, "The Science and Art of Prayer: Making Prayer Effective," *East-West*, July 1933.
3 Yogananda, "On the Throne of Omnipresence," *Inner Culture*, January 1936.
4 Yogananda, "Recipe Messages," *East-West*, November-December 1928.
5 Yogananda, *Super-Advanced Course No. 1*, Lesson 2.
6 Kriyananda, *The New Path*, 437-438.
7 Yogananda, *The Essence of Self-Realization* 17:3.
8 Yogananda, "The Surest Way to Prosperity," *East-West* magazine, October 1932.

Chapter Three
1 Yogananda, *The Essence of Self-Realization* 17:2.
2 Yogananda, "Your Most Important Engagement," *East-West*, January–April 1927.
3 Yogananda, *Super-Advanced Course No. 1*, Lesson 2.
4 Yogananda, *New Super Cosmic Science Course*, Lesson 5.
5 Yogananda, "Absorbing the Rivers of Desires into the Ocean of Inner Peace," *Spiritual Interpretation of the Bhagavad Gita, Inner Culture*, October 1941.
6 Yogananda, "Can Faith Alone Save Us?" *Inner Culture*, January 1941.
7 Yogananda, *The Essence of Self-Realization* 10:1.
8 Yogananda, *Super-Advanced Course No. 1*, Lesson 2.
9 Yogananda, "Prayer, or Loving Demand," *Inner Culture*, April 1936.
10 Yogananda, *The Essence of Self-Realization* 17:2.
11 Yogananda, "Loving Demand," *Inner Culture*, April 1936.
12 Yogananda, "The Science and Art of Prayer: Making Prayer Effective," *East-West*, July 1933.
13 Yogananda, *The Essence of Self-Realization* 11:6.
14 Yogananda, 17:6.
15 Yogananda, "Recipes," *East-West*, November-December 1926.
16 Yogananda, "Hints to the Reader," *Whispers from Eternity*, 9-17.
17 Yogananda, "Key to Demands, *Whispers from Eternity*, 6.

18 Kriyananda, *The New Path*, 437.
19 Yogananda, *The Essence of Self-Realization* 17:1.
20 Kriyananda, "What Do We Pray For?"
21 Yogananda, *Super-Advanced Course No. 1*, Lesson 2.

Chapter Four

1 Yogananda, *Advanced New Super Cosmic Science Course*, Lesson 2.
2 Kriyananda, *Intuition for Starters*, 35.
3 Yogananda, *Advanced New Super Cosmic Science Course*, Lesson 2.
4 Kriyananda, *Intuition for Starters*, 103, 104.
5 Kriyananda, *Awaken to Superconsciousness*, 252.
6 Kriyananda, *Intuition for Starters*, 50-51.
7 Kriyananda, 103, 104.
8 Kriyananda, 50.
9 Kriyananda, 48.
10 Kriyananda, 49.
11 Kriyananda, 49-50.
12 Kriyananda, 55-56.
13 Yogananda, *Advanced Course on Practical Metaphysics*, Lesson 3.
14 Kriyananda, *Intuition for Starters*, 50-51.
15 Kriyananda, 64.
16 Kriyananda, 72-73.
17 Kriyananda, 67, 79.
18 Kriyananda, 72.

Chapter Five

1 Yogananda, *Super-Advanced Course No. 1*, Lesson 11.
2 Yogananda, "Second Coming of Christ," *Inner Culture*, September 1938.
3 Kriyananda, *Awaken to Superconsciousness*, 176.
4 Kriyananda, unpublished article, "Divine Will Healing—How to Channel the Divine Light."
5 Kriyananda, "A Special Dispensation."
6 Kriyananda, "Divine Will Healing."
7 Yogananda, "Steps Toward the Attaining of Consciousness," "Second Coming of Christ," *Inner Culture*, August 1937.
8 Kriyananda, *The Art and Science of Raja Yoga*, 296.
9 Kriyananda, "Divine Will Healing—How to Channel the Divine Light."
10 Kriyananda, "Divine Will Healing."
11 Yogananda, *Scientific Healing Affirmations*, 92.
12 Kriyananda, "Divine Will Healing—How to Channel the Divine Light."
13 Yogananda, *Super-Advanced Course No. 1*, Lesson 11.
14 Yogananda, *Advanced Course on Practical Metaphysics*, Lesson 2.
15 Kriyananda, *Awaken to Superconsciousness*, 159-160.
16 Yogananda, *Super-Advanced Course No. 1*, Lesson 11.
17 Yogananda, "Steps Toward the Attaining of Consciousness," "Second Coming of Christ," *East-West*, April 1933.
18 Yogananda, *Autobiography of a Yogi*, 163.
19 Kriyananda, *Conversations with Yogananda* No. 101.
20 Kriyananda, Swami, from a talk at the Whole Life Expo, San Francisco in 1994.

Life is a Dream

*Life is a dream,
time like a stream,
carries our burdens away.*

*Never despair,
joy's everywhere,
love can befriend you today.*

*Free from all care
like birds on the air,
Soar above griefs and worries:
seek joy and be gay!*

*Often on earth
things of great worth
worldly ambitions defy;*

*Sometimes a friend
helps us ascend,
up from life's cares to the sky.*

*Love is a star:
though shining afar,
It can guide us and help us
toward light to draw nigh.**

---

*Kriyananda, from *A Tale of Songs*.

GLOSSARY

Ahankara. The ego, from the Sanskrit, meaning "I act."

Aum. The all-pervading sound emanating from Cosmic Vibration, also known as the Pranava, the Amen, and the Amin.

Babaji. Called "Mahavatar" ("Great Avatar") by Yogananda, Babaji reintroduced the ancient science of Kriya Yoga in the modern age. In *Autobiography of a Yogi*, Yogananda writes: "Babaji's mission in India has been to assist prophets in carrying out their special dispensation."

Bhagavad Gita. The major scripture of Hinduism, the teachings of Lord Krishna to his disciple Arjuna, delivered on the battlefield of Kurukshetra, as told in the epic story, Mahabharata.

Chakras. Plexuses or centers in the spine, from which energy flows out into the nervous system, and through that system into the body, sustaining and activating the various body parts.

Chitta. The feeling aspect of consciousness.

Christ Consciousness. Consciousness of Spirit as immanent in every unit of vibratory creation.

Cosmic Consciousness. Consciousness of Spirit transcending finite creation.

Day of Brahma. The aeons-long period of cosmic manifestation. At the dawn of a Day of Brahma, all creation, remanifested, emerges from a state of unmanifestation – the Night of Brahma.

Dharana. One-pointed concentration.

Dharma. Virtue, righteousness, right action.

Dhyana. Absorption in deep meditation.

Ego. The soul identified with and attached to the material body and the material creation.

Gunas. The three basic qualities that comprise the universe: *sattwa guna*, the elevating quality, that which most clearly suggests divinity; *rajas*, the activating element in nature; *tamas*, the darkening quality, that which obscures the underlying unity of Life.

Guru. The spiritual preceptor who introduces the disciple to God and guides his inner journey from the darkness of ignorance to the light of Self-realization.

Ida. One of the two parallel nerve channels in the astral spine, *iḍa* begins and ends on the left side of the spine. The energy passes upward through it and causes inhalation.

Karma. Action that is motivated by the ego, and which at some time, in one form or another, returns to the one who initiated it.

Krishna. One of the incarnations of Lord Vishnu, Krishna was a king at the time of the war of Kurukshetra, as told in the epic, Mahabharata. He is the guru of the warrior Arjuna, and his instructions to his disciple at the beginning of the war form the Bhagavad Gita, India's principle scripture.

Kriya Yoga. An ancient science developed in India for the use of all God-seekers. Its technique is referred to and praised by Krishna in the *Bhagavad Gita,* and by Patanjali in the *Yoga Sutras.* It consists of the careful, conscious circulation of energy around the spine in order to magnetize it and redirect the mental tendencies toward the brain.

Kundalini. Life Force which lies dormant at the base of the sushumna in the astral body. Spiritual enlightenment requires that this force be awakened and through specific practices caused to rise upward and reunite with Spirit at the *sahasrara chakra,* the thousand-petalled lotus.

Kutashta Chaitanya. The state of Christ Consciousness, or the awareness of the presence of Spirit in every atom of creation. Located at the Spiritual Eye, the Kutastha, is a reflection of the medulla oblongata: a field of dark blue light surrounded by a golden halo, in the center of which is a five-pointed star. The golden aureole represents the astral world; the blue field inside it, the causal world and the omnipresent Christ consciousness; the star in the center, the Spirit beyond creation.

Lahiri Mahasaya. Yogananda's "param guru," Lahiri Mahasaya was the guru of Swami Sri Yukteswar. He initiated thousands into the practice of Kriya Yoga.

Mahabharata. One of the two major Sanskrit epics of ancient India, the Mahabharata is both historical and allegorical. It contains an account of the war of Kurukshetra and also the Bhagavad Gita.

Maya. The instrument with which material manifestation was created, separating the creation from the Creator. It is a conscious force that perpetuates creation and keeps its inhabitants in ignorance of their true identity. Often referred to as Maha Shakti.

Medulla oblongata. The approximate physical location of the negative pole of the sixth chakra. It is the point at which cosmic energy enters the physical body.

Nadis. Subtle channels of life force in the astral body, comparable to the nervous system in the physical body.

Patanjali. An enlightened sage who described the science of Raja Yoga in his *Yoga Sutras.* He lived approximately in the second century BCE and is reputed to have written numerous spiritual treatises. Yogananda refers to him as an ancient Indian avatar, "the greatest of Hindu Yogis."

Pingala. One of the parallel nerve channels in the astral spine, pingala begins and ends on the right side of the spine. Energy passing downward through it causes exhalation.

Prana. Life force as it manifests in the human body and in all living creatures.

Pranayama. Control of the senses through withdrawal of energy.

Sanatan Dharma. The "Eternal Religion." The immutable truths that form the basis of religious and spiritual theologies, and moral and ethical codes.

Satchidananda. The description of the state preceding and beyond manifestation by India's great philosopher-saint, Swami Adi Shankaracharya: *Ever-existing, ever-conscious, ever-new Bliss.*

Swami Sri Yukteswar. Yogananda's guru, and a direct disciple of Lahiri Mahasaya, often mentioned in *Autobiography of a Yogi.*

Samadhi. Divine ecstasy. Union of the individual soul with the infinite Spirit.

Samskaras. Past tendencies. The traces of past karmas, both positive and negative, that carry over from life to life.

Spiritual Eye. The point midway between the eyebrows, within the frontal lobe of the brain, is described as the seat of the intellect, of willpower, and—in superconsciousness—of ecstasy and spiritual vision.

Sushumna. The astral spine, through which kundalini, having been magnetized to flow upward, begins its slow ascent toward enlightenment.

Vasana. A tendency or talent from past incarnations that influences current behavior.

Vedas. The four ancient scriptural texts of Sanatan Dharma: Rigveda, Samaveda, Yajurveda, and Atharvaveda.

Vritti. Eddies or whirlpools of energy that accompany ego-motivated thoughts and actions.

Yugas. Ages or cycles of time. The four ages are Kali Yuga (the age dark with ignorance), Dwapara Yuga (an age of energy), Treta Yuga (an age of awareness of the power of mind), and Satya Yuga, also called Krita (an age of high spiritual awareness).

Yamas and Niyamas. Described by Patanjali in his Yoga Sutras, the first two branches of the soul's journey to enlightenment, which consist of guidelines for conserving vital energy and directing it into constructive attitudes and actions.

BIBLIOGRAPHY

Becker, Robert. *The Body Electric: Electromagnetism and The Foundation of Life.* New York: William Morrow Paperbacks, 1998.

Clarity Magazine. Ananda Church of Self-Realization, Nevada City, California. Winter 2011.

East-West. Self-Realization Fellowship. Monthly and bimonthly issues, November/December 1925–March 1934.

Graeber, Nalini. *Transitioning in Grace: A Yogi's Approach to Death and Dying.* Nevada City, CA: Crystal Clarity Publishers, 2019.

Inner Culture. Self-Realization Fellowship. Monthly issues, April 1934–December 1941.

Kriyananda, Swami. See also Walters, J. Donald.

   Affirmations for Self-Healing. Nevada City, CA: Crystal Clarity Publishers, 2005.

   Ananda Yoga for Higher Awareness. Nevada City, CA: Crystal Clarity Publishers, 2004.

   Art as a Hidden Message. Nevada City, CA: Crystal Clarity Publishers, 1997.

   "Astral Ascension Ceremony." Online Appendix.

   Awaken to Superconsciousness. Nevada City, CA: Crystal Clarity Publishers, 2000.

   "Baptism Ceremony." Online Appendix.

   Cities of Light: A New Vision for the Future. Gurgaon, India: Ananda Sangha Publications, 2009.

   Conversations with Yogananda. Nevada City, CA: Crystal Clarity Publishers, 2003.

   Eastern Thoughts, Western Thoughts. Nevada City, CA: Crystal Clarity Publishers, 1975.

   Education for Life. Gurgaon, India: Ananda Sangha Publications, 2006.

   "A Festival of Light." Online Appendix.

   God Is for Everyone. Nevada City, CA: Crystal Clarity Publishers, 2003.

   "Grace vs. Self-Effort." Speaking Tree, *Hindustan Times,* January 29, 2004. https://www.hindustantimes.com/india/grace-vs-self-effort/story-CiQ5zfaJykdwz8uOKUeprN.html

   Guidelines for Conduct of Members of the Ananda Sevaka Order. Nocera Umbra, Italy: Ananda Sangha Publications, 2020.

A Handbook on Discipleship. Nevada City, CA: Crystal Clarity Publishers, 2010.

The Hindu Way of Awakening: Its Revelation, Its Symbols. Nevada City, CA: Crystal Clarity Publishers, 1998.

Hope for a Better World! Nevada City, CA: Crystal Clarity Publishers, 2002.

"How Old Are You?" Speaking Tree, *Times of India*, date unknown.

"How Well Do You Get Along with Others?" *Clarity Magazine*, Ananda Church of Self-Realization, Winter 2011.

In Divine Friendship: Letters of Counsel and Reflection. Nevada City, CA: Crystal Clarity Publishers, 2008.

Intuition for Starters. Edited by Devi Novak. Nevada City, CA: Crystal Clarity Publishers, 2002.

Keys to the Bhagavad Gita. Nevada City, CA: Crystal Clarity Publishers, 1979.

"Lahiri Mahasaya's Birthday." Talk at Ananda Village, California, September 30, 1995.

Letters to Truth Seekers. Nevada City, CA: Crystal Clarity Publishers, 1973.

The Light of Superconsciousness. Edited by Devi Novak. Nevada City, CA: Crystal Clarity Publishers, 1999.

Living Wisely, Living Well. Nevada City, CA: Crystal Clarity Publishers, 2010.

Material Success Through Yoga Principles. Nevada City, CA: Crystal Clarity Publishers, 2005.

Meditation for Starters. Nevada City, CA: Crystal Clarity Publishers, 1996.

Money Magnetism: How to Attract What You Need, When You Need It. Nevada City, CA: Crystal Clarity Publishers, 1992.

The New Path: My Life with Paramhansa Yogananda. Nevada City, CA: Crystal Clarity Publishers, 2009.

Out of the Labyrinth. Nevada City, CA: Crystal Clarity Publishers, 2001.

A Place Called Ananda. Nevada City, CA: Crystal Clarity Publishers, 1996.

The Promise of Immortality. Nevada City, CA: Crystal Clarity Publishers, 2001.

"Radiant Health and Well Being." YouTube video, Ananda Sangha Worldwide. https://www.youtube.com/watch?v=jRx_U2JS8HE

Rays of the One Light. Nevada City, CA: Crystal Clarity Publishers, 2007.

Rays of the Same Light. Nevada City, CA: Crystal Clarity Publishers, 1988.

Religion in the New Age. Gurgaon, India: Ananda Sangha Publications, 2010.

A Renunciate Order for the New Age. Nevada City, CA: Crystal Clarity Publishers, 2010.

The Road Ahead. Nevada City, California: Ananda Publications, 1973.

The Road Ahead. Nevada City, CA: Crystal Clarity Publishers, 1974.

Sadhu, Beware! A New Approach to Renunciation. Gurgaon, India: Ananda Sangha Publications, 2005.

"The Science of the Future." Talk at Unity in Yoga Conference, May 27, 1995.

Self-Expansion Through Marriage. Nevada City, CA: Crystal Clarity Publishers, 2012.

Space, Light, and Harmony: The Story of Crystal Hermitage. Nevada City, CA: Crystal Clarity Publishers, 2005.

Twenty-Six Keys to Living with Greater Awareness. Nevada City, CA: Crystal Clarity Publishers, 1989.

"Wedding Ceremony." Online Appendix.

"Whisper to God." Speaking Tree, *Times of India*, date unknown.

"You Don't Have to Be Sick." YouTube video, Ananda Sangha Worldwide. https://www.youtube.com/watch?v=V9ApjBHI29U&abchannel=AnandaSanghaWorldwide

Your Sun Sign as a Spiritual Guide. Nevada City, CA: Crystal Clarity Publishers, 2013.

Yours—the Universe! Nevada City, CA: Hansa Publications, 1967.

Laubach, Frank. *Letters by a Modern Mystic.* London, United Kingdom: SPCK Publishing, 1937.

Sivananda, Swami. *Japa Yoga.* Rishikesh: The Sivananda Publication League, 1942.

Walters, J. Donald. *How to Be a Channel.* Nevada City, CA: Crystal Clarity Publishers, 1987.

Secrets of Friendship. Nevada City, CA: Crystal Clarity Publishers, 1992.

Secrets of Health and Healing. Nevada City, CA: Crystal Clarity Publishers, 2018.

Secrets of Success and Leadership. Nevada City, CA: Crystal Clarity Publishers, 2017.

Yogananda, Paramhansa. *The Attributes of Success.* Los Angeles, CA: Self-Realization Fellowship, 1944.

Autobiography of a Yogi. Gurgaon, India: Ananda Sangha Publications, 2004. Reprint of the 1946 first printing, published by The Philosophical Library, Inc., New York, New York.

The Bhagavad Gita According to Paramhansa Yogananda. Edited by Swami Kriyananda. Nevada City, CA: Crystal Clarity Publishers, 2008.

The Essence of the Bhagavad Gita, Explained by Paramhansa Yogananda, As Remembered by His Disciple Swami Kriyananda. Nevada City, CA: Crystal Clarity Publishers, 2006.

The Essence of Self-Realization: The Wisdom of Paramhansa Yogananda, Recorded, compiled, and edited by his disciple Swami Kriyananda. Nevada City, CA: Crystal Clarity Publishers, 1990.

How to Love and Be Loved. Nevada City, CA: Crystal Clarity Publishers, 2007.

The Rubaiyat of Omar Khayyam Explained. Edited, with occasional comments, by J. Donald Walters. Nevada City, CA: Crystal Clarity Publishers, 1994.

"Spiritual Interpretation of the Bhagavad Gita." *Inner Culture,* August 1938–December 1941.

Whispers from Eternity. Edited by Swami Kriyananda. Nevada City, CA: Crystal Clarity Publishers, 2008.

Yogananda, Swami. "Advanced Course on Practical Metaphysics, 1926." Lessons 1-12. Los Angeles, CA: Self-Realization Fellowship, 1926.

"Advanced Super Cosmic Science Course, 1934." Lessons 1-6. Los Angeles, CA: Self-Realization Fellowship, 1934.

Cosmic Chants. Los Angeles, CA: Self-Realization Fellowship, 1938.

"Interpretation of the Bhagavad Gita." *East-West,* April 1932–March 1934.

"Interpretation of the Bhagavad Gita." *Inner Culture,* April 1934–February 1936.

Metaphysical Meditations. Los Angeles, CA: Self-Realization Fellowship, 1932.

"New Super Cosmic Science Course, 1934." Lessons 1-6. Los Angeles, CA: Self-Realization Fellowship, 1934.

Praecepta Lessons, Volumes 1-5. Los Angeles, CA: Self-Realization Fellowship, 1934–1938.

Psychological Chart. Los Angeles, CA: Self-Realization Fellowship, 1925.

Scientific Healing Affirmations. Los Angeles, CA: Self-Realization Fellowship, 1924.

Songs of the Soul. Los Angeles, CA: Self-Realization Fellowship, 1923.

"Spiritual Interpretation of the Bhagavad Gita." *Inner Culture,* May 1937–July 1938.

"Super Advanced Course No. 1, 1930." Lessons 1-12. Los Angeles, CA: Self-Realization Fellowship, 1930.

"Yogoda Course, 1925." Lessons 1-12. Los Angeles, CA: Self-Realization Fellowship, 1925.

Yogoda, Tissue-Will System of Body and Mind Perfection. Boston, MA: Sat-Sanga, 1923.

Yogoda, Tissue-Will System of Body and Mind Perfection. Boston, MA: Sat-Sanga, 1925.

PHOTO & ILLUSTRATIONS

Cover Background: Blenze, Freepik
p. 3: Ananda Image Bank
p. 10: Ananda Image Bank
p. 11: Ananda Image Bank
p. 12: Storyset, Freepik
p. 14: Ananda Image Bank
p. 16: AlexeyZhilkin, Freepik
p. 21: Public Domain, Wikimedia
p. 24: ElisaRiva, Pixabay
p. 32: Storyset, Freepik
p. 33: PikiSuperstar, Freepik
p. 42: Storyset, Freepik
p. 47 : Freepik
p. 48: Barbara Bingham
p. 52: Dooder, Freepik
p. 58: Jigsawstocker, Freepik
p. 60: Fahmiruddinhidayat111198, Freepik
p. 64: Freepik
p. 73: User5638775, Freepik
p. 74: Freepik
p. 76: Johannes Plenio, Unslpash
p. 80: KJPargeter, Freepik
p. 83: pch.vector, Freepik
p. 86: PikiSuperstar, Freepik
p. 88: Werezu_official, Freepik
p. 91: drynvalo, Freepik
p. 95: Storyset, Freepik
p. 100: Ananda Image Bank
p. 104: 8icons, Freepik
p. 110: rawpixel.com, Freepik
p. 113: Freepik
p. 116: Drew Dizzy Graham, Unsplash
p. 127: WayHomeStudio, Freepik
p. 131: pch.vector/StudioGStock, Freepik
p. 134: ZBoroda77, Freepik
p. 141: Macrovector, Freepik
p. 146: Master1305, Freepik
p. 151: CallMeTak, Freepik
p. 155: Macrovector, Freepik
p. 162: Macrovector, Freepik
p. 166: Darius Bashar, Freepik
p. 169: Ananda Image Bank
p. 170: Freepik
p. 174: JComp, Freepik
p. 187: Ananda Image Bank
p. 194: IrynaShek, Freepik
p. 197: Storyset, Freepik
p. 201: Tusya111, Freepik
p. 203: SipleLine, Vecteezy
p. 204: Stocknick, IStockPhoto
p. 204: Umit Yildirim, Unsplash
p. 205: JuliaWhite, Shutterstock
p. 206: Tejindra Tully
p. 208: Paul Skorupsas, Unsplash
p. 218: Jyotirmoy Gupta, Unsplash
p. 220: Giorgio Majno
p. 221: Vecstock, Freepik
p. 224: Ananda Image Bank
p. 227: Andrea Roach
p. 228: Babumon, Unsplash
p. 232 (all): Stephen Sturgess
p. 233: OlgaRai, Vector Stock
p. 234: Brown, Freepik
p. 245: Warren, Unsplash
p. 251: Suwant, Freepik
p. 254: BillionPhotos, Freepik
p. 260: Gursimrat Ganda, Unsplash
p. 264: JComp, Freepik
p. 281: Tiverets, Vector Stock
p. 287: Umit Bulut, Unsplash
p. 296: Woodhouse, Freepik
p. 302: Rudall30, IStockPhoto
p. 305: Stephen Sturgess
p. 310: Freepik
p. 313: Volodymyr Hryschenko, Unsplash
p. 319: Ananda Image Bank
p. 328: Ananda Image Bank
p. 329: Ananda Image Bank
p. 330: Andrea Roach
p. 331: photographeeasia, Freepik

PARAMHANSA YOGANANDA

Born in 1893, Paramhansa Yogananda was the first yoga master of India to take up permanent residence in the West.

He arrived in America in 1920 and traveled throughout the country on what he called his "spiritual campaigns." Hundreds of thousands filled the largest halls in major cities to see the yoga master from India. Yogananda continued to lecture and write up to his passing in 1952.

Yogananda's initial impact on Western culture was truly impressive. His lasting spiritual legacy has been even greater. His *Autobiography of a Yogi*, first published in 1946, helped launch a spiritual revolution in the West. Translated into more than fifty languages, it remains a best-selling spiritual classic to this day.

Before embarking on his mission, Yogananda received this admonition from his teacher, Swami Sri Yukteswar: "The West is high in material attainments but lacking in spiritual understanding. It is God's will that you play a role in teaching mankind the value of balancing the material with an inner, spiritual life."

In addition to *Autobiography of a Yogi*, Yogananda's spiritual legacy includes music, poetry, and extensive commentaries on the Bhagavad Gita, the Rubaiyat of Omar Khayyam, and the Christian Bible, showing the principles of Self-realization as the unifying truth underlying all true religions. Through his teachings and his Kriya Yoga path millions of people around the world have found a new way to connect personally with God.

His mission, however, was far broader than all this. It was to help usher the whole world into Dwapara Yuga, the new Age of Energy in which we live. "Someday," Swami Kriyananda wrote, "I believe he will be seen as the avatar of Dwapara Yuga: the way shower for a new age."

"As a bright light shining in the midst of darkness, so was Yogananda's presence in this world. Such a great soul comes on earth only rarely, when there is a real need among men."

– HIS HOLINESS THE SHANKARACHARYA *of* KANCHIPURAM –

SWAMI KRIYANANDA

A prolific author, accomplished composer, playwright, and artist, and a world-renowned spiritual teacher, Swami Kriyananda (1926–2013) referred to himself simply as a close disciple of the great God-realized master, Paramhansa Yogananda. He met his guru at the age of twenty-two, and served him during the last four years of the Master's life. He dedicated the rest of his life to sharing Yogananda's teachings throughout the world.

Kriyananda was born in Romania of American parents, and educated in Europe, England, and the United States. Philosophically and artistically inclined from youth, he soon came to question life's meaning and society's values. During a period of intense inward reflection, he discovered Yogananda's *Autobiography of a Yogi*, and immediately traveled three thousand miles from New York to California to meet the Master, who accepted him as a monastic disciple. Yogananda appointed him as the head of the monastery, authorized him to teach and give Kriya initiation in his name, and entrusted him with the missions of writing, teaching, and creating what he called "world brotherhood colonies."

Kriyananda founded the first such community, Ananda Village, in the Sierra Nevada foothills of Northern California in 1968. Ananda is recognized as one of the most successful intentional communities in the world today. It has served as a model for other such communities that he founded subsequently in the United States, Europe, and India.

> "Not only did Kriyananda walk in the footsteps of an enlightened master, it [is] obvious that he himself became an embodiment of Yogananda's teachings."
> – MICHAEL BERNARD BECKWITH, author, *Spiritual Liberation* –

> "Swami Kriyananda is a man of wisdom and compassion in action, truly one of the leading lights in the spiritual world today."
> – LAMA SURYA DAS, Dzogchen Center, author of *Awakening the Buddha Within* –

ABOUT THE AUTHOR

SHIVANI LUCKI left her legal studies and a promising career in Washington, D.C. when she realized her quest for truth and justice would not be fulfilled in the classroom or courtroom. Her gypsy journey across the United States eventually led to California where she began a serious practice of yoga and meditation with Swami Kriyananda, who introduced her to the idea of intentional communities through his book, *Cooperative Communities— How to Start Them and Why*.

With a small backpack, a sleeping bag, and a heart full of hope, she arrived on June 22, 1969, at the fledgling Ananda community. She was twenty-four years old. Recognition was instantaneous: This was the way of life she had long been seeking. She resolved to dedicate her life to Yogananda's ideal of "World Brotherhood Colonies," for "plain living and high thinking."

Her special passion has always been the self-healing techniques of Yogananda, taking as her unique mission to find and share these mostly out of print or never published teachings. One day she hoped to found an institute for healing based on Yogananda's methods.

Shivani has earned a worldwide reputation as one of the foremost teachers of meditation, specifically Kriya Yoga, an ancient method Yogananda re-introduced to the world in modern times. She helped establish two Ananda communities—one in California, and one near Assisi, Italy—and the Yogananda Academy of Europe. Fulfilling her dream, she founded the Life Therapy School for Self-Healing. Since 1985 she and her husband have lived in the Ananda Assisi community.

"Shivani possesses a luminosity that disperses all self-doubt and fear. To know her is to exchange endless ego traps for clarity, joy, and inner security."

—*Jagadish*, *Thailand*

~ In Appreciation ~

Every creative endeavor is a journey. We may believe we know where we are headed and how to get there – but it doesn't always work out that way. Inspiration is never static, and the creative process, like life itself, develops through many stages.

While my goal was crystal clear for me at the outset – to present the full scope, depth, and practical healing power of Paramhansa Yogananda's techniques for achieving physical vitality, mental peace, and spiritual realization – the path to the goal became a profound process or personal discovery. Discoveries came, of course, through meditating on the principles and practicing the techniques, and through the many people who kindly commented on the text, and shared their personal stories of healing. As the book grew from infancy to adulthood, it gradually discovered its destiny as a trilogy instead of a single encyclopedic tome.

I have acknowledged the true authors of these books in the Dedication. Here, I add my deep appreciation to **Nandini Cerri**, director of Yogananda Edizioni in Italy, who for years encouraged me to write, and supported me at every step of the way.

Many friends, teachers, and healthcare practitioners read parts of the book, offering their thoughtful insights and suggestions. My thanks to them all, especially to: **Jagadish Photikie, Jennifer Hansa Black, Hana Mukti Božanin, Dr. Donatella Caramia, Dr. Abhilash Kumar, Latha Gupta, Nayaswami Lakshman**, and **David Sanjaya Connolly**.

Of exceptional note, I offer my deepest appreciation to my Aquarian brothers: **Rambhakta Beinhorn**, who sensitively and expertly edited the books; and **Tejindra Scott Tully**, whose inspired design for the covers and text makes the book a pleasure to read and a brilliant examplar of graphic artistry.

Let me not forget my husband, **Arjuna Lucki**, who endured long absences while I was sequestered in my writing hideaway; and my many friends and colleagues who, during my absence from usual duties, took the helm and taught my classes with masterful skill.

May I presume to thank you as well, **dear reader**, for sharing the inspiration you garner from these pages with those in need of healing?

Together may we bring Light and Healing to the world!

HEALTHY LIVING with CRYSTAL CLARITY

Autobiography of a Yogi
Paramhansa Yogananda

Autobiography of a Yogi is one of the world's most acclaimed spiritual classics, with millions of copies sold. Named one of the Best 100 Spiritual Books of the twentieth century, this book helped launch and continues to inspire a spiritual awakening throughout the Western world.

Yogananda was the first yoga master of India whose mission brought him to settle and teach in the West. His firsthand account of his life experiences in India includes childhood revelations, stories of his visits to saints and masters, and long-secret teachings of yoga and Self-realization that he first made available to the Western reader.

This reprint of the original 1946 edition is free from textual changes made after Yogananda's passing in 1952. This updated edition includes bonus materials: the last chapter that Yogananda wrote in 1951, also without posthumous changes, the eulogy Yogananda wrote for Gandhi, and a new foreword and afterword by Swami Kriyananda, one of Yogananda's close, direct disciples.

Also available in Spanish and Hindi from Crystal Clarity Publishers.

Scientific Healing Affirmations
Paramhansa Yogananda

Yogananda's 1924 classic, reprinted here, is a pioneering work in the fields of self-healing and self-transformation. He explains that words are crystallized thoughts and have life-changing power when spoken with conviction, concentration, willpower, and feeling. Yogananda offers far more than mere suggestions for achieving positive attitudes. He shows how to impregnate words with spiritual force to shift habitual thought patterns of the mind and create a new personal reality.

Added to this text are over fifty of Yogananda's well-loved "Short Affirmations," taken from issues of East-West and Inner Culture magazines from 1932 to 1942. This little book will be a treasured companion on the road to realizing your highest, divine potential.

How to Achieve Glowing Health and Vitality
THE WISDOM OF YOGANANDA SERIES, VOLUME 6
Paramhansa Yogananda

Yogananda explains principles that promote physical health and overall well-being, mental clarity, and inspiration in one's spiritual life. He offers practical, wide-ranging, and fascinating suggestions on having more energy and living a radiantly healthy life. Readers will discover the priceless Energization Exercises for rejuvenating the body and mind, the fine art of conscious relaxation, and helpful diet tips for health and beauty.

Meditation for Starters
Swami Kriyananda

Have you wanted to learn to meditate, but just never got around to it? Or tried "sitting in the silence" only to find your mind wandering? Do you wish you had a meditation guidebook that explained clearly what to do, step-by-step? If so, *Meditation for Starters* is for you.

Learn meditation from a true expert, with more than 60 years of experience. Swami Kriyananda has helped tens of thousands of people successfully start a regular meditation routine.

This award-winning book provides everything you need to begin a meditation practice. Easy-to-follow instructions teach you how to relax the body, focus your attention, and interiorize your mind. With only a little practice you will experience the enhanced awareness and joyful calmness that was missing in your life.

The Hindu Way of Awakening
ITS REVELATION, ITS SYMBOLS:
AN ESSENTIAL VIEW OF RELIGION
Swami Kriyananda

Hinduism, as it comes across in this book, is a robust, joyful religion, amazingly in step with the most advanced thinking of modern times, in love with life, deeply human as well as humane, delightfully aware of your personal life's needs, for the teaching in this book is no abstraction: It is down-to-earth and pressingly immediate.

This book brings order to the seeming chaos of the symbols and imagery in Hinduism and clearly communicates the underlying teachings from which these symbols arise - truths inherent in all religions, and their essential purpose - the direct inner experience of God.

Intuition for Starters
HOW TO KNOW & TRUST YOUR INNER GUIDANCE
Swami Kriyananda

Is there a way to know how to make the best choice? Yes! through developing our faculty of intuition.

Often thought of as something vague and undefinable, intuition is the ability to perceive truth directly not by reason, logic, or analysis, but by simply knowing from within.

This book explains how within each of us lies the ability to perceive the answers we need and shows how to access the powerful stream of creative energy which lies beneath the surface of our conscious mind: the superconscious.

Step-by-step exercises, advice, and guidance reveal intuition to be an ally and an accessible fountain of wisdom to be found within each of us.

Living Wisely, Living Well
Swami Kriyananda
Winner of the 2011 International Book Award for Self-Help: Motivational Book of the Year.

Learn the art of spiritual living, and discover hundreds of techniques for self-improvement. Living Wisely, Living Well contains 366 practical ways to improve your life—a thought for each day of the year.

• A step-by-step guidebook for manifesting your higher Self • The distillation of a lifetime of wisdom • A call to dynamic inner growth

Take a year off from the "same old you." Read this book, put into practice what it teaches, and in a year's time you won't recognize yourself.

Affirmations for Self-Healing
Swami Kriyananda

These 52 affirmations—one for each week of the year—will help you strengthen positive qualities in yourself such as willpower, forgiveness, happiness, courage, contentment, and kindness.

This inspirational book is the ultimate self-help manual—a powerful tool for personal transformation. Swami Kriyananda teaches that negative thoughts exist in the subconscious mind, mentally whispering thousands of times each day, "I am afraid, I am tired, I am angry . . ." To be successfully overcome, these thoughts must be faced in their own territory.

Affirmation is a proven method of influencing the subconscious mind and replacing those negative thoughts with positive statements of well-being. Each affirmation and prayer combination in this book is a tool that reaches the depths of the subconscious in a language it can hear and understand. Where other methods fail, these affirmations can succeed.

Kriya Yoga
SPIRITUAL AWAKENING FOR THE NEW AGE
Nayaswami Devarshi

Both instructive and inspiring, *Kriya Yoga: Spiritual Awakening for the New Age*, is a roadmap for the already practicing Kriya Yogi. Through real-life stories from long-time Kriyabans, you will learn what attitudes and practices can help or hinder your progress on the spiritual path.

Simultaneously, this book is a signpost to the aspiring devotee on how and why to take up the lifelong practice of Kriya Yoga. You will discover what pitfalls to look out for along the way, and how to reach ultimate success on your journey to Self-realization.

He added, "The time for knowing God has come!"

APPENDICES
A treasure trove of inspiration awaits you!

The online Appendices for this volume are reserved just for you. Scan the QR code or enter the internet address below, and discover many additional resources to help deepen your understanding on your path to self-healing and Self-realization.

Included are:

- *Instruction videos in Life Force healing techniques, taught by the author*
- *Instruction and guided practice of pranayama and meditation*
- *Articles—many of them available for the first time—from the original writings of Paramhansa Yogananda and from the writings and talks of Swami Kriyananda.*

www.healinglifeforces.com/volume-1/

HEALING LIFE FORCE COMMUNITY
Sign up today and you will receive:

- *Healing Tips videos by the author*
- *Live sessions with the author*
- *Blogs on healing techniques in daily life*
- *Insights, invitations and much more.*

Scan the QR code or enter this internet address to join!
www.healinglifeforces.com

Your **Healing Journey** with **Paramhansa Yogananda** continues!

HEALING WITH LIFE FORCE
VOLUME ONE

Prana

Volume One, *Prana*, takes us back to the very beginning, when Life Force becomes the power that fashions creation. Yogananda shows us how to harness that power and use it to infuse our bodies with vitality. That force also gives rise to the eternal struggle between the soul and the ego, the root cause of all disease. Through the pages and practices of this book, you will learn how to reconcile these two protagonists through techniques of meditation; how to regenerate the cells and organs of your body with **Yogananda's Energization Exercises**; and how to nourish yourself and keep your body free from impurities with his dietary and detox recipes. A fascinating section in this volume presents Yogananda's techniques for utilizing the sun's power for self-healing.

"All methods of healing are really indirect ways of rousing the life energy, which is the real and direct healer of all diseases."
—Yogananda

"The greater the will, the greater the flow of energy."

"Remember it. Emblazon it in your mind. Repeat it to yourself several times a day. This single truth can revolutionize your life."
—Kriyananda

HEALING WITH LIFE FORCE
VOLUME THREE

MAGNETISM

This volume reveals how the Law of Attraction operates in our lives: how it draws us into contact with friends from past lives; and how we can use it to attract the economic and human resources for a successful career. The final chapter of the trilogy demonstrates how we can attune ourselves to the subtle, vibratory healing frequencies of mantra and music; of nature, holy places, and inspiring people.

Important techniques are given to reinforce the magnetic aura which protects us from negative influences that threaten our physical, mental, emotional, and spiritual health and well-being. *Chapters include:*

- **The Relationships Challenge**
- **Characteristics of Healthy and Unhealthy Relationships**
- **Soulmates**
- **Separation and Divorce**
- **Prosperity and Success**
- **Healing Habitats**
- **Transition and Transcendence**

> "A strong, positive magnetic aura around your body will prevent not only people's negative thoughts from affecting you, but also negative § or harmful circumstances and happenings, even disease."
> —YOGANANDA

AVAILABLE AT CRYSTALCLARITY.COM IN OCTOBER, 2024

www.ingramcontent.com/pod-product-compliance
Lightning Source LLC
Chambersburg PA
CBHW050201240426
43671CB00013B/2208